THE STRONG FAMILY

Over 250,000 in Print • Now with Discussion Guide

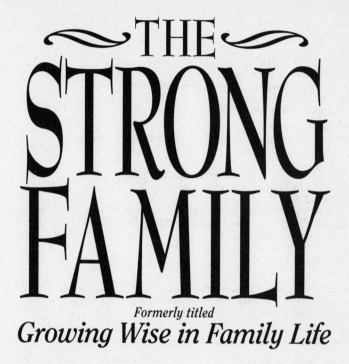

THE STRONG FAMILY

Formerly titled
Growing Wise in Family Life

Charles R. Swindoll

ZondervanPublishingHouse
Grand Rapids, Michigan

A Division of HarperCollinsPublishers

THE STRONG FAMILY
© 1991 by Charles R. Swindoll
Requests for information should be addressed to:
Zondervan Publishing House
Grand Rapids, Michigan 49530

Swindoll, Charles R.
  The strong family : growing wise in family life / Charles R.
Swindoll.
    p.   cm.
  Rev. ed. of: Growing wise in family life. c1988.
  Includes bibliographical references (p.   º and indexes.
  ISBN 0-310-42191-8 (paper)
  1. Family—Religious life. 2. Christian life—1960– 3. Family—United States.
I. Swindoll, Charles R. Growing wise in family life. II. Title. III. Title:
Growing wise in family life
  [BV4526.2.S78   1994]
  248.4—dc20   94–2808
                                                                   CIP

Scripture quotations, unless otherwise marked, are taken from the New American Standard Bible, © The Lockman Foundation 1960, 1962, 1963, 1968, 1971, 1972, 1973, 1975, 1977 and are used by permission.

Scripture references marked TLB are taken from The Living Bible, © 1971 by Tyndale House Publishers, Wheaton, Illinois and are used by permission.

Scripture references marked NIV are taken from the Holy Bible, New International Version®. NIV®. Copyright ©1973, 1978, 1984 by International Bible Society. Used by permission of Zondervan Publishing House. All rights reserved.

Scripture references marked Amplified are from The Amplified New Testament, © 1954, 1958, 1987 by The Lockman Foundation. Used by permission.

Scripture references marked Good News are from the Good News Bible, © American Bible Society, 1976.

Cover design by Mark Veldheer
Cover photo by Superstock
Interior design by Rick Devon
Discussion guide written by Lee Hough

Printed in the United States of America

04 05 /❖ DC/ 18 17 16 15 14

CONTENTS

PART ONE

Laying the Foundation

PART TWO

Building the Structure

PART THREE

Weathering the Storm

Introduction

The family is "in." Everything I read tells me more and more moms and dads, kids and grandkids, pals and pets are moving into the limelight as we press toward the end of the twentieth century.

Millions of us prefer the films and the TV channels that portray slices of modern life. Whether they are performances about personal heroism or neighborhood crime, silly sitcoms or serious docudramas, family-related shows get our vote the highest percentage of the time.[1]

But wait. Even though the family is "in" and enjoying a prominent place in the theater spotlight and the media sun, who says that the domestic scene being portrayed on page and stage is an accurate one? The models on display may be entertaining, endearing, upbeat, even funny, but would most of us agree they represent the truth . . . I mean, the whole truth? Does their message really equip us to handle life?

Reading popular bestsellers or watching an intriguing movie or even a wholesome, humorous television show several times a week may be relaxing—even stimulating. But is it sufficient to counteract the garbage today's real world is slinging in our direction? Hardly.

Something terribly important is missing: a consistent dose of biblical truth mixed with God-given wisdom. By substituting the entertaining for the eternal, a shortcut to happiness and satisfaction is suggested. What disturbs me is the false impression we are left with, namely, that the family who laughs together hangs in there together. Nothing wrong with laughing, understand. It just isn't enough.

Let's not kid ourselves—much has eroded, even in this so-called "family-oriented" era. The family may be before the public more than ever, but its lifestyle is a long way from the time-honored truths of the Judeo-Christian ethic which formed our nation's roots. The inescapable fact is that we've drifted far from that heritage.

Need some examples of erosion? For starters, how about the divorce epidemic and wholesale departure from lifelong monogamy? As the country-and-western tune laments, "What's forever for?" And how about parental authority? And let's not omit the unpopular philosophy of sacrificing one's greedy goals for the good of one's marriage and family. (When's the last time you met someone who had the audacity to do that?) Or upholding the dignity of motherhood and fatherhood. And how about decreasing the number of folks today who still believe in the distinctive differences between masculinity and femininity? While we're at it, how many people do you know who consider one of life's highest honors to be that of bearing, nurturing, training, and finally releasing children of rock-like character into society?

It's rare these days to meet folks who take the blessing of Genesis 1:28 at face value—a blessing which calls us to be fruitful, multiply, and fill the earth. Most people I meet would question and place conditions on that foundational statement in Scripture. All this brings me back to the fact that what is being portrayed about the family is heavy on fantasy and light on truth. As Malcolm Muggeridge correctly observed, "We human beings have a wonderful faculty for thus snatching fantasy from the jaws of truth."[2]

If we hope to do more than fantasize about family life, we need to sink our teeth into stuff that will stick to our ribs. What good is it if the family is "in" but God's timeless wisdom is "out"? By that, I mean an understanding of the family that goes beyond a list of shallow rules and rigid regulations, a knowledge that supersedes theoretical opinions from psychological jargon. Our greatest need is fresh insight from our ever-relevant Lord, whose Word is still unsurpassed as reliable counsel in any generation. In a day when the family is gaining popularity, resulting in decisions being made that will have lasting effects, scriptural truth is essential for survival.

That, in a nutshell, explains why I have chosen to dedicate my time and attention to another book on the family—one that places proper emphasis on wisdom in family living.

Solomon said it best centuries ago:

> *By wisdom a house is built,*
> *And by understanding it is established;*
> *And by knowledge the rooms are filled*
> *With all precious and pleasant riches*
>
> *(Proverbs 24:3–4).*

If you (and ultimately your family) benefit from these pages, it will not be accidental. It will occur because wisdom, understanding, and knowledge will slowly but surely replace vague opinions, wonderings, and hunches. To put it straight, my desire is that the following pages will intensify your interest in building a strong family . . . a wise family.

But a writer's desire is not a reader's guarantee. No invisible magic wand is hidden between the lines or among the pictures in this book. Truth may be presented; but, unless you apply them with diligence, my words will do little more than arouse a few emotions, then wind up collecting dust on your book shelf along with a half dozen other family books you own. I'm saying this: much will depend on you. Your willingness to accept God's counsel, and your determination to alter your attitudes and actions so that they begin to square with Scripture will have everything to do with the effect of this book on your life. I will do everything in my power to keep this literary journey interesting and enjoyable, but I cannot promise you a quick 'n' easy trip. Wisdom doesn't work like that. But the good news is this: The effort you exert to put the principles into action will lead to some very rewarding results, both in your life and in your home. Count on it!

Before we begin, I must pause and express sincere feelings of gratitude. First, my thanks to Larry Libby, who gave me insightful editorial assistance. Second, another round of applause is due my long-time secretary, Helen Peters, who began typing my books and researching my references many years ago. She's done them all—this one included—with incredible speed, accuracy, and diligence. Third and finally, I am again thankful to Cynthia, my wife. She has not only accepted the reality that I am hopelessly addicted to pen and paper, she has affirmed it! It's a shame all authors are not as encouraged as I am! Her interest in my writing motivates me like nothing else on earth. Furthermore, she holds my feet to the fire when it comes to putting into action what I write about the family. Such accountability breeds openness and honesty, two traits that make for a happy home.

And now let's get under way. Our families need to be strong . . . and time is of the essence.

Chuck Swindoll
Fullerton, California

PART ONE

LAYING

THE

FOUNDATION

1

An Endangered Species?

Despite the pessimistic headlines announcing that the strong family in America is an endangered species, I refuse to sigh and give up hope. Who says "endangered" means *doomed?* If we're ingenious enough to preserve the bison, whooping crane, and humpbacked whale, I'm convinced we can preserve the family. The "want to" is certainly there with a lot of us.

My research confirms two findings: (1) a fulfilling and happy family is as strong today as it was fifty years ago—maybe even stronger, and (2) effective family life does not just happen; it's the result of deliberate intention, determination, and practice. In fact, there are many strong, happy families all over the country, but unfortunately they are not the ones who make front-page news. Furthermore, not much research is done on strong, happy families. Most professional authorities focus their attention on families that are fractured by internal struggles.

Professor Nick Stinnett is an exception. Dr. Stinnett, chairman of the Department of Human Development and the

Family at the University of Nebraska at Lincoln, launched a fascinating "family strengths research project" a number of years ago. His study included strong black families as well as white, strong ethnic families, and strong single-parent families. He and his research team observed and interviewed strong families in South America, Switzerland, Austria, Germany, South Africa, and the United States. There was only one criterion for being included in the sample of strong families: the families had to rate themselves very high in marriage happiness and in their satisfaction in parent-child relationships. I should also point out that the project was not limited to Christian families.

What Makes a Family Strong?

All sorts of questions were asked of these families, such as, "How do you deal with conflict?" and, "Do you experience power struggles?" and, "How do you communicate?" The researchers asked questions that provided information about and insight into the entire range of human relationship patterns within each family. The goal? Very simply, to discover what makes families strong.

Dr. Stinnett writes of his findings:

All together, we studied 3,000 families and collected a lot of information.

But when we analyzed it all, we found six main qualities in strong families.

Strong families:

- **are committed to the family,**
- **spend time together,**
- **have good family communication,**
- **express appreciation to each other,**
- **have a spiritual commitment,**
- **and are able to solve problems in a crisis.**[3]

Look back over that list. There is enough there to fill the rest of the pages of my book! When I first came across this information, I used it not only as the basis for a miniseries of pulpit messages on the family, I also posted it in my home. It became the topic of numerous conversations among the Swindoll tribe. I would suggest you try the same experiment with your family.

Where Does Domestic Strength Begin?

To get to the heart of the issue, we need to blow the dust off the most reliable and ancient record on the subject of the family. It is not the result of some professor's research, interesting and helpful as that may be. It is the Genesis account. In some of the earliest lines of the Bible, the family is brought into clear focus.

Immediately after the Lord God created the first man and woman, He blessed them (placed His favor upon them), and then He spoke to them. In fact, the first command in all the Scriptures appears in this section. Interestingly, it had to do with the family:

> *Be fruitful and multiply, and fill the earth . . .*
>
> *(Genesis 1:28)*

It doesn't take a degree from Harvard to realize how far we've drifted from that original game plan. Our generation has rewritten the whole idea of married couples being fruitful and multiplying. We now have the OINK family—"One Income, No Kids." And if you really want to be in style, you're a DINK family—"Double Income, No Kids." The income can flex, no problem. But, for sure, bail out on the idea of having kids if you hope to make it to the top in a hurry. That may make social or economic sense, but the theology of it stinks!

In the final verses of Genesis 2, the zoom lens of Scripture again picks up the subject of the family as God planned it.

> *For this cause a man shall leave his father and his mother,*
> *and shall cleave to his wife; and they shall become one*

flesh. And the man and his wife were both naked and were not ashamed (24–25).

Look closely. Woven into the fabric of those two sentences are four timeless one-word principles that give a marriage (as well as a family) its strength.

- **Severance: "leave his father and . . . mother."**
- **Permanence: "cleave to his wife."**
- **Unity: "they shall become one flesh."**
- **Intimacy: "both naked and were not ashamed."**

From earliest time, God has cared so much about the family that He provided the foundational guidelines that would make it solid and keep it strong. Stop and think. Before He said much about work or anything at all about civil government, the church, the school, the law, the races, or maintaining our health, God spelled out the primary principles of domestic health and happiness. To Him, that deserved top priority. And He didn't forget about it once He set everything in motion.

How Can Domestic Strength Be Sustained?

Many years later, long after He had given birth to a new nation of people (the Hebrews) who would bear His name in a unique way, He reminded them of the importance of maintaining strong families. I'm thinking of that brief period of time just before the Hebrews invaded Canaan to take up residence in the Promised Land. The events are recorded in the sixth chapter of Deuteronomy.

It is really a family scene. Husbands, wives, and children by the tens of thousands are on the edge of enemy territory. Before these families can occupy Canaan, they must invade and conquer. Once that is accomplished, they can settle down and begin living normal lives. It is *that* fact which most concerns the Lord. Once they "settle in," if they're not careful, they will become soft, indulged, and indifferent. In order to survive their success, they must sustain family solidarity. How? Moses spells it out in Deuteronomy 6.

He begins with an affirming word to families:

> *Now this is the commandment, the statutes and the judgments which the LORD your God has commanded me to teach you, that you might do them in the land where you are going over to possess it, so that you and your son and your grandson might fear the LORD your God, to keep all His statutes and His commandments, which I command you, all the days of your life, and that your days may be prolonged. O Israel, you should listen and be careful to do it, that it may be well with you and that you may multiply greatly, just as the LORD, the God of your fathers, has promised you, in a land flowing with milk and honey (Deuteronomy 6:1–3).*

Is God still interested in the family? You bet. He wants fathers, sons, and grandsons to live wisely . . . to multiply greatly . . . to enjoy divinely provided prosperity. He still does. With all that in mind, Moses shouts:

> *"Hear, O Israel! The LORD is our God, the LORD is one!" (Deuteronomy 6:4).*

If you are Jewish, those words have a familiar ring to them.

6:4 This verse has been called the *SHEMA* from the Hebrew word translated *Hear.* The statement in this verse is the basic statement of faith in Judaism. The verse means that THE LORD (Yahweh) is totally unique. He alone is God. The Israelites could therefore have a sense of security that was totally impossible for their polytheistic neighbors. The "gods" of the ancient New East rarely were thought of as acting in harmony. Each god was unpredictable and morally capricious. So a pagan worshiper could never be sure that his loyalty to one god would serve to protect him from the capricious wrath of another. The monotheistic doctrine of the Israelites lifted them out of this insecurity since they had to deal with only one God, who dealt with them by a revealed consistent righteous standard.[4]

Once Moses set forth the foundational uniqueness of their faith, based on a monotheistic concept of their Lord, he gave them four ways their families could survive. Remember, they were soon to invade a culture that had no place for the living God of heaven, the Creator Himself. Those four guiding principles, by the way, are as potent today as they were in the days of Moses. We would continue to develop a strong family if we would remind ourselves and our families of these four statements on a regular basis. Open your Bible and circle four words in Deuteronomy 6: *hear* (v. 4), *love* (v. 5), *teach* (v.7), and *fear* (v. 13). They form the basis of the four principles that keep a family strong.

Hear the Truth Continually

Let's look again at the *SHEMA.*

"Hear, O Israel! The Lord *is our God, the* Lord *is one!"*
(Deuteronomy 6:4).

Notice what formed the foundation of the Hebrews' faith. Two primary truths: (1) Jehovah is unique, unlike any and all other deities, and (2) He is unity. One in essence, one in harmony. The ancient Israelis were commanded to hear such truth on a continuing basis. They were to repeat this as a statement of their faith.

Strong families lean hard on certain unshakable facts, and this is a major one. To amplify the credo: "The Lord is our God. We acknowledge His presence, His uniqueness, His place, His right to rule over us. We seek His will, we endeavor to walk in His way."

Cynthia and I have made such statements to our children from their earliest years. When times were hard and our future uncertain, we would repeat words like those above, affirming confidence in our God and our determination to trust in Him. Over and over, we would underscore His reliability.

"The Lord is our God, children. We must trust Him without reservation. There is no one more reliable. His will is perfect.

All that is happening fits beautifully into His wise plan for us."

Families who hear the truth continually don't float and drift aimlessly. They pull together. It is essential for survival in a day like ours.

Love the Lord Fervently

> And you shall love the LORD your God with all your heart and with all your soul and with all your might. And these words, which I am commanding you today, shall be on your heart (Deuteronomy 6:5–6).

Let me suggest you read that again. This time, more slowly. Do you know what stands out in my mind as I meditate on those lines? "All . . . all . . . all. . . ." Such repetition emphasizes *totality*. The parents' love for God is total not partial; unquestionable not casual. There is fervency here. Invincible confidence.

Our love for God must be complete. It is impossible for me to transfer to my child a principle I do not personally embrace, that is, a love for God that permeates all my heart. It is impossible for me to convince my child of the value of honesty, for example, if I am dishonest. Impossible for me to convey to my child the necessity of clean lips if I habitually practice profanity. It is impossible for children to grasp the importance of care and compassion for others if their parents run roughshod over others. Our love for God must be an all-encompassing love, a deep-down dedication. It will be "on your heart," not simply a nice-sounding religious idea washing around in your mind.

I can still remember reading Howard Taylor's moving biography of his father, James Hudson Taylor, early missionary to inland China. Howard's impressions of the importance of God, his earliest convictions, were first formed as he witnessed his dad's devotion. The same with Corrie ten Boom. It was from "Papa ten Boom" she received her first and deepest realizations that God mattered . . . that He was worth her trust. Truth is more permanently transferred from a parent's life than his lips. Modeling the truth far outweighs preaching it to the young.

But there is a place for actual teaching. In fact, the very next principle addresses the importance of verbal communication.

Teach the Young Diligently

And you shall teach them diligently to your sons and shall talk of them when you sit in your house and when you walk by the way and when you lie down and when you rise up. And you shall bind them as a sign on your hand and they shall be as frontals on your forehead. And you shall write them on the doorposts of your house and on your gates (Deuteronomy 6:7–9).

This was not the first time such an exhortation was given to the Hebrews. Earlier, Moses had said:

Only give heed to yourself and keep your soul diligently, lest you forget the things which your eyes have seen, and lest they depart from your heart all the days of your life; but make them known to your sons and your grandsons (Deuteronomy 4:9).

The task of "indoctrinating" children was a responsibility of the home, not of some institution or the combined efforts of a group of professionals. And the teaching was to be deliberate. The root term translated "teach" in the Deuteronomy 6 passage suggests "repeating," telling over and over again as well as modeling a consistent message.

I'm rethinking a lot of things these days about how we teach Christianity. You and I are seeing many Christians who were taught an enormous amount of biblical facts—but later defected. They learned theology, but somehow it lacked authenticity. Perhaps the thing that was omitted was the diligence . . . "you shall teach them diligently to your sons."

The word *diligently* in English is actually an adverb, but in Hebrew the root term is a verb that means "to sharpen." So if read literally, the statement would be ". . . and you shall sharpen your sons." The New International Version doesn't miss it far when it renders the verse, "You shall impress them on your children." The term appears in a particular stem in the Hebrew language that adds intensity to the verb. "You shall *intensely* sharpen your sons." It's a strong command. So it isn't a passive action; it is a very aggressive and assertive involvement in the educational process . . . all within a family setting.

God's desire is that there be a conscious, consistent, transfer of God's truth from the older to the younger in the family. If there is an unconscious mistake Christian parents make, it is thinking that our children automatically capture our zeal for Christ. Quite the contrary; the only thing automatic is that our children automatically get turned off to spiritual things. Never forget, living in enemy territory can easily take its toll. If there is going to be a capturing of the heart for God and the cultivation of inner zeal, there needs to be the process described here of an authentic training session. Look at how it happens:

> *Sharpen your sons when you talk of them, as you sit in your house, when you walk by the way, when you lie down and when you rise up (Deuteronomy 6:7).*

The Hebrews had a term for making a formal proclamation, as in delivering a lecture. It is not used here. There's also a term for just talking. That's the one used here. That is extremely significant! We are to talk of spiritual things just as we would talk about anything else in our home. You talk together about how the Dodgers played last night. No big deal, you just talk about that. You talk about what you're going to do next week. You don't lecture on it. You don't make a big announcement, you simply talk about it. You talk about the pressure you felt today from so-and-so. You talk about what you're going to have for supper. You may talk about what you plan to watch on television that evening. You don't hold classes on it, you merely talk about it. There is an easy-going, natural flow of conversation. That's the word used here. That is what will make your Christianity authentic. It isn't a Sunday lifestyle! It is a Monday, Tuesday, Wednesday, Thursday, Friday, Saturday, Sunday, Monday, Tuesday, and on and on in the cycle-of-living lifestyle. So much so, that Christ fits naturally into the regular conversation and lifestyle of the home.

You know what's helped us in the Swindoll home? To think of where we live as a training place, not a showplace. The home is a laboratory where experiments are tried out. It is a place where life makes up its mind. The home is a place where a child is free to think, to talk, to try out ideas. In a scene like that, God fits very comfortably into the entire conversation. And at any place where His name is inserted, it fits. That's authentic. It's a nonstructured style.

> ... and you ... shall talk of them when you sit in your house and when you walk by the way and when you lie down and when you rise up (v. 7).

Isn't that comfortable? Ready for a shocker? It's *supposed* to be comfortable! Christianity is designed for everyday living. Society has made it a "Sunday religion." But true-to-life Christianity is designed for Tuesday afternoon just as beautifully as Saturday morning or Sunday evening. You don't put on some special garb. You don't have to wear some kind of hat. You don't have to put on a collar. You don't have to wear a coat. Thank goodness, you don't have to dress up for it. It fits after a meal as well as before bedtime. That's what makes the "teaching" in the home so authentic.

Sometimes it hurts. I can still remember a particularly irritating morning a few years back. No need to describe the details, it just happened. I got a little convicted about it later in the day while my youngest son and I were out doing a little target practice together. It seemed a great moment for us to relax and enjoy a few honest moments together. So I said, "Chuck, I was a little impatient this morning."

"Uh huh," he grunted, as he sited in on his next shot. He squeezed another round off and took aim again.

I said, "Uh . . . I realize I was a little hard to be around."

"Uh huh," he responded again, unfortunately affirming what I was saying at the time.

"I . . . I want you to know that, uh . . . I feel badly about it,"
I continued. "But you know, Son, there are times that I'm like
that."

He paused. "Yes, yes, there are, Dad. There are times that
you're like that."

And then the line that just fractured me.

"You know, Dad," he added, "God uses you to teach all of
us patience in our family!"

Ouch!

I'm certainly not the first to point out that the teaching is
to permeate every sphere of life (note in verses 7–9: "when . . .
when . . . when . . . when . . ."). Whether resting or working,
formally instructing or casually relating, fishing, hunting, driving, or watching television, truth is to be deposited into the
lives of our young.

Will it pay off? Let's let Solomon, the wise, answer that for us:

> *My son, observe the commandment of your father, and do
> not forsake the teaching of your mother; bind them continu-
> ally on your heart; tie them around your neck. When you
> walk about, they will guide you; when you sleep, they will
> watch over you; and when you awake, they will talk to you.
> For the commandment is a lamp, and the teaching is light;
> and reproofs for discipline are the way of life (Proverbs
> 6:20–23).*

God promises that our growing children will later be able
to use what they learn. They will be guided when they walk . . .
protected when they sleep . . . encouraged when they awaken.
Such are the dividends of parental investments.

Why be so consistent? What's the big deal? We find an
extremely important answer back in Deuteronomy 6.

> *So the LORD commanded us to observe all these statutes, to
> fear the LORD our God for our good always and for our sur-
> vival . . . (v. 24).*

I love the way that reads: *"for our good always and for our
survival."* God never asks something of parents that will bring

harm to the home. And it won't weaken the child, it will help that boy or girl ultimately survive. Strong families survive from generation to generation because diligence is applied to the teaching process. And remember, the teaching weaves very naturally and comfortably into the fabric of everyday life. True religion is not something to be forced into or tacked onto life. It should flow through it.

I like the way Charlie Shedd described it in one of his original promises, to his tiny son, Peter:

> I hope that I will be able to make religion natural to you. It is natural. In fact, I think this relationship with God is the only thing that is one hundred percent natural. We will pray together until it is easy for you to put your arms on the window sill of heaven and look into the face of God.
>
> Before I put you back in your crib, I want to tell you something Philip said.
>
> We had been out in the country for a ride. It was evening and we ran out of gas. We were walking along after we had been to the farm house, and I was carrying a can of gas. Philip was only four. He was playing along, throwing rocks at the telephone poles, picking flowers, and then, all of a sudden it got dark. Sometimes night comes all at once in the country. Philip came over, put his little hand in mine and said, "Take my hand, Daddy. I might get lost."
>
> Peter, there is a hand reaching to you from the heart of the universe. If you will lay your hand in the hand of God and walk with Him, you will never ever get lost.[5]

We have pondered three principles thus far: (1) hear the truth continually, (2) love the Lord fervently, (3) teach the young diligently. Let's consider one more:

Fear the Lord Greatly

> *Then it shall come about when the LORD your God brings you into the land which He swore to your fathers, Abraham, Isaac and Jacob, to give you, great and splendid cities which you did not build, and houses full of all good things which you did not fill, and hewn cisterns which you did not dig, vineyards and olive trees which you did not plant, and you*

shall eat and be satisfied, then watch yourself, lest you for-
get the LORD who brought you from the land of Egypt, out of
the house of slavery. You shall fear only the LORD your God;
and you shall worship Him, and swear by His name. You
shall not follow other gods, any of the gods of the peoples
who surround you, for the LORD your God in the midst of
you is a jealous God . . ." (Deuteronomy 6:10–15).

Again, I remind you that God is looking out for His own.
He's got our good at heart. After giving, giving, giving so many
things, He warns us about forgetting Him. How easy, when
blessed, to adopt a presumptuous, arrogant spirit. Indulgence
begins an erosion within that leads to indifference, which ultimately results in independence. "Who needs God any longer?"
It is an attitude often found among the self-sufficient. The
secret of keeping that from happening? "You shall fear only the
Lord your God and you shall worship Him."

When family members maintain a sincere fear of God,
something wonderful occurs within the ranks. Self-made pride
and presumption continue to decrease as a fear of God increases. Don't misunderstand. By "fear of God" I do not mean fright
. . . feeling uneasy and afraid in His presence. The right kind of
fear is reverence for His holy name, a wholesome respect for
His sovereign will, holding Him in highest regard. It is the ever
present realization that God is the Almighty, Holy God. It is
remembering (in today's terms) that He doesn't mess around.
He means what He says. We respect Him too much to disregard
His ways or disobey His will.

What calm assurance, what quiet confidence this gives a
family! And the longer this attitude persists, the more the Lord
honors it by lengthening the shadows of stability. It is as if He
wraps an invisible shield of protection around your family.
Perhaps that is what He meant when He gave the Hebrews this
command:

You shall not follow other gods, any of the gods of the peo-
ples who surround you (Deuteronomy 6:14).

In a very real sense we, too, are surrounded by gods. They may not be as obvious as wood, stone, or metal, but they are there, nonetheless. Let's not assume that simply because the surrounding gods are invisible, they are inconsequential.

To name a few, families today must face the gods of materialism, money, and meism . . . gods of sensuality, immorality, and hedonism. And we must not forget the gods of fame, celebrity, popularity, and power. The gods of mind-bending drugs and alcohol are always there as well . . . to say nothing of the gods of intellectualism, humanism, false philosophies, and man-made religions.

How dangerous . . . *enemies all!*

Strong families remain that way because they are always aware that "the name of the LORD is a strong tower; the righteous runs into it and is safe" (Proverbs 18:10).

We're Back to Wisdom

There is no school that families can attend and earn a degree in family strength. It doesn't work like that. Families become strong, not because they have gone to a school and learned the rules, but because parents pay the price to be different . . . because they inculcate biblical truth in everyday life, conducting their relationships in the realm of wisdom, understanding, and knowledge.

Remember that key scripture? It brings us back to the basic ingredients:

> *By wisdom a house is built, and by understanding it is established; and by knowledge the rooms are filled with all precious and pleasant riches (Proverbs 24:3–4).*

To have a place that is built, established, and filled with such solid materials as these doesn't just happen. It's the result of domestic determination and commitment, both of which are rare.

No wonder the strong family is an endangered species. Frankly, it always will be.

2

Masculine Model of Leadership

Changes occur when we get involved, when we face the music.

My interest is not in writing a few, nice, safe chapters on family life, hoping everyone will nod, smile sweetly, dream a little, then live happily ever after. Times like ours call for honest admissions, accurate evaluations, and tough decisions. That means we cannot simply skate along, enjoying the scenery. We must get beneath the veneer of fantasy and dreams if we hope to build a strong family.

The role of the parent is a logical place to begin when talking about how to strengthen the family. To be even more specific, the role of the father. When I think of that role, I envision the masculine model who gives the home the leadership and security it must have in order to survive. Immediately, I'm bothered by a trend I see occurring: preoccupation and passivity among fathers. It is equally disturbing to observe an increasing number of men whose masculinity seems unimportant to them.

A Vanishing Masculinity

Remember when men were men? Remember when you could tell by looking? Remember when men knew who they were, liked how they were, and didn't want to be anything but what they were? Remember when it was the men who boxed and wrestled and bragged about how much they could bench press? Remember when it was the women who wore the makeup, the earrings, and the bikinis? Remember when it was the men who initiated the contact and took the lead in a relationship, made lifelong commitments, treated a woman like a lady, and modeled a masculinity that displayed security and stability?

I'm not thinking about the half-crazed Rambo types who suffer from macho mania . . . those who look for a fight, walk with a swagger, never apologize, and give that "make my day" stare. Those guys may be able to destroy half of North Vietnam single-handedly, but they make terrible neighbors, horrible business partners, and brutal husbands and dads. Being a man is not the same as living like a panther ready to pounce.

Neither do I have in mind the Archie Bunker-type loud-mouth who slouches in his chair, barks out orders, and thinks the world gravitates around him. Since when do dogmatism, prejudice, and selfishness mean masculinity? This type of fellow lives in a fantasy world, only imagining he's running the show. In actuality, he's a frightened child inside a man's body, the object of sarcastic ridicule among friends and family alike.

True manhood calls for discipline of character, strong determination to set a course of action, and courage to stay at a task. But brutality? Vulgarity? Lack of courtesy? Hardly. Authentic men aren't afraid to show affection, release their feelings, hug their children, cry when they're sad, admit it when they're wrong, and ask for help when they need it. Vulnerability fits beautifully into mature manhood. So does integrity.

I am concerned about a vanishing masculinity that was once in abundance. I mean honest-to-goodness *men* who are distinctly that—discerning, decisive, strong-hearted men who know where they are going and are confident enough in themselves (and their God) to get there. They aren't afraid to take the lead, to stand tall and firm in their principles even when the going gets rough.

Such qualities not only inspire the respect of women, they engender healthy admiration among younger men and boys who hunger for heroes. We need fewer spineless wimps who've never disentangled themselves from mama's apron strings, and more clear-thinking, hardworking, straight-talking men who, while tender, thoughtful, and loving, don't feel the need to ask permission for taking charge. I'm convinced that most single ladies would love to have men like that to spend time with . . . and most wives long to have men like that to share life with. Children especially like having dads like that.

Over the last three decades there has been an assault on masculinity. The results are well represented in the arts, the media, the world of fashion, and among those who have become our youths' heroes. There are exceptions, I realize, but therein lies the problem . . . they are *exceptions*. Androgynous individuals now prance to and fro on rock-concert stages across America. Poster-size portraits of male celebrities paper the walls in thousands of boys' bedrooms. Many of the performers no longer even pretend to be masculine. Sex roles are deliberately being blended. Female impersonations are the hot ticket in show places all around the world, performing before mainly male audiences.

A number of years ago, *People* magazine included a dialogue between a psychologist and his seven-year-old nephew. The professional asked the boy, "Is Michael Jackson a boy or a girl?" The boy thought for a moment, then answered, "Both." If you don't think it's now cool to wrap both sexes into one package, you've not checked out the stores that handle the chic designer labels. We're talking "Who's What?"

This reminds me of a book I read about on being a man.[6] The author, Weldon Hardenbrook, referred to a line of women's lingerie released by Calvin Klein. The lingerie is modeled after men's undershirts and jockey shorts. The ladies' undies are not slinky satin or frilly nylon, but 100 percent cotton, available in six varieties of tops, eight types of bottoms, in twenty-five colors. And get this: the briefs are cut high on the leg, but the string bikini resembles a jockstrap and the boxer shorts actually have a fly. Was there any question whether or not it would sell? Are you kidding? That line of Klein's underwear line was expected to gross $70 million in its first fourteen months. Unisex used to be limited to a few kinky beauty salons and off-the-wall jewelry stores—now it's as close to us as undergarments. Don't kid yourself, gender blending is not a passing fad on society's bizarre edge. It is here, and it is neither subtle nor silent.

Author Alvin Toffler saw all this happening years ago in his book, *The Third Wave,* where he announced:

> . . . the role system that held industrial civilization together is in crisis. This we see most dramatically in the struggle to redefine sex roles. In the women's movement, in the demands for the legalization of homosexuality, in the spread of unisex fashions, we see a continual blurring of traditional expectations for the sexes.[7]

Toffler is on target but too soft.

The separate distinction of male and female is not merely a "traditional expectation," it's a biblical precept ("male and female He created them," Genesis 1:27b). And it isn't simply a "role system that held industrial civilization together." It is a foundational block upon which any healthy civilization rests. When the roles get sufficiently blurred, confusion and chaos replace decency and order. When effeminate men begin to flood the landscape, God's longsuffering reaches the length of its tether, ushering in the severest judgment imaginable . . . a la Sodom and Gomorrah. Romans 1:24–27 is still in the Book, isn't it? Worst of all, because more and more men care less about being men, the family is thrown into confusion. Leadership is shifted to the wife and mother, and the children understandably reverse the roles, tragically perpetuating the unnatural trend.

A Portrait Worth Examination

Tucked away in Paul's first New Testament letter, we find one of those biblical pen portraits no one could improve. Even though the original purpose of the writer was not to describe the role of a father in the family, I think there is room for us to apply his words along those lines.

Read the following paragraph slowly and deliberately. I want to use it as the basis of some suggestions on how we men can become the kind of dads that wives appreciate and children admire.

> *But we proved to be gentle among you, as a nursing mother tenderly cares for her own children. Having thus a fond affection for you, we were well-pleased to impart to you not only the gospel of God but also our own lives, because you had become very dear to us. For you recall, brethren, our labor and hardship, how working night and day so as not to be a burden to any of you, we proclaimed to you the gospel of God. You are witnesses, and so is God, how devoutly and uprightly and blamelessly we behaved toward you believers; just as you know how we were exhorting and encouraging and imploring each one of you as a father would his own children, so that you may walk in a manner worthy of the God who calls you into His own kingdom and glory (1 Thessalonians 2:7–12).*

I don't know if you observed a rather bold contrast at the beginning and end of those verses. Paul, the writer, initially admits he was gentle "as a nursing *mother*," then later he writes that he exhorted, encouraged, and implored them "as a *father*." When I first saw that contrast, it occurred to me there might very well be some hints for the home in a context that mentions both mother and father. In fact, I find no less than five wonderful traits in this portrait of a father in the home.

A Fond Affection

"Having thus a fond affection for you . . ." (v. 8).

Paul had at his fingertips a half dozen or more Greek terms of affection he could have used that were familiar to the people in that day. He picked one, however that is found nowhere else in all the New Testament. Gerhard Kittel, in his massive, nine-volume set on New Testament words, tells us that the term translated *affection* means "to feel oneself drawn to something or someone."[8] There is a strong intensity implied in the term. Zahn, a Greek scholar of German descent, says it is a term of endearment taken from the nursery, one that is both masculine and tender. It is the picture of a father who holds and treats a child tenderly, feeling himself affectionately drawn to that little one.

As I write these words, I remember (as many of you who are dads also remember) the first time I held our first child in my arms. Ours happened to be a curly-haired little boy whom we named Curtis. That was way back in September of 1961. I remember carefully holding that little fella, afraid I would break him—or drop him. I had this incredible fear he would somehow fall out of my arms. I noticed right away he couldn't hold his head up. It kept falling. I said stuff like, "Hold your head up, Curt!" and, "Straighten up, boy!" It didn't help a bit. You see, I had never held a baby that tiny and fragile before. It's amazing how mothers have a built-in knack for knowing how to do all the right things. Even though Cynthia had never had her own baby before Curt, she seemed to know what to do. Moms know, but dads don't! And so what do we do? We hold them very carefully, very tenderly . . . at least at first. Unfortunately, much of our tender affection fades rapidly if we're not careful.

As the years pass, work increases, pressures mount, and the demands and deadlines grapple for more of our time and energy. In the meantime our child grows—no longer little and able to be held in our arms. Before we know it he's about our height or even taller. In fact, we find our arms are no longer able to reach around his broad shoulders.

But don't kid yourself. That "fond affection" is still needed! And I would add, it is especially needed from dad. I don't mean that we simply think it, but that we *demonstrate* it. That is especially true as our children spread their wings and begin to break close ties with their parents. Such attempts at independence require a great deal of wisdom on the parents' part.

I am reminded of the prodigal son. It's the story of a boy who reaches the age when he says, "I'm going to make it on my own. Give me what I've got coming, Dad, because I'm leaving." Off he goes. Perhaps it was a rather stormy, rapid departure. The young man hits the streets and lives there for an undetermined period of time. While he's away there is no contact with home. The boy doesn't write. He doesn't attempt to get in touch. Who knows how long he stayed away. As times got hard the boy sank lower and lower. He wound up humiliated, bankrupt, and depressed. Finally, at the very bottom, he comes to his senses and says to himself:

> *How many of my father's hired men have more than enough bread, but I am dying here with hunger! I will get up and go to my father . . . (Luke 15:17–18).*

By the way, he never once thought his father would not let him return home. Interesting, isn't it? Our kids know us. They can usually predict our response.

> *I will get up and go to my father, and will say to him, "Father, I have sinned against heaven, and in your sight; I am no longer worthy to be called your son; make me as one of your hired men" (vv. 18–19).*

Sounds to me like he is rehearsing his speech. He is now living with the scars of all those terrible memories. Awash in feelings of guilt, he tries to imagine stumbling back to the front door of his home, facing a dad who is liable to be ashamed of him. So he plans to say with sincerity, "I'm not worthy to be called your son." He expects to encounter the wrath of Khan. But that's not what he finds back home. The boy's return is one of the most moving scenes imaginable! I never tell this story without having to fight back the tears.

And he got up and came to his father. But while he was still a long way off, his father saw him, and felt compassion for him, and ran and embraced him, and kissed him (v. 20).

Wow! That's what I call demonstrating tender affection. No hesitation. No inquisition. No probation. Only compassion. In fact (if you read the rest of the story), there was a celebration! We'll examine the story in greater detail in chapter 10.

To those of us who bear the name "Dad," I cannot impress upon you enough how imperative it is that we show our affection. We can do that in two ways. First, we affirm who our child is; and second, we appreciate what our child does. This twofold assurance, however, must be given in more than words. Affection—the nonverbal communication of closeness, touching, and even kissing—is among the most important experiences we share with one another.

Many a young woman who opts for immoral sexual relationships does so because she can scarcely remember a time when her father so much as touched her. Unaffectionate dads, without ever wishing to do so, can trigger a daughter's promiscuity. All this leads me to write with a great deal of passion, dads . . . *don't hold back your affection!* Demonstrate your feelings of love and acceptance to both sons and daughters, and don't stop once they reach adolescence. They long for your affirmation and appreciation. They will love you for it. More importantly, they will emulate your example when God gives them their own family.

Between 1961 and 1970, God gave Cynthia and me four children. The one ingredient she and I have discovered that has held us close together has been the open expression of our affection for one another. Interestingly, what we demonstrated to them, they began to demonstrate to one another. The investment of "fond affection" throughout their growing-up years has resulted in wonderful dividends. It is a great delight to see our married kids now carrying on the same affectionate tradition with their little ones.

A *Transparent Life*

Next, we read of the value of giving ourselves—our whole lives.

> *Having thus a fond affection for you, we were well-pleased to impart to you not only the gospel of God but also our own lives, because you had become very dear to us (1 Thessalonians 2:8).*

Talk about being transparent! Look at the words, my fellow father. "Not only the gospel, but our own lives."

Question: Isn't the gospel important? *Absolutely.* Well then, when it comes to the Christian family, isn't the gospel *alone* enough? *Absolutely not!* To hear the gospel is a necessity for children. If they are to come to know the Savior whom you love, Dad, they need to have you tell them of Him. I have no greater joy than the memory that our four children heard early in their lives the gospel concerning Jesus Christ from their dad's lips. They heard that God loved them through His Son and sent the Savior for them. And that He died for them, paying the penalty for their sins. And if, as a child, they would simply trust themselves to the Savior, by faith in His death and resurrection, they would be given the gift of eternal life.

They heard . . . and each one responded. That is imparting the gospel. How terribly important to impart the gospel! But when it comes to rearing those children, how valuable it is to impart our own lives to them as well. The term *impart* carries with it the idea of making a contribution, sharing fully.

What would that include? I can think of several things that might be "imparted." Our children want to learn a proper scale of values from us. They also want to discover how to make good decisions. It intrigues them to think we are able to stand alone and unintimidated. They want to know the techniques of such security (not just that you do it, but *how* you do it). They want to know how to handle their finances. They also need your approval . . . the assurance that you value them. I would also include a well-exercised sense of humor, a positive, contagious attitude toward life. Few memories are more pleasant than a father who laughed and had fun with his family. And how about including freedom from worry and stress? Or when stress comes, admitting your struggle with it. They'll understand. In fact, you'll be amazed. Your stock will go up several points in their minds whenever they see you under stress and observe your willingness to talk about it. Our children learn from our failures as well as from our successes. This is all part of living a transparent life.

Few experiences are more endearing than having one of your children lean over and tell you he loves you . . . that he understands and cares. Children find great security in finding us open and vulnerable. My kids, hopefully, are learning through a transparent life that their dad has needs. Sometimes my need is to be forgiven—so I must be willing to admit failure and wrong. Then and only then do I become *real!* Do not fear that transparency will cause a child to lose respect for you.

Several years ago an understandably proud father slipped into my study. His daughter had written a letter that had won a blue ribbon prize at school. She had written a paper on her dad. Among other things, she wrote:

> My dad has not always been "Pop" to us. We, my brothers and sister, as well as Mom, called him "Daddy" when we were young. He was able to make even folding clothes on Saturday fun with tickle fights amidst freshly washed garments strewn all over the living room floor. He would roll and pretend at vulnerability on the carpet and grab each tiny, groping hand that attempted to tweak his ribs. We seldom won, of course. Daddy could mercilessly tickle the toes off a dead giant, not to mention take on four lively kids.
>
> And, yes, there were serious times as well. We knew of them, too. He could spank the tears out of any of us, not

because the physical pain was so incredible, but because it hurt us to think that we had brought him pain by having earned that spanking.

Looking back, I can see that my parents, by joint effort, have done an exceptionally good job raising us. High moral values, spiritual priorities, academic excellence—all these have been held out to us as important. My pop has instilled in us kids a sense of trust. He's been available, especially in emergencies. He has done what he thinks best for us, even when we might not agree. My dad has a corner on the upper echelons of fatherhood.

Wow! There is no question in my mind that her dad is imparting his life, not just the gospel.

A fond affection . . . a transparent life, two qualities a family needs in a dad. There is a third, according to this biblical passage.

An Unselfish Diligence

Hardworking men will especially appreciate this verse:

For you recall, brethren, our labor and hardship, how working night and day so as not to be a burden to any of you, we proclaimed to you the gospel of God (v. 9).

Focus your attention on eleven words: "working night and day so as not to be a burden. . . ." It's an obvious picture of hard work, responsible diligence.

Many of you who read this page have no better memory (perhaps for some, no other memory!) of your father than that he was a hard worker. But before you poo-poo that mental image, pause long enough to appreciate it in contrast to an irresponsible, indolent father. Those of us fortunate enough to have had a dad who was a diligent model of hard work have much for which to be grateful. Dads sometimes get the blast of preachers and authors who decry all that time at work. While it can certainly be taken to an unwholesome extreme, many a family has a hardworking dad to thank for their survival.

And so I say to you men who are models of diligence in your work, stay at the task . . . but don't quit there. Help your child discover what it means to be diligent and devoted and dedicated to a job. Help him know what motivates you. Help her know what spurs you on to do a quality piece of work and to get the job done. There are numerous lessons to be learned from hard work. Happy is the family who has a model of diligence in the man of the home. And *happier* is the family when dad keeps the right perspective on his diligence.

When the Chaplain of the Senate, Richard Halverson, wrote his book *Perspective,* he dedicated it "to faithful Christian laymen who with silent heroism under relentless secular pressure fight the economic battle as stewards of the living God . . ." I join Dr. Halverson with a hearty round of applause.[9]

Hats off to you guys! And to all of you with fathers who have distinguished themselves as men of diligence and commitment, I urge you to say, "Thank you. Thanks for the years you invested that we might have a few things. Maybe you didn't give us all of yourself, and maybe we don't know you as well as we would like, but how greatly we've benefited from your work. You have taught us to appreciate what it means to be responsible. We love you, Dad!"

It is easy to let things you buy for your family take the place of giving yourself. In our affluent era, how easy to provide too much too soon! Maybe a simple principle I learned will help you, too. Your child will not fully appreciate something unless he knows he deserves it. He won't assess its value and have fun with something if it is just dumped on him. So help your child work hard, too. There are times you would be wise to restrain yourself . . . to keep your hands off and allow the child to work things through on his own.

A little fella was sitting at the kitchen table, trying to draw a pony. (If you've ever tried to draw a pony, you know how difficult it is, especially if you're not an artist.) To make matters worse, his dad, standing near, was blessed with artistic skill. He found himself biting his lip as he watched his son struggle to make the legs look like legs, to put the ears in just the right places, and make it all look proportionate. The kid just about wore the eraser down to zip as he reworked his drawing. Finally, the father could restrain himself no longer. In a moment of impatience, he grabbed the paper, flipped it over, and drew a beautiful young colt, running at full gallop. He included some shading, even added a few leafy trees in the background, then pushed the paper across the table and said, "Here, Son, here's your pony."

The boy looked down, frowned, and said rather dejectedly, "But, Daddy, . . . I wanted a pony *I* drew."

For all the right reasons, diligent dads can lavish upon their children so many things that the child becomes indulged and, ultimately, irresponsible. We need to work at keeping the balance.

There is yet another quality worth our consideration.

A Spiritual Authenticity

> *For you recall, brethren, our labor and hardship, how working night and day so as not to be a burden to any of you, we proclaimed to you the gospel of God. You are witnesses, and so is God, how devoutly and uprightly and blamelessly we behaved toward you believers (vv. 9–10).*

Pay close attention to the one side, "we proclaimed," followed by the other side, "we behaved." Like a coin, a life needs both sides before it is considered authentic. When it comes to being a father, few things are more significant than authenticity.

As difficult as it is to write the words that follow, I must. How rare are those families where the father is truly the spiritual leader! Usually, it's the mother. Isn't it about time we changed that, men? It is refreshing when the dad is the one who sets the pace, who takes the lead, who, more than anyone in the family, "hungers and thirsts after righteousness." I'm not thinking about big talk and little walk, not that . . . but rather a life that is lived in beautiful balance, where Christ is truly living out His life in the man of the house . . . where the wife and the children learn from the man's example what it means to truly love God.

Cynthia and I are very close friends with a family who live in another state. There are four girls in that family, all very close in age and relationships. They attended the same high school, even the same university. All four are now happily married. What stands out in all four young women's minds is the authentic model of true Christianity they witnessed in their dad. No question, if you asked any one of them, each would say their father set the pace, spiritually, in their home.

To give you an idea of his leadership, I want to quote from a letter he wrote them during their college years.

Dear girls of mine:

I'm enclosing this article I've read. It is one of the finest I have seen with regard to pinpointing the necessity for proper family relationships. I am hopeful that it will be worth your time to not only read it but also study and keep it for future use.

Now listen to his counsel. Notice how obviously yet graciously he takes the leadership:

The men you girls marry need to fit into the mold of the husband as outlined in this article. I don't know of the author's spiritual understanding, but he is using biblical principles in describing the family relationships.

Now, your heart can play tricks on you with regard to looking for a husband. There is so much romanticism beamed at you from every direction, it is easy to fall prey to the secular version of the husband and happiness. I am confident that each of you girls will allow the Lord to choose your husband. He will pick a man who fulfills the scriptural mandates for the head of the house.

I love each of you.
Daddy

That's what I'd call being spiritually authentic. Isn't it amazing, men? We watch our daughters grow, begin to date, move closer and closer to making life's second most significant decision—marriage—and we virtually take hands off the whole thing. It is our tendency to back away and leave most (if not all) of the counsel up to the wife . . . when, in fact, the girl is marrying one like us—a man. And because she doesn't quite know how to ask for our input, she waits for us to take the initiative. She longs to have that behavior that is marked by devoutness and uprightness of heart. It is so easy to let the eternal slip by unnoticed, isn't it? We can do the same with our sons. I thought of that when I read these lines from a modern translation of *Augustine's Confessions,* as he speaks of his own father:

> No one had anything but praise for my father who, despite his slender resources, was ready to provide his son with all that was needed to enable him to travel so far for the purpose of study. Many of our townsmen, far richer than my father, went to no such trouble for their children's sake. Yet this same father of mine took no trouble at all to see how I was growing in your sight or whether I was chaste or not. He cared only that I should have a fertile tongue, leaving my heart to bear none of your fruits, my God, though you are the only Master, true and good, of its husbandry.[10]

A Positive Influence

> *Just as you know how we were exhorting and encouraging and imploring each one of you as a father would his own children, so that you may walk in a manner worthy of the God who calls you into His own kingdom and glory (vv. 11–12).*

Paul refers to his ministry in Thessalonica as being one of active encouragement, "as a father." Isn't that interesting? When the apostle searched for an example of someone who brought a positive influence, "a father" came to his mind.

Would you think of a father as best fulfilling this role? Does *your* dad come to mind, for example? It has been my observation that fathers in our generation seem to have lost sight of this trait. More often than not, we focus on the negative, the wrong, rather than the positive.

Dan Benson, in his book *The Total Man,* verifies that fact with a rather disturbing statistic. After an extensive survey was taken, it was found that for one positive statement made in the homes that were surveyed, there were ten negatives—ten to one![11]

Let me refer to Charlie Shedd's words again. He is addressing the importance of a positive influence in a home. In another promise to his son, Peter, he writes:

> I promise you that I will never say "No" if I can possibly say "Yes."
>
> We see it often. Babies raised in a positive atmosphere develop much better personalities than those who constantly hear the words "No," "Stop," "Don't."
>
> Let me show you what I mean. This has to do with a dirty old bale of binder twine. When we moved from Nebraska to Oklahoma, we brought it along. I had used it there to tie sacks of feed and miscellaneous items. It cost something like $1.15. So I said, "Now, Philip, you see this binder twine? I want you to leave it alone." But it held a strange fascination for him and he began to use it any time he wanted. I would say, "Don't," "No," and, "You can't!" But all to no avail.
>
> That went on for six or eight months. Then one day I came home, tired. There was the garage, looking like a no-man's land with binder twine across, back and forth, up and down. I had to cut my way through to get the car in. And was I provoked! I ground my teeth as I slashed at that binder twine. Suddenly, when I was halfway through the maze, a light dawned. I asked myself, "Why do you want this binder twine! What if Philip does use it?" So when I went in to supper that night, Philip was there and I began, "Say, about that binder twine!" He hung his head, and mumbled, "Yes, Daddy." Then I said, "Philip, I've changed my mind. You can use that old binder twine any time you want. What's more all those tools out in the garage I've labeled 'No'—you go ahead and use them. I can buy new tools, but I can't buy new boys." There never was a sunrise like that smile. "Thanks, Daddy," he beamed. And guess what, Peter? He hasn't touched that binder twine since![12]

It's amazing, isn't it, how kids are put together. We scream, "Quit!" "Stop!" "Don't!" and they do. Then we finally learn to relax and say, "Go ahead, it's fine, do!" and, lo and behold, they're no longer interested.

Oh, dads, when will we learn? How long will it take? Each day of our lives we make deposits into the memory banks of our children. By remembering that, I find I am more likely to work on the qualities that build a lasting relationship between my children and me. Naturally, there are times when I blow it, and my family must forgive me. But when I focus on the traits I've mentioned in this chapter, I'm motivated to become the dad God wants me to be.

I want to close this chapter by having us step into the time tunnel for a few moments.

Looking back . . . Looking ahead: A Plea

As you look back and stand in the shadow of *your* father, what one word would you use to describe him? As you remember the man, what do you call him? Think back. . . .

> If he's wealthy and prominent, and you stand in awe of him, call him "Father." If he sits in his shirt sleeves and suspenders at a ball game and picnic, call him "Pop." If he wheels the baby carriage and carries bundles meekly, call him "Papa" (with the accent on the first syllable). If he belongs to a literary circle and writes cultured papers, call him "Papa" (with the accent on the last syllable).
>
> If, however, he makes a pal of you when you're good, and is too wise to let you pull the wool over his loving eyes when you're not; if, moreover, you're quite sure no other fellow you know has quite so fine a father, you may call him "Dad."[13]

Now it's your turn. What do you call yours! Or if he's gone on to glory, what did you call him? A lot of people I know would answer without hesitation, "Absent." Much as I would prefer to soften the blows or speak in defense of all dads, there's a growing number of folks who refuse to be ignored any longer. They miss their dad! They don't want substitutes: things to play with, a car for graduation, their own room, money for tuition, or a Hawaiian honeymoon. No, not nearly as much as they wanted the presence and influence of a dad. Not all day, you understand (they're realistic enough to realize that can't be), but time with him . . . to talk to, listen to, laugh with, mess around with, learn from, and grow alongside the man who loved their mother enough to conceive them.

"Where is he now?" they ask.

I hear more loneliness than bitterness in their voices. More "I wish" than "I hate." Somehow, some way . . . there's a longing for those strong arms and that familiar voice. Emotional distance does a number on relationships, even when adulthood replaces adolescence. Singer Barry Manilow sang of that in a song of yesteryear.

> *We walked to the sea, just my father and me;*
> *And the dog played around on the sand.*
> *Winter cold cut the air, hangin' still everywhere,*
> *Dressed in gray . . . did he say "hold my hand"?*
>
> *I said, Love's easier when it's far away;*
> *We sat and watched a distant light.*
>
> *We're two ships that pass in the night,*
> *We both smile and we say it's all right;*
> *We're still here—it's just that we're out of sight*
> *Like those ships that pass in the night.*
>
> *There's a boat on the line where the sea meets the sky,*
> *There's another that rides far behind;*
> *And it seems you and I are like strangers*
> *A wide ways apart as we drift on through time.*
>
> *He said, it's harder now, we're far away,*
> *We only read you when you write;*
> *We're two ships that pass in the night. . . .*[14]

Dad, it is possible you've gotten overly committed, so involved in your work or some away-from-home project or hobby that it is draining your time and energy with your family. I understand, believe me, I do. Maybe it is hard for you to come up close and be vulnerable—even with your kids. You may really prefer "Father" to "Pop" or "Dad." Again, I can't fault you for the way you've been put together. You can't be someone you're not . . . nor should you try to fake it. But surely between a distant patriarch and a down-home, easygoin' daddy there's a common ground . . . a place to meet, time to be, room to hear, to feel, to care, to touch. Yes, I'm pleading.

How easy to get squeezed into a system that began with the Industrial Revolution. A mass migration brought people from quiet, family-oriented farms to busy cities, big factories, and tight living quarters. Urban fathers left home early and returned late. By the mid-twentieth century, even the grand-fathers, once the revered, wise sages of homesteads, were shunted off to retirement villages or old folks' homes. Imperceptibly, dads have become shadows in dark rooms, leaving home before dawn and returning after bedtime.

Instead of challenging fathers to give of themselves, the system encourages them to give the stuff their increased salaries can buy: a better education, a membership at the club, material possessions, nicer homes, extra cars, personal TVs, credit cards, and computers—the list goes on.

But what about dad himself? And that priceless apprentice-ship learned in his presence? And that healthy masculine influence? And that integrity which rubs off the older onto the younger? It's gotten lost in the shuffle. The adversary has won a tragic victory, which no church, no school, no occupation, no coach, no therapy group, no hobby can fully overcome. The Absent Father has emerged. It's time for you and me to cut a new course.

C'mon, dads, let's lead a revolt! Let's refuse to take our cues from the system any longer. Let's start saying no to more and more of the things that pull us farther and farther away from the ones who need us the most. Let's remember that the great-est earthly gifts we can provide are our presence and influence while we live and a magnificent memory of our lives once we're gone.

You're not perfect? So, what else is new?

You don't know exactly how to pull it off? Welcome to the club!

A piece of graffiti usually comes to my mind when I hear such excuses: "Life ain't no exact science." Which, being interpreted, means, "You ain't Clark Kent, so don't sweat it." Your family doesn't expect profound perfection, command performances, or a superhuman plan. Just you—warts and all—your smile, your affirmation, your gentleness, your support, your leadership, your involvement . . . *you!*

C'mon, dads! Let's get started before all our children have is a memory of us—the shadowy memory in the back of their minds of two ships that once passed in the night.

3

Positive Partner of Support

There is no more influential or powerful role on earth than a mother's. As significant as political, military, educational, or religious public figures may be, none can compare to the impact made by mothers. Their words are never fully forgotten, their touch leaves an indelible impression, and the memory of their presence lasts a lifetime.

I ask you, who else is anywhere near that influential?

If you were blessed with a good mother, you will reap the benefits the rest of your days. If your mother neglected your needs and failed to support your dad, unfortunately, much of what you suffered cannot be erased. For good or ill, a mother's mark is permanent.

Abraham Lincoln was right: "No one is poor who had a godly mother." Instead of camping on the negatives and emphasizing how far many mothers have drifted from this magnificent calling to shape the future of our country, I want to throw out a positive challenge. Ladies, this is your hour . . . your distinct opportunity to soar! A harmonious marital partnership and a solid, unselfish commitment to motherhood have never been of greater importance to you or, for that matter, to our nation. Talk about a challenge worth your effort! In spite of what you may have heard, this role is the most dignified, the most influential, and the most rewarding in all the world.

I am not surprised to see that our society puts down the role of motherhood. Since when did society ever pull for the highest ideals?

Homemakers have been disrespected and ridiculed for years. Women who find fulfillment in being supportive partners alongside their husbands and encouraging mothers to their children have often been the brunt of jokes and sordid humor. Many mothers let that negative propaganda get to them—and begin to entertain feelings of disenchantment. Some have gone so far as to resent the child-rearing years of their past. You may have heard about the poll taken by one of the syndicated columnists who posed the question, "If you had it to do over again, would you have a family?" As I recall, somewhere around 70 percent of those who answered responded, "No!" Remember, that's the percentage of those *who responded* . . . certainly not in any sense representing *all* who are engaged in the responsibilities (and delights!) of motherhood.

A Return to Scripture

So much for popular opinions and societal trends. I find far more help and motivation from God's eternal counsel. I have two scriptures in mind which will provide us much food for thought: First, Proverbs 24, and then 2 Timothy 1.

We looked at Proverbs 24:3–4 earlier, but another examination would be worthwhile. These two verses have to do with the building, the establishing, the firming up of the home. It's not a reference to hammer and nails, a trowel with brick and mortar. Not matching carpets and drapes, new paint and room additions. It's not that kind of building. The tools Solomon mentions are relational, which are far more valuable.

> *By wisdom a house is built, and by understanding it is established; and by knowledge the rooms are filled with all precious and pleasant riches.*

Every time I read those words, I am impressed anew with their beauty. Solomon is suggesting that homes are built with three primary tools: wisdom, understanding, and knowledge.

Wisdom is the ability to see with discernment, to view life as God perceives it.

Understanding is the skill to respond with insight.

Knowledge is the rare trait of learning with perception—discovering and growing.

In a book on marriage, I paraphrased these two verses from Proverbs 24 in this way:

> By means of *wisdom*—the skill to see with discernment, maintaining a broad yet accurate view of life—a house is rebuilt, restored so that those within it don't simply exist, they flourish, they reach their full potential. By means of *understanding*—the ability to respond with insight, gaining a full awareness of situations that result in an insightful response rather than a surface reaction—one brings order and an upright condition back to a marriage and home.
> By means of *knowledge*—the willingness to learn with perception, becoming acquainted with the facts, and grasping their significance so that ignorance is dispelled and truth is continually pursued—one causes each life to be filled to overflowing with riches that can never be destroyed, like memories, positive attitude, mutual respect, and a depth of character.[15]

Now you can see why I place such a premium on wisdom, understanding, and knowledge. And, mothers, God can give you all three. In fact, you have a nine-month jump on the children's father! There is something about that forty-week advance you have on us dads that gives you a perspective, an insight, we don't have. You felt the child and knew the child before we, the fathers, ever had a chance to feel and know them. The jolt of responsibility hit us when we saw that little baby for the first time, but you felt it months before. When that child arrived, when you began to cradle it, love it, nurse it, and cuddle it, you already had the beginning of wisdom, knowledge, and understanding. Instinctively, you could sense the child's needs. You understood and knew how to respond properly to his cries, his looks, and all those unutterable infant hints. God gave you that inner reservoir of knowledge to help you invest yourself for the next fifteen, eighteen, twenty or more years. Actually, for the rest of your life!

And the benefits of your investment? The home becomes established, strengthened, and ultimately filled with "precious and pleasant riches."

Can you imagine what those "riches" are? To name only three: character traits, unerasable memories, and lasting, deep relationships. These and other precious treasures embellish a home where the mother invests herself. What a superlative opportunity to model the truth!

I heard about four scholars who were arguing over Bible translations. One said he preferred the King James Version because of its beautiful, eloquent old English. Another said he preferred the American Standard Bible for its literalism, the way it moves the reader from passage to passage with confident feelings of accuracy from the original text. A third man preferred Moffatt because of its quaint, penetrating use of words, the turn of a phrase that captures the attention of the reader. After giving the issue further thought, the fourth scholar admitted, "I have personally preferred my mother's translation." When the other scholars chuckled, he responded, "Yes, she translated it. She translated each page of the Bible into life. It is the most convincing translation I ever saw."

There was another man who saw such a translation in his lifetime. He lived in the first century. His name was Timothy. We don't hear much about Timothy's mother. We hear a lot about Timothy and a lot about Paul, his older friend and mentor. These two men were so close that the elder sought the younger in his last few weeks on earth. As a result of his Christian witness in a hostile world, Paul was thrust into a Roman dungeon. He would soon be killed. Shortly before he was beheaded, he wrote Timothy a letter. In doing so, he began to drift back into the pools of his memory.

Second Timothy is dripping with nostalgia. You can't read it properly without putting yourself into a dungeon in Rome and feeling what it was like to be facing your last days. Paul is old. His life is spent. He has finished his course. And at times like that, when your life is spent and death is inevitable, you draw on your memory. While thinking of their friendship, he goes back to more pleasant days with Timothy.

> *I thank God, whom I serve with a clear conscience the way my forefathers did, as I constantly remember you in my prayers night and day . . . (1:3).*

That's what you do when you're alone and life is ending. You thank God. You review your memories. You pray a lot. You even recall the tears of the past.

> *. . . longing to see you, even as I recall your tears, so that I may be filled with joy (v.4).*

A Mother's Contributions

I find in that statement and in those that follow, five distinct contributions a mother makes in her home. The very first thing Paul remembers about his friend Timothy is his tears—"as I recall your tears." Timothy had his mother to thank for that!

Transparent Tenderness

Dads, let's face it. Most of us learn tenderness from our children's mother. Boys and girls, likewise, learn tenderness from their mothers. Isn't it interesting that if we had a chance to state what we learned from which parent, most of us would say we learned tenderness from our mother and diligence from our dad. From dad we discovered the value of a dollar, the necessity of hard work, the significance of honesty, the importance of standing alone when everything or everyone seems to turn against us; but we learned transparent tenderness from our mother.

Something happened in our family several years ago that reminds me of the value of a tender mother. Cynthia and I had gone to our church on a Friday evening to attend a parents' appreciation banquet, sponsored by the high schoolers. It was well publicized, and the room was packed with parents who came to be appreciated for a change! Just after the prayer had been offered for the meal, Cynthia got a little tap on her shoulder and one of those serving leaned over and whispered, "Your two younger children are at the door and want to see you." She went and conversed for a moment and then returned to the table, looking rather serious. She picked up her purse and got ready to leave to take care of some need at home. Without knowing all the details, I said, "For a change, honey, why don't you just sit down and enjoy the banquet. I'll go instead. You're always the one who has to give . . . who gets up in the night . . . always the one giving up. For a change, let me. Please, sit down."

After hesitating to calm her mother's heart, she sat back down.

I left, not knowing exactly what had happened. At the door I found two tear-stained children with tiny red spots on their clothing. Lifting their bikes into the back of our station wagon, I heard the story. Chuck, our nine-year-old, had wanted a little canary very, very badly. We discussed it. Like a good father, I checked the price, and told him we would have to talk about this investment for a while longer.

He worked with us, we worked with him, and we came up with enough to buy the canary and the cage. He loved this little canary. He named it Twit. He talked with this little bird and fed it regularly. In return Twit chirped and sang and won its way into the heart of our family. Its presence added to the fun in the upstairs part of our home.

Within the last few days, Chuck had creatively strung some little string perches across the cage—in fact, he had gotten a little carried away and put perches all over the inside of the cage. Cynthia had told him, "You need to clip those off and give the bird more room." When we left for the banquet, he was looking for the scissors. Well . . . in the process of cutting the strings, the little bird fluttered down too close to the scissors and, much to his surprise, Chuck clipped the bird's toe. The bird began to bleed. Neither Chuck nor Colleen knew what to do. Desperately, he attempted to calm the frightened creature by reaching into its cage to cradle it, thinking that somehow it would live if he could hold it. Suddenly, the bird flew out of his cage, into the bathroom, and fluttered around the room in a flying frenzy. Within less than a minute it gasped and fell to the floor—dead.

Our two children stared in disbelief. Horrified and alone, they simply did not know what to do. Tiny dots of blood were sprinkled on the bathroom wall and on them . . . and worst of all, the delightful little pet was gone. They rode their bikes to the church to ask for help. When I arrived home with them, I picked up the little bird, wrapped it in tissue and went outside. We found a shovel and dug a deep hole. And with tear-stained eyes, we placed that little bird in the ground and pushed the dirt over it.

Without a word, Chuck left my side. He found a small branch on the ground in the backyard, broke it in two, and made a little cross with some Elmer's glue. Then he got a piece of paper and with his own hand he drew little hearts all over the paper. In the middle of it he wrote, "Chuck's Beloved Bird." With tenderness, he took that little message and placed it at the foot of the cross. The three of us knelt there, arm in arm, and prayed. And, yes, we wept.

Life stood strangely still. A banquet and all of its significance, and a ministry with all of its involvements faded in the distance as two little children and their dad genuinely and openly grieved. You see, you don't get over your grief until you express it fully.

I relate this little story, not to show what a hero I was in that circumstance, but to illustrate what our whole family has learned from Cynthia. It occurred to me later that evening that our little tribe has learned much of its tenderness from the mother in our home. It is she, much more than I, who taught our children to be demonstrative, caring, and full of compassion. To grieve when they lose something or someone special to them. By giving permission for those emotions to emerge, by exemplifying them, she has introduced a whole new dimension into the Swindoll home. That little incident with the canary showed me what an influence she has had on all of us—especially old dad.

Moms, that's one of your greatest contributions. Don't lose your tenderness. If you buy into the feminist message of today, you'll become masculine and militant, rough, harsh, and even a little *mean!*

Those little hands that keep lifting up, keep looking for a mother's tenderness they fail to find in the fast lane, will keep coming back to you. Timothy found tenderness in his home, and that is the first thing Paul remembers about him. He was man enough to shed tears.

That's not all. Paul adds:

> *For I am mindful of the sincere faith within you, which first dwelt in your grandmother Lois, and your mother Eunice, and I am sure that it is in you as well (2 Timothy 1:5).*

Paul knew Timothy's heritage. He knew the man's roots. He knew about Grandma Lois and about Timothy's mother, Eunice. He realized that the things which characterized the grandmother and the mother characterized Timothy. That's the way sincere faith works.

Authentic Spirituality

You'll appreciate the word *sincere.* If I were to transliterate the Greek term, it would read *anhupocritos,* or "unhypocritical."

"As I think of you, Timothy," Paul is saying, "I think of a man who is unhypocritical in his Christian life. You got it from your mom. She got it from hers." There's no mention of a significant grandfather in his past—or even of his father. Just the maternal grandmother and mother. Often, that's the avenue through which sincere faith comes, though not exclusively.

Listen to this, moms! Please read my words carefully. A church, a Christian school, a circle of Christian friends can deposit facts into heads. But they cannot translate truth into authentic living. Those avenues can't make it "real." Truth doesn't weave itself into real fleshed-out life until it flows through you. Kids gather the facts. They learn them from the books. They see it in print on a page. But then they look to you to see it modeled into an *anhupocritos* kind of faith. Believe me, we can give them the words to say, we can convey Christian concepts until we turn a deep shade of blue, but they won't fit reality until our young see the reality of such truths in the home.

For years our family has been going to Mount Hermon Christian Conference Center in the Santa Cruz, California area. We've been doing this each year since 1972, so it's now a treasured family memory. I heard a true story from one of the fellows up there who works with teenagers at their Ponderosa Camp, a beautiful facility nestled in the woods. He was working with a group of preteen kids who had been raised in church. Actually, several churches were represented, and most—maybe all—of these kids had been in a church throughout their lives. On top of that, many of them attended private Christian schools. They knew all the church songs, church cliches, all the religious words.

My friend, who had the task of being their leader that week, decided he would cut through the veneer and add a little reality to their very first session together. So he thought he would ask a down-to-earth question. He began, "Hey, let's loosen up and get acquainted, okay? I'll ask you some questions, and you answer them. Ready?"

Nobody responded. They had heard it all. He glanced outside and then blurted out, "What's small and gray, has four legs, climbs trees, has a big bushy tail, and hides nuts for the winter?"

Not a word came from anybody in the room. Nothing. A few frowned, looked at each other, but no one responded. He asked it again. "What's small and gray, has four legs, climbs trees, has a big bushy tail, and hides nuts for the winter?"

Again, no answer. Finally, one brave little gal in the back stuck her hand into the air, and in all seriousness answered, "I think it's a squirrel, but I'll go ahead and say Jesus Christ."

I hope your faith is not too fragile to see the point. When he told me that story, I cracked up! Can you believe the unreality of that child's faith? Isn't it incredible . . . so full of religious words and standard church talk, she was afraid to venture outside the realm of the expected and call a squirrel a squirrel!

Mothers, one of your major contributions to a family is realism. Let the truth be known. Talk truth. Model truth. Reward honest seeking. Have a little fun with it. Live it up! Make sure the kiddos understand that asking questions is all right, because when they reach college age and we deposit them into some university, they will then know what to expect. Their faith won't backfire and leave them with a massive head wound.

Transparent tenderness, authentic spirituality. The third one is in the same context. It's in 2 Timothy 1:6–7a:

> *And for this reason I remind you to kindle afresh the gift of God which is in you through the laying on of my hands. For God has not given us a spirit of timidity, but of power . . .*

Inner Confidence

The term *dunamis* (power) has in mind "inherent strength, inner might." Don't think of timidity as a helpful trait in this context—it's not. It's insecurity. It's inferiority. Once you become real, moms, and once the reality of your life begins to flow through, it's amazing how your child will begin to sense security and confidence and will begin to emulate such.

Apparently, when Timothy reached the age of thirty-five or forty and began his ministry in Ephesus, he did it with confidence and not with fear, timidity, and inferiority. Let me suggest he quite likely learned that from his mom as well. Who can ever measure the benefit of a mother's inspiration?

The Lazy B Ranch is comprised of 260 square miles of scrub brush on the New Mexico and Arizona border and has been in the Day family since 1881. When Harry and Ada Mae Day were ready to have their first child, they traveled 200 miles to El Paso for the delivery, and Ada Mae brought her baby, Sandra, home to a difficult life. The four-room adobe house had no running water and no electricity. There was no school within driving distance. One would have thought that with such limited resources, Sandra's intellectual future was slim.

But Harry and Ada Mae were dreamers who did not allow themselves to be limited by their surroundings. Harry had been forced by his father's death to take over the ranch rather than enter Stanford University, but he never gave up hope that his daughter would someday study there. And Ada Mae continued to subscribe to metropolitan newspapers and to magazines such as *Vogue* and *The New Yorker*. When Sandra was four, her mother started her on the Calvert method of home instruction and later saw that she went to the best boarding schools possible. Sandra's brother, Alan, says that one summer their parents packed them in the car and they drove to all the state capitols west of the Mississippi. "We climbed to the dome of every building until finally we had to come home," he said.

Sandra did go to Stanford, then on to law school, and eventually on to become the first woman Supreme Court justice in the United States. On the day of her swearing in, the Day family was there, of course. During the ceremony Alan watched her closely as she put on her robe, then walked to her seat among the justices. "She looked around, saw the family and locked her eyes right into ours!" said Alan. "That's when the tears started falling."

What causes a woman like Sandra Day O'Connor to go so far? Intelligence, of course. And lots of inner drive. But much of the credit goes to a determined little ranch woman sitting in her adobe house at night, reading to her children hour after hour, and to parents scampering the stairways of capitol domes, their children in tow.[16]

We have thought about a mother's transparent tenderness, authentic spirituality, and inner confidence. As you would expect, we must include love.

Unselfish Love

For God has not given us a spirit of timidity, but of power and love and discipline (v. 7).

Love—the kind of love mentioned here—has to do with seeking the highest good of the other person. It is a selfless love. Love when it hurts. Love when you're weary. Love when it means discipline. Love when it means staying at the task . . . washing . . . fixing meals . . . driving those miles . . . "scampering up the stairways" . . . planning for the future . . . dreaming big dreams. Love when it means caring for those whom you had not planned on giving birth to as much as those whose births were planned.

I said hello to four mothers who came to a Mother's Day service a couple of years ago. Two of them spoke back to me. The other two were too weary and hassled to worry about who was saying hello to whom. I fully understood. They looked a little . . . well, their hair was in an unusual shape—not like they had planned it to be. One mother had a baby hanging over her shoulder and the other had a child stumbling along behind her. And I thought, *May the Lord give those great ladies strength and a lot of love*. There are times when mothering wears thin!

This reminds me of a different kind of Mother's Day card I saw recently. My kids and I were looking for one for their mom. We landed on one that was great. So appropriate! It was a great big card written in a small child's printing—you know, that first-grade block printing. On the front of the card was a little boy who had on dirty sneakers. They were untied, naturally. His cap was twisted to one side, his jeans were torn, and he was obviously soiled and sweaty from playing hard. He was holding onto the handle of a little wagon. Toys were everywhere. He had a Band-Aid stuck on his arm, and there were smudges all over the card. We're talking typical six-year-old! On the front it read:

> MOM, I REMEMBER THAT LITTLE PRAYER YOU USED TO SAY FOR ME EVERY DAY.

Then, inside:

> GOD HELP YOU IF YOU EVER DO THAT AGAIN!

I laughed out loud in the gift shop. Sometimes a mother gets so exasperated she just can't express herself any other way.

Let me tell you when your love comes through. Your love comes through when you listen when we hurt and when you hear what we don't say. Your love comes through when you laugh while under pressure, even though it doesn't seem to fit. Those are two ways that you tell us you really love us—your sense of humor and your sense of insight.

In her book *On Death and Dying,* Elisabeth Kubler-Ross tells the moving account of a young girl under an oxygen tent. She is dying. Nurses and attendants have waited on her time and again, day after day. Because she is not a demanding kind of patient, she suffers quietly through the day. Finally, it was one of those hurry-up-and-turn-out-the-light nights. A weary yet understanding nurse (who was also a mother) reached over and turned out the light. And for a change the girl said something. Speaking from under the tent, she asked softly, "What would happen if this hospital suddenly caught on fire?"

The preoccupied nurse momentarily didn't realize what was really being asked. She said, "Oh, you'd be all right, honey. We'd take care of you." Then, before she reached for the door to leave, she suddenly understood. Lovingly, the nurse went back, unzipped the tent, and reached in. Wrapping her arms around the frail, frightened girl, she held her close, and whispered in her ear, "Does this help?"[17]

There's not a mother reading those lines who doesn't understand such a response. It is at those times that you declare your love most eloquently . . . when you detect a need, spontaneously reach out, embrace, and say, "Does this help?" That's *wisdom* at work. There are times when a child doesn't know what he or she needs. And that's when your love provides the essential insight. God calls such a response *understanding*. God has given you a sixth sense. You know when someone is afraid, yet doesn't know how to say it. When acting upon it, your unselfish love prompts you to do the right thing. When you do, you reveal God-given *knowledge*.

Remember the Skin Horse in *The Velveteen Rabbit?* All his stuffing was starting to come out, his hair had been "loved off," but how valuable he was! Mothers, maybe you're becoming like that. Your hair's getting a little loved off, huh! Your eyes are falling out. You're weak at the joints and you feel kind of shabby, but you're so very valuable. You're learning so much . . . and, believe me, so are your kids. Carefully kept mothers don't have secure kids. Carefully kept, untouchable "velveteen mothers" turn out fragile, selfish, untouchable children. But unselfish, giving, secure moms somehow manage to deposit healthy, wholesome kids into our lonely, frightened society.

You really must model the tenderness we need. Our world can't find it anywhere else. It is to you we look for that sense of sincere (unhypocritical) faith. It is from you we get rid of timidity and learn confidence.

When all of that is woven together, it becomes a beautiful tapestry of love. And if I may add one more quality, mothers—

Self-Control

Again, look at this seventh verse:

For God has not given us a spirit of timidity, but of power and love and discipline.

Moms who get the job done are moms who set wise parameters and say, "Now, that's it." There is a vital element of disciplined self-control that accompanies the role of the mother, and it forms a needed balance to the love and the tenderness. It is so hard to be consistent—yet love needs the balance that discipline provides.

Dr. Stanley Coopersmith, associate professor of psychology at the University of California studied 1,738 normal middle-class boys and their families, beginning in the preadolescent period and following them through to young manhood.

After identifying those boys having the highest self-esteem, he compared their homes and childhood influences with those having a lower sense of self-worth. He found three important characteristics which distinguished them: (1) The high-esteem children were clearly more loved and appreciated at home than were the low-esteem boys. The parental love was deep and genuine, not just an empty display of words. The boys knew they were the object of pride and interest, increasing their own sense of self-worth.

(2) The high-esteem group came from homes where parents had been significantly more strict in their approach to discipline. By contrast, the parents of the low-esteem group had created insecurity and dependence by their permissiveness. Their children were more likely to feel that the rules were not enforced with discipline because no one cared enough to get involved. ("If you are left without discipline—then you are illegitimate children and not sons.") Furthermore, the most successful and independent young men during the latter period of the study were found to have come from homes that demanded the strictest accountability and responsibility. And as could have been predicted, the family ties remained the strongest—not in the wishy-washy homes—but in the homes where discipline and self-control had been a way of life.

(3) The homes of the high-esteem group were also characterized by democracy and openness. Once the boundaries for behavior were established, there was freedom for individual personalities to grow and develop. The boys could express themselves without fear of ridicule, and the overall atmosphere here was marked by acceptance and emotional safety.[18]

Self-control pays rich dividends.

Believe it or not, mothers, you are part of the answer—a major part of the answer—in building guys and gals who can keep control of themselves. Never (repeat, *never*) sell yourselves short.

Who hasn't nodded in agreement with Dorothy Nolte's words:

> If a child lives with criticism, he learns to condemn.
> If a child lives with hostility, he learns to fight.
> If a child lives with ridicule, he learns to be shy.
> If a child lives with shame, he learns to feel guilty.
> If a child lives with tolerance, he learns to be patient.
> If a child lives with encouragement, he learns confidence.
>
> If a child lives with praise, he learns to appreciate.
> If a child lives with fairness, he learns justice.
> If a child lives with security, he learns to have faith.
> If a child lives with approval, he learns to like himself.
> If a child lives with acceptance and friendship, he learns
>   to find love in the world.[19]

Five Cheers for Motherhood!

What does motherhood require? Transparent tenderness, authentic spirituality, inner confidence, unselfish love, and self-control. Quite a list, isn't it? Almost more than we should expect. Perhaps that explains why Erma Bombeck says motherhood takes 180 movable parts and 3 pairs of hands and 3 sets of eyes . . . and, I might add, the grace of God. If you happen to be a mother, here's one guy who applauds your every effort. Five cheers for all you do!

Since confession is good for the soul, maybe I should conclude this chapter by admitting that many of us who are sons and fathers have been guilty of an attitude of presumption. We have taken you for granted much too often, giving you far too little credit for the load you carry and the endless responsibilities you live with. We owe you so much!

Jimmy Dean, country and western singer of some renown, released an album back in the late seventies. One of the songs on that album is unique since Dean doesn't sing it, he says it. It's titled, "I Owe You."

He's at a nostalgic place in his life. While thumbing through the things in his wallet, he inadvertently comes across a number of longstanding "I owe yous" to his mother, which he names one after another. By the time he's through, there's a big knot in your throat.

Borrowing that idea, I'd like to make up another list of "I owe yous" which apply to mothers all over the country, all of which are long overdue. Let's stop after each one and consider the priceless value of the one who made your life possible—your mother.

Dear Mom:

As I walk through my museum of memories,

I owe you . . . for your *time*. Day and night.
I owe you . . . for your *example*. Consistent and dependable.
I owe you . . . for your *support*. Stimulating and challenging.
I owe you . . . for your *humor*. Sparky and quick.
I owe you . . . for your *counsel*. Wise and quiet.
I owe you . . . for your *humility*. Genuine and gracious.
I owe you . . . for your *hospitality*. Smiling and warm.
I owe you . . . for your *insight*. Keen and honest.
I owe you . . . for your *flexibility*. Patient and joyful.
I owe you . . . for your *sacrifices*. Numerous and quickly
                   forgotten.
I owe you . . . for your *faith*. Solid and sure.
I owe you . . . for your *hope*. Ceaseless and indestructible.
I owe you . . . for your *love*. Devoted and deep.

May I end as I began this chapter? There is no more influential or powerful role on earth than a mother's. Stay at it, dear lady. Never doubt the value of your calling. Without your positive supportive partnership, the family simply could not survive.

4

Your Baby Has the Bents!

Mark Twain had a homey philosophy on how to rear children. It went something like this:

> Things run along pretty smoothly until your kid reaches thirteen. That's the time you need to stick 'em in a barrel, hammer the lid down nice and snug, and feed 'em through the knot-hole. And then, about the time he turns sixteen, *plug up the knot-hole*.

As much as I admire the writings of the man, it doesn't sound to me like he knew very much about raising kids. Having reared four active children through their teenage years, I would take issue with anyone who thinks they could even get a thirteen-year-old boy into a barrel . . . to say nothing of ever being able to feed him through a single knot-hole. A creature who can consume an entire refrigerator full of food in a dozen minutes or less would never survive that knot-hole routine. Furthermore, things do not run along pretty smoothly until the age of thirteen. Get serious! Those can be some of the most energy-draining, frustrating (dare I say maddening?) years of a family's existence.

One mother described her son as a human jet engine, flying at top velocity during every waking hour. Trying to get him to hold still, she said, was like trying to sew a button on a poached egg.[20] That's a funny statement. Not all parents are laughing, however, when they look back on those days. Columnist Ann Landers received this letter from a painfully honest New York mother.

> I've lived seventy years, and I speak from experience, as a mother of five. Was it worth it?
>
> No. The early years were difficult. Illness, rebellion, lack of motivation (we called it shiftlessness and laziness in our day).
>
> One was seriously disturbed—in and out of mental hospitals. Another went the Gay Lib route. Two are now living in communes (we never hear from them). Another has gone loony with the help of a phony religious leader who should be in jail.
>
> Not one of our children has given us any pleasure. God knows we did our best, but we were failures as parents and they are failures as people.[21]

She signed it "Sad Story."

As I sit here late tonight, I try to imagine what life must have been like during the stormy years in that powder-keg home in New York. It's hard to believe her comment: "Not one of our children has given us any pleasure."

Parents aren't the only ones without mirth; there are a lot of little kids who aren't laughing either. The number one killer of children under five? Child abuse. Not accidents. Or crib death. Or leukemia. Two-thirds of all child abuse occurs with children under age four . . . and one-third of *that* number, six months or less! And those are the ones that are reported.

Obviously, child-rearing is demanding, difficult, discouraging, and on certain occasions confusing. But it is not impossible! And it is worth every bit of the effort and sacrifice. Do not let anyone convince you you've got more important things to do or personal projects that rate a higher priority. As Cynthia and I glance back over our shoulders and pick out the most important achievements of our past, nothing comes close to the joys of rearing our children and now reaping the benefits.

Was it easy, free of conflict, and consistently rewarding? Of course not. Did it require flexibility, availability, sacrifice, and cooperation? You bet. Still does. But, believe me, when we think of other involvements and projects, neither of us can come up with *anything* that comes close by comparison. Hardly a day passes without one or both of us verbally giving God thanks for the family He has enabled us to have and enjoy. And when you toss in grandkids . . . oops, better not get me started!

The Most Basic Place to Begin

Many people I meet don't share my excitement about the family. Sometimes they ask questions like "What's wrong? How come rearing children is such a hassle! Where does a parent begin?"

At the risk of sounding simplistic, yes, there is a place to begin. When it comes to rearing children, developing a strong home where happiness and harmony can flourish, there is a primary starting point: *knowing* your child. This is the most profound insight, the single most helpful secret I can pass on to you on the subject of child-rearing.

Do not think that just because you have conceived, carried, and finally given birth to your little one, you automatically know your child. Nor can you say you know him or her just because you live in the same house. I must say, categorically, *you do not*. Knowing your child takes time, careful observation, diligent study, prayer, concentration, help from above, and, yes, wisdom. Notice I did not include in that list a high IQ or some course in school. The two essential ingredients are desire and time. If you really want to know, and if you're willing to invest the time, God will honor your efforts. He will enable you to know your child.

The scriptural basis of that statement takes us back to Solomon's words of wisdom.

> *Train up a child in the way he should go, even when he is old he will not depart from it (Proverbs 22:6).*

What a wonderful, insightful statement! And yet, how misunderstood, how misquoted! The common interpretation of that verse goes something like this: Be sure your child is in Sunday school and church at an early age. Teach him a lot of Bible verses and hymns. Make sure he learns the Ten Commandments, a few prayers to be used at mealtimes, at bedtime, and in case of emergency. If possible, send him to a Christian school, see that he attends a Christian camp each summer, and enforce your rules and regulations with unbending strictness. Because, after all, the kid is going to grow up and rebel. For sure, he will sow some wild oats. But when he is finished with his fling, when he's old and gray-haired, he will finally come back to God. You can count on it!

I don't know how you respond to that popular interpretation, but I know how it strikes me. Forget it! Who needs it? Who really cares if your grown-up son finally sees the error of his ways at, let's say, age sixty . . . or seventy. Big deal! Furthermore, that whole concept isn't necessarily true. You and I know any number of rebels who were forced into a restricted, parent-dominated, externally religious lifestyle during their early years in the home. And when they got free of all that, they split the scene and ran wild. I mean, *really* wild! And they never did stop running. In fact, they didn't return to the Lord, even when they grew older. I know some, in fact, who died while running from Him.

Worst of all, this interpretation can't hold water exegetically. I've been studying the verse for many years, which allows me to write with a measure of confidence; that is *not* what the biblical text teaches.

I am prepared to introduce a new approach to this age-old verse of Scripture. All I ask is that you keep an open mind to some rather innovative ideas. Please do not stop short of hearing me out. Even though my approach may differ from what you have been taught or have believed all your life, please stay with me and think clearly. What you are about to read could be the breakthrough you have needed to begin the process of knowing your child.

Allow me to "dissect" various parts of Proverbs 22:6. To begin with, "Train up a child . . ." deserves careful examination. The Hebrew term behind "train up" is derived from the palate or the roof of the mouth. In the days of Solomon it was employed in a couple of ways. The original term was used to describe a rope placed in the mouth of the horse so as to give it direction while the rider was breaking it. It's the thought of bringing a wild spirit into submission by using a rope in the mouth.

It was also used to describe an intriguing action of a Hebrew midwife after she assisted the mother in the birth of her infant. The midwife, shortly after helping in the birth process, would hold the tiny newborn in her arms, take her index finger and dip it in a tiny pool of crushed grapes or dates. Placing that finger into the mouth of the child, she would massage the gums, palate, and roof of the mouth, encouraging a sucking response. It was believed to have a cleansing effect as well. Taking that action to its final result, the term carried the idea of cultivating a sensation within the mouth, cleansing, and creating a thirst.

Now, let's go on. "Train up a child in the way he should go."

As parents look at that statement, they think, *I know the way he should go. After all, I'm the parent. I know what's right because I'm older and more mature. And because I know the way he should go, I'm gonna see he goes my way!* You may be surprised to know it doesn't mean that at all. In fact, it means quite the opposite!

Look at the margin in a New American Standard version of the Bible. It is suggested that the verse should literally be read, "Train up a child according to *his* way."

YOUR BABY HAS THE BENTS!

Now, I promised you some eye-opening insights into this passage, so here goes! A child who is properly trained is trained in keeping with his or her own way, *not our way,* parents. Admittedly, you and I may know the proper path very well. But the verse is not just referring to the ultimate goal of bringing a child into right relationship with God and ultimately into a happy and prosperous future. It refers to the makeup of a child—his unique characteristics and mannerisms, which Scripture calls "his way." The Hebrew word is *dereck.* It is used in Proverbs 30, for example, to describe the manner or way of four things:

> *There are three things which are too wonderful for me, four which I do not understand: the way of an eagle in the sky, the way of a serpent on a rock, the way of a ship in the middle of the sea, and the way of a man with a maid (vv. 18–19).*

Take time to notice that "the way" is used four times in those verses. An eagle, for example, does not fly three miles north, stop, and take a right. Its style is far more coordinated and beautiful. The eagle has unique mannerisms. It soars unlike any other bird of the sky. If you've ever seen an eagle in flight, you know what I mean. You find yourself intrigued by "the way" of an eagle in the sky.

Repulsive though it may seem to some, we are also intrigued by the presence of a serpent on a rock. There is nothing quite like the slithery, silent movements of a snake.

If you have ever been on a ship in the middle of the sea, then you know the romance between the two—it's almost mysterious! On the other hand, if you have ever found yourself in a little boat when a huge ship comes nearby, you know the feeling of the enormous, awesome presence of that ship in the sea.

And, certainly, there is no handbook of romance for the way of a man with a maid. Such a relationship is altogether unique, depending on the man and his bride. No rule book is to be followed by all. It isn't a cut-and-dried process. That's what makes marital intimacy so exciting!

So it is with children. There is no precise rule book for rearing kids. Hence, Solomon writes, "Train up a child in keeping with or accordance to *his* mannerisms, *his* characteristics, *his* way." Wise are the parents who believe that and adapt their training accordingly.

For half their lives some parents have thought that children are born into their families like pliable, little, soft hunks of clay; they can push them, mold them, stretch them, poke them, twist them, roll them, press them down, and stamp them out in a one-two-three process. They then stick 'em in the kiln, make sure they get good and hard, and finally send them on their way. Wrong! Children come to us from the womb with a prescribed set of characteristics. In fact, I think the word *bent* says it best. (The same Hebrew term is used in the eleventh chapter of the Book of Psalms where we read of the "bending" of a bow.) Solomon's point is clear: No baby is a pliable piece of clay. All babies have bents . . . including yours. Wise are the parents who learn their children's bents and train them accordingly.

The Amplified Bible translates the verse:

> *Train up a child in the way he should go [and in keeping with his individual gift or bent], and when he is old he will not depart from it.*

If it is true that each child has his own unique bent, it should be illustrated in Scripture. Indeed it is!

Let's take the case of the first child ever born into a family, according to the biblical record. Remember his name? Cain. He was born to the original couple, Adam and Eve. Sometime later, they had a second son. His name was Abel. Were Cain and Abel a lot alike? No, in no way. As a matter of fact, Abel was a lover of God, whose heart was warm and sensitive toward God, whose spirit was willing to adapt to God's way. But Cain was self-willed and stubborn, determined to go his own way. The two boys (from the same womb) were opposites.

YOUR BABY HAS THE BENTS!

If that sounds like a set-up, let's make it more difficult and look at a set of twins. I'm thinking of the two sons of Isaac and Rebekah. The firstborn was named Esau. His twin brother was named Jacob. Surely those twins were similar, right? (You're smiling.) Two boys could not have been more different. Esau was rugged, strong, and masculine. He was a hunter. He was even hairy. He liked to go out in the field and bring back the venison. And how his dad loved him! Jacob? Well, he hung around the kitchen with mom. He liked to cook more than hunt. Esau was a black-and-white kinda guy. Not Jacob. He was a deceiver type. He even managed to rip off his brother's *birthright*. By the way, while Isaac preferred Esau, Jacob was his mom's favorite. How common! When you have a child that's like you, it is so easy to make that one your favorite. Without even realizing it, that's the one you pour your life into; that's the one to whom you give more of your time, which only complicates the conflict.

What about *your* children? Can you believe how different they are? How about your original family . . . the one in which you were raised. You were not a lot like your brother or sister, were you? Down inside you knew it, but your parents ignored it, right? That's when you started to rebel, wasn't it? Why? Well, more than likely because you sensed that your parents didn't really understand how you were put together.

I hardly need to remind you that some children are strong and determined, while others are weak, easily influenced by peer pressure. Some are creative and dreamy, others are more objective and pragmatic. Some are confident and secure, others are unsure of themselves, seemingly unable to stand alone. Some are stubborn and aggressive, others are cooperative and willing. Some are just naturally humorous and happy-go-lucky. Most families usually have at least one joyful optimist in the brood. And then there are children who are melancholy and pessimistic, sort of like Eeyore in *Winnie the Pooh*.

One of ours would wake up bright and cheery, having a terrific time, walking around with dirty diapers for almost an hour, and we didn't even realize it (for a while!). I've known other babies who come unglued over the slightest irritation—and stay ticked off all afternoon. Why? Because each child is *different!* Remember, we must train a child "according to his way."

Thoughtless, preoccupied, and unwise parents tend to make two major mistakes: (1) We tend to rear the way we were reared. Dads are usually the worst offenders. "I was raised this way, and that's the way I'm gonna raise my kids!" (2) We tend to compare our children with each other. Right? Illustration—report cards. My brother had the most boring report card that anyone would ever, ever want to see. Not I, pal. I had *variety.* I offered a choice of letters! Take your pick. But invariably, my grades were compared to young Einstein. I think you've got the point.

Each child is born with a prescribed set of bents. The verse goes on to say:

> . . . and when he is old he will not depart from it.

Do you know what *old* means? It means "when they are old enough to grow a beard . . . old enough to have facial hair." In other words when they reach adulthood, having been known and uniquely trained by their parents, they will not depart from the path of obedience. Now I call *that* a promise worth claiming! I like the way the Modern Language Bible renders Proverbs 22:6:

> *Educate a child according to his life requirements; even when he is old he will not veer from it.*

A Brief, Personal Interlude

One of my first books was *You and Your Child.* In it I presented some of these principles in greater detail than I have attempted to do here. If you want to dig deeper into the whole idea of rearing your children according to this unique concept, you may wish to use that volume as a guide.

I mention that because over twenty years have passed since I first put those ideas into print. Back then our four were small.

YOUR BABY HAS THE BENTS!

The principles I suggested were in a somewhat embryonic and theoretical stage as Cynthia and I were in the process of putting them to work. All four of our children are now in their twenties and thirties (three of them married and rearing their own children), and our youngest is continuing his education. Our four are no longer little children. We have had occasion to see if the ideas I presented way back then still hold water. I am so grateful to report *they work!* Now that we have had ample opportunities to try these things out in the crucible of everyday living, it is a great joy (and relief!) to announce that the truth of God's counsel has paid off. The principles are paying off . . . *so far!*

Our family, while made up of independent-thinking, strong-minded people, is still close. All of us are imperfect and in the process of learning and growing. But the good news is this: We are still having fun, still communicating openly, and still committed to each other. God gets all the glory. As we enjoy each other, our family knows it is because He is the One who has honored our commitment to principles that broke the mold of traditional parenting.

If parents were to ask me, "What is the greatest gift we could give our young child?" I would answer rather quickly: a sensitive spirit. That is especially rare among busy parents who live under the demand of hurried schedules, constantly doing battle with the tyranny of the urgent. Nevertheless, my counsel to you would be, give your child the time it takes to find out how he or she is put together. Help your child know who he or she is. Discuss those things with your children. Help them know themselves so that they learn to love and accept themselves as they are. Then, as they move into a society that seems committed to pounding them into another shape, they will remain true to themselves, secure in their independent walk with their God.

I have begun to realize that secure, mature people are best described in fifteen words: they know who they are . . . they like who they are . . . they are who they are. They are *real*.

All through those early years of child-rearing, Cynthia and I deliberately invested the effort required to discover how our four were designed by God . . . and then to pass along what we saw. That included both the pleasant and the unpleasant . . . the things that needed to be changed as well as those things they should cultivate.

Proverbs 20 tells us we are to "observe" our child.

> *It is by his deeds that a lad distinguishes himself if his conduct is pure and right. The hearing ear and the seeing eye, the LORD has made both of them. Do not love sleep, lest you become poor; open your eyes, and you will be satisfied with food (vv. 11–13).*

Don't sleep, parents! In other words, don't passively shrug your shoulders and hope for the best. Get involved. Open your eyes. Perk up your ears. Watch your child in action. Learn the bents, the abilities, the characteristics, the good, the bad, and then adapt your training accordingly. When you discover healthy, wholesome traits, cultivate, commend, and affirm. When you encounter unwholesome and unwise traits, deal firmly as you counteract those damaging bents.

I can just hear some dads who are thinking, *Wait a minute, Chuck. I wasn't given all that special attention, and I turned out pretty good. I mean, I think if you sort of let kids alone, they'll make it okay on their own.* I have another proverb for you, my friend. If your philosophy is sort of a lie-back-and-let-it-happen style, listen to the other side of that story.

> *The rod and reproof give wisdom, but a child who gets his own way brings shame to his mother (Proverbs 29:15).*

If you look in the margin of the New American Standard Bible, you will notice it says, "But a child left to himself brings shame." Left in his room? No. Left alone on the playground at school? No. Left to fend for himself in college? No, not that. The idea means "left in the condition in which he was born." Left untouched. Left undisciplined. Left without an authority figure to respect. Left without affirmation and direction. Neglected! *Left!* If we adopt a hands-off policy and leave our children to find their own way through the maze from childhood to adulthood, God's Word says quite openly they will bring shame.

As Cynthia and I look back, we see that God has honored our efforts (though some of them were, at times, inconsistent and feeble) to stay involved with our children as they matured. We kept our eyes open, and we refused to look the other way. It is such a pleasure to be able to write years later that those efforts paid off . . . in spades! Because the test of time has added credence to our theories, I am all the more excited about sharing them. When you find something that works, you are anxious to pass it on.

A Simple Analysis of the Bents

No doubt you are asking, "What do I look for? What are the things I should open my eyes to see . . . or perk up my ears to hear?" At the risk of appearing oversimplified, I will answer that there are two different sets of bents: bents toward *good* and bents toward *evil*.

The Good Bents

Psalm 139 addresses the subject of good bents better than any scripture I have ever read. It begins:

> O LORD, *Thou hast searched me and known me. Thou dost know when I sit down and when I rise up; Thou dost understand my thought from afar (vv. 1–2).*

Talk about knowing your child! God knows even the *thoughts* of His own. Before I ever know the thought myself, He already knows it and has analyzed it. That's almost spooky, isn't it? Before I am thinking a thought, God has intercepted those promptings, those mental, unseen images, and He has analyzed them perfectly. He knows why they are in my head as well as what I am going to do with them. That isn't all . . . He also observes us.

> *Thou dost scrutinize my path and my lying down, and art intimately acquainted with all my ways (v. 3).*

Someone has said that a secret sin on earth is open scandal in heaven. A secret life on earth is no secret at all—it's an open book (in living color!) in heaven. Since God knows everything, we can be sure that such knowledge began before we ever existed. And that takes us down to verse 13 of this grand psalm.

Let me remind you that we are about to enter into a secret place where no human eyes have ever entered. It is the place within a mother-to-be, her womb that houses her unborn child for nine (or less) months. We are going to enter into that special chamber created by God. As we visit this place of our original residence, we are going to discover some things about the good bents He prescribed within us as He put us together while we were only in fetal form.

> *For Thou didst form my inward parts; Thou didst weave me in my mother's womb (v. 13).*

The "Thou" is a pronoun that is in great emphasis in the Hebrew text. "Lord, You and no other. . . ." Mother Nature didn't make me. Fate did not shape me. Nor was it just a biological combination of mother and dad in a moment of sexual passion. Nor was I conceived through blind chance. You, God (and no other), made me! Your child needs to know that, especially your child who wrestles with how he or she has been made. There is no exception. God takes full responsibility, and He is not at all ashamed of His workmanship. "Lord, *You* made me."

The psalm goes on to say that the One who made me "formed my inward parts." The word literally means "originated or created." God reached into my life when I was merely a tiny embryo and began to shape me within. He originated me. He began to put me together while I was still in the soft silence of my mother's womb. It was there my inward parts were originated by God. "Inward parts" literally (and surprisingly) means "kidneys." It was not uncommon for the Hebrews to use the name of one vital organ as a representative of all the vital organs. "You made my vital organs, like my kidneys, liver, lungs, heart, brain, spine, and even the remarkable fluid that moves within my spine. Furthermore, You gave me my personality, my temperament. You began to make those parts that were vital for life." That seems to be an accurate amplification of this statement. By the way, all those who question whether an unborn child is truly alive need only read this psalm.

The next line is an intensified statement in Hebrew poetry: "Thou didst weave me in my mother's womb." Weave. *Sha-nak.* It means "to knit together so as to interweave into a mass, as in a thicket." It is like the interweaving of a vine. He began to weave my being together, this organ with that organ, these arteries and those veins and vital organs—kidneys and liver and lungs and heart and brain. "All of that was created in just the way You planned, Lord—like the mass of a thicket—You wove all of me together. The nine-month interweaving work of God included my likes and dislikes, my personality as well as my perspective on life.

A paraphrase might read, "For God alone, and none other, originated my vital organs. You alone were the One who knitted together all the things that made me who I am in my mother's womb."

We're not surprised that his response in verse 14 is a spontaneous burst of praise. He looks up and says:

I will give thanks to Thee, for I am fearfully and wonderfully made; wonderful are Thy works, and my soul knows it very well.

As I analyze my body and see the way I have been put together, I join the psalmist in praise and gratitude to God, my Creator.

He returns to describing God's workmanship in verse 15: "My frame was not hidden from Thee. . . ." The "frame" means "bony substance." It's another way of saying "my skeleton." In this statement God declares He had a hand in the internal structure of every baby—the length, the shape, right down to the size of the bones.

Before you discount the importance of this detail, think about the impact it could have on your child to know that God takes full responsibility for his or her height. For example, what if you have a twelve-year-old who is six-foot-three-inches tall . . . who is a *girl?* Your daughter needs to know that her size is from God. She is shaped exactly as God would have her shaped. Think of it! God spent nine months in His genius plan to give us our size, our shape . . . our face! And some spend their lifetime denying their unique identity or trying to change all that.

He continues . . .

My frame was not hidden from Thee, when I was made in secret, and skillfully wrought in the depths of the earth (v. 15).

"Skillfully wrought" originally means "variegated." It's a divine picture of multicolored organs, muscle, bone, blood—and even personality. Like multicolored tapestry. Like fine needlepoint, God interwove my person within my body and made me exactly as He would have me be, like no one else on earth, including personality, mental ability, drive, size, interest, and shape. And He did it all before we were born . . . talk about a case against abortion!

A paraphrase might read, "My skeleton, my bones, that which determines my physical appearance, was not hidden from You, God, when I was concealed in that place of protection inside my mother's womb, when my veins and arteries, even my personality, were interwoven and miraculously embroidered together like fine needlepoint."

The next time you pick up your little baby or grandbaby, look into the face of that marvelously made child and say, "You are fearfully and wonderfully made." And it wouldn't hurt to repeat that statement throughout their childhood. Children need to know how valuable they are in God's sight—and ours. Nothing gives them greater security than a strong sense of self-esteem.

Hear this well, busy parents—especially you who tend toward impatience, who are always on the run, who have determined that the school, church, or some tutor will do what you haven't time to do. Your child has been put together in an altogether unique fashion, like no one else on earth. I don't care if there are quadruplets in your home, they need you to help convince them they are unique persons, each one different, each one his or her own person. Children arrive in our arms longing to be known, longing to accept themselves as they are, to be who they are. So when they wade into the swift current of their times, they will be able to stand firm, and won't depend on peer pressure to give them their standard. They won't need to be accepted by the group nearly as much.

That, you see, is the parent's primary job. Which is why you need to be *available*.

The psalmist says:

Thine eyes have seen my unformed substance; and in Thy book they were all written, the days that were ordained for me, when as yet there was not one of them (Psalm 139:16).

God has set out a plan that is moving under His perfect direction. Wise is the parent who cooperates with that plan. It takes prayer. It takes time with God. It takes concentration. It takes thought. It takes observation. It takes caring. And it takes communication. It also takes watching reactions and responding when the reaction comes.

Here are some ways this will work out. Early on you will see certain things emerging in your child's makeup. You will notice that some children are, by nature, extremely careful. Others, much more casual and rather messy. One will be quiet and contemplative, another loud and boisterous as an assault tank! One will be practical, having a mechanical mind, the other musical and artistic. All that needs to be noticed, talked about, and cultivated.

My wife tells me her mother told her she could tell she had interests in music when she was just a little girl in a playpen. Recorded music would be playing in the background, and Cynthia's little foot or hand would be tapping to the beat of the music. She has a love for music to this day. Her parents observed and encouraged this good bent.

Parents, we need to cooperate with those good bents as we see them emerging. We need to pass on our observations. As your child grows older, talk with the child about what you notice.

Some children, as I said earlier, are creative and artistic and messy. Making messes goes with being artistic. I didn't know I was creative until I was in high school. The reason is now quite clear to me. One of life's primary rules in our home was: UNDER NO CIRCUMSTANCE DO YOU MAKE A MESS! Problem is, you can't be creative and clean at the same time. You gotta be messy. And the very meticulous (dare I say neurotic?) parent who doesn't want anything out of place or any stuff to clean up is going to frustrate a creative kid. They'll have to discover it on their own later on, as I did from a high school teacher who saw dramatic gifts in me I didn't know I had. But, parents, the downside of that up-tight approach is that you'll miss out on all the fun!

Some kids are made for the ballet floor. Some are made for a violin. Some are made to play a horn. Some are made to paint. Some are made to dribble a ball all over the court, jump like crazy, and stuff that round pill into the hoop. Some are made for the gridiron—they're linebackers. But don't try to make a linebacker into a ballet dancer. Can you imagine a guy like Banks or Butkus on a ballet floor! Can you imagine Baryshnikov as a tight end for the Chicago Bears? Get serious.

So what have we learned about dealing with the good bents? Cooperate with them! Observe how the Lord put your child together, cultivate those skills and abilities, and watch them blossom and flourish.

One final word about this—a warning: Do not try to force your child to fulfill what was never fulfilled in *your* life. Dads who didn't quite make it into the professional football ranks, watch it. Your son may not even *like* the game. And the mother who modeled but didn't make it to the cover of *Glamour* magazine, guard against pushing and manipulating your daughter into that field. Good bents emerge quite naturally and are to be observed, enjoyed, and cultivated . . . not forced and hurried. Wise are the parents who train up their children according to the way God has put them together.

The "Bad" Bents

Since I prefer good news to bad, I wish I could stop the chapter right here. But that would be premature. We need to turn to the flip side of every child's makeup. There are not only good bents in all kids, there are bad bents as well. Psalm 51 clearly states this. Believe me, this applies to that precious, delightful, soft, loving, wonderful, beautiful granddaughter (or grandson) of yours, or that brand new baby who is soon to be born into your family. Both parents and grandparents need to hear—I mean really hear—the psalmist's words:

> Behold, I was brought forth in iniquity, and in sin my mother conceived me (Psalm 51:5).

"Brought forth" means "born." "Iniquity" simply means "with a sinful nature." Paraphrased, the statement is saying:

> Behold, I was born with a sinful set of bents in my nature, and in sin my mother conceived me.

This doesn't mean the act of my conception was wrong or sinful. It means that from conception on there was a depraved nature passed on from parent to child; a nature that is sinful to the core. The Amplified Bible captures the thought:

> Behold, I was brought forth in [a state of] iniquity; my mother was sinful who conceived me [and I, too, am sinful].

The hard, cold fact cannot be denied: children are born spiritually dead. They may be sweet, adorable, and innocent at birth, but it isn't long before they demonstrate their sinful nature. A bit later the psalmist adds:

> No, in heart you work unrighteousness; on earth you weigh out the violence of your hands. The wicked are estranged from the womb; these who speak lies go astray from birth. They have venom like the venom of a serpent; like a deaf cobra that stops up its ear, so that it does not hear the voice of charmers, or a skillful caster of spells (Psalm 58:2–5).

Isn't that vivid? Your little one is like a cobra that slithers out of a jug as some guy plays music . . . only this cobra emerges with his fingers in his ears, thinking, I'll go where I want to go. And when it bites (hissssss), there's poison in those fangs. That is the way it is with your child. Need a little convincing? Just stop and think; your child never has to be taught to do wrong. He comes by that naturally. This is called the "Adamic nature" or the universal depravity of mankind. To put it bluntly, it's your child's bent toward badness. In spite of all I have written about the good bents and all the cultivation that needs to go into bringing the good to the surface, I assure you, your child also has evil bents. You must cooperate with the good. But the bad calls for counteraction. If you ignore dealing with the bad, you are in for serious trouble. I am not alone in my warning.

Dr. Albert Siegel said in the *Stanford Observer*:

> When it comes to rearing children, every society is only twenty years away from barbarism. Twenty years is all we have to accomplish the task of civilizing the infants who are born into our midst each year. These savages know nothing of our language, our culture, our religion, our values, our customs of interpersonal relations. The infant is totally ignorant about communism, fascism, democracy, civil liberties, the rights of the minority as contrasted with the prerogatives of the majority, respect, decency, honesty, customs, conventions, and manners. *The barbarism must be tamed if civilization is to survive.*[22]

YOUR BABY HAS THE BENTS!

The Minnesota Crime Commission released a report a number of years ago which sounds a lot like Dr. Siegel's warning:

> Every baby starts life as a little savage. He is completely selfish and self-centered. He wants what he wants when he wants it: his bottle, his mother's attention, his playmate's toy, his uncle's watch. Deny these and he seethes with rage and aggressiveness which would be murderous were he not so helpless. This means that all children, not just certain children, are born delinquent. If permitted to continue in the self-centered world of infancy, given free reign to his impulsive actions, every child would grow up a criminal, a thief, a killer, a rapist.

If you read those words and think your youngster is excluded, you make a grave error. Every child has the potential of becoming a study in hostility . . . a heartache . . . a model of wickedness.

There's no denying it—parents must deal with the evil that rests in their children's lives. Those who fail to do so consistently and wisely will face a future of misery.

Specifically, how do I respond to the evil bent in my child? You must counteract it. You don't dare leave it alone! Too many parents have chosen to do that. That's why you read of ten-year-olds scheming the death of their parents, or twelve- and fifteen-year-olds committing heinous crimes.

First, to get the "inside help" you need, you need to lead the child to a knowledge of Jesus Christ as Lord and Savior. That spiritually dead nature needs life. Only personal faith in Jesus Christ can make that happen. Salvation is of highest priority!

Second, you need to deal with wrong as it occurs. Deal with it sufficiently until the child learns that wrong won't be permitted. Your child must learn to respect authority. Your child must also learn to obey. You don't shrug and say, "I just can't do anything with my five-year-old." You stay at it until your little one gets the message. If you need professional help, pursue it. Your desire is to shape that stubborn will with wisdom. I will develop this more fully in the next chapter.

Let me remind you of the statement we examined earlier in Proverbs 29:15:

> *The rod and reproof give wisdom, but a child who gets his own way brings shame to his mother.*

Look again at Proverbs 20:11–12:

> *It is by his deeds that a lad distinguishes himself if his conduct is pure and right. The hearing ear and the seeing eye, the LORD has made both of them.*

Moms and dads, before we can expect to claim the promise of Proverbs 22:6, we must pay attention (open our eyes and ears), and we must discipline when self-will attempts to take charge. Doing so pays rich dividends. Ignoring the signs of rebellion results in tragic consequences. For example, read this true study in contrasts very carefully.

> The father of Jonathan Edwards was a minister and his mother was the daughter of a clergyman. Among their descendants were fourteen presidents of colleges, more than one hundred college professors, more than one hundred lawyers, thirty judges, sixty physicians, more than a hundred clergymen, missionaries and theology professors, and about sixty authors. There is scarcely any great American industry that has not had one of his family among its chief promoters. Such is the product of one American Christian family, reared under the most favorable conditions.
>
> The contrast is presented in the Jukes family, which could not be made to study and would not work, and is said to have cost the state of New York a million dollars. Their entire record is one of pauperism and crime, insanity and imbecility. Among their twelve hundred known descendants, three hundred ten were professional paupers, four hundred forty were physically wrecked by their own wickedness, sixty were habitual thieves, one hundred thirty were convicted criminals, fifty-five were victims of impurity, only twenty learned a trade (and ten of these learned it in a state prison), and this notorious family produced seven murderers.[23]

Trust me, it makes all the difference in the world when parents counteract the bad. Kids are pretty smart cookies. They may learn how to cover up their wicked ways, but their attitudes will finally emerge.

Several years ago I delivered a commencement address at a college in mid-America. I sat on the platform following my address and watched over two hundred graduates walk by and receive their degrees . . . many bachelor's, some master's. It was a prestigious and sophisticated moment as each graduate walked by. The academic dean requested that we please hold our applause until all the graduates passed by and then we would applaud them all at once. But I noticed, when the dean announced the salutatorian, everyone automatically applauded. When they announced the valedictorian (graduating 4.0), another thunderous ovation occurred. I didn't think the audience would ever stop applauding.

I found myself thinking we should also applaud those who had a healthy, secure self-esteem. But people aren't trained to applaud that. I wanted to applaud the one who had the best attitude of any student in his four years at school. But, again, who ever applauds that? The more I thought about it, I really wanted to applaud the ones who had the best response to difficult and demanding teachers . . . to students who stayed loyal to a teacher in spite of repeated weaknesses. But, again, you don't applaud that. We applaud beauty. We applaud intelligence. We applaud a well-coordinated body on a basketball court or a baseball diamond or a football field. But who applauds good self-esteem or a sweet, servant spirit of submission or a willingness to give rather than receive? No, we don't do that. We don't mean wrong by it, it's just the way the system works. I have a bone to pick with our system, by the way.

Interestingly, one of the faculty members sitting beside me that day prompted my thinking about all this. As everyone else was applauding Miss Genius, he leaned over and mentioned that she may be tops in her grade-point average, but (to quote him precisely) "her attitude stinks." Immediately, I tried to imagine the home in which she was reared. Someone became overly impressed with her brilliance but failed to give her the help she needed with her attitude. They cultivated the good but took hands off the bad. I admire her intelligence, but, frankly, I fear for her future.

As Leonardo da Vinci once put it, "He who does not punish evil, commands it to be done."

Three Practical Suggestions

To help some of what I have mentioned "stick," let me make three practical suggestions to you who are parents.

First, *determine your priorities*. Ask yourself how high the family rates on your list of involvements. How about your children in particular—just how serious are you regarding time with each? Have you told them or your mate? Are you willing to alter your schedule in order to "know your child"?

Second, *record your observations*. If a child reveals his or her bents in everyday life, those things are worth writing down. Keep a journal on each child. Make sure it is handy so you can get to it in a hurry. As you write, pray for wisdom. Ask God to guide your thoughts. Please remember, each child is unique. No comparisons! Cultivate the good. Counteract the bad.

Third, *share your findings*. Children long to know themselves better. They respect your counsel, and will long remember your remarks. Be candid and honest as you help them "see" who they really are. Let me repeat those words that enable us to live a happy, healthy life: Know who you are. Like who you are. Be who you are.

Few things are more basic to parenting than what we have dealt with in this chapter. Those who take these tasks seriously will do more for our nation than any other task they could undertake.

Theodore Roosevelt put it this way:

> There are exceptional women, there are exceptional men, who have other tasks to perform in addition to, not in substitution for, the task of motherhood and fatherhood, the task

of providing for the home and of keeping it. But it is the tasks connected with the home that are the fundamental tasks of humanity. After all, we can get along for the time being with an inferior quality of success in other lines, political or business, or of any kind; because if there are failings in such matters we can make them good in the next generation; but if the mother does not do her duty, there will either be no next generation, or a next generation that is worse than none at all. In other words, we cannot as a Nation get along at all if we haven't the right kind of home life. Such a life is not only the supreme duty, but also the supreme reward of duty. Every rightly constituted woman or man, if she or he is worth his or her salt, must feel that there is no such ample reward to be found anywhere in life as the reward of children, the reward of a happy family life.[24]

PART TWO

BUILDING

THE

STRUCTURE

5

Shaping the Will with Wisdom

I struggle with any argument that bases its logic on the extreme. Invariably, such thinking leads to ridiculous conclusions.

Consider, for example, the subject of automobile accidents. Some drivers on the road today are careless, thoughtless, and downright irresponsible behind the wheel. Their reckless actions cause countless accidents. With people like these on our backstreets and freeways, driving can be dangerous. You could be seriously injured while driving your car, maybe even killed. How foolish it would be, however, for someone to suggest that the best solution to our high accident rate is that no one drive a car!

Or look at all the unhappy marriages around us. Many who marry struggle with their partners. Wills clash. Arguments abound. Disharmony persists. The courts are choked with divorces. In spite of this dilemma, I've never heard anyone suggest we pass legislation making marriage illegal—even though that would immediately solve all future marital conflicts.

Yet, when it comes to the physical discipline of children, that's the sort of logic you hear being advanced these days. Because corporeal punishment has been taken to brutal extremes by some parents or guardians, the tendency on the part of many is to "throw the baby out with the bath water." That's the way it is when diplomacy and expediency become substitutes for discernment and accuracy.

Years ago I learned a principle that has never once failed me: *Never make the extreme your standard.* The flip side of that principle? Balance and wisdom must prevail when the possibility of risk or danger is present. To remove *all* corporeal punishment because some parents have misused and abused it is to embrace an extreme position that defies logic and common sense . . . and, much more importantly, it denies the counsel of Holy Scripture.

Before proceeding one line further, let me clarify that I abhor and deplore any form of abuse, especially child abuse. I have no place in my philosophy or theology for domestic discipline taken to that extreme. As a parent who has reared four children of my own and as a pastor who has been forced to deal with domestic abuses of every variety imaginable, I have seen both the rewards of fair discipline and the horrors of uncontrolled abuse. There is, admittedly, no way to remove the risk, but in light of the ultimate benefits that accompany the proper discipline of children, I am now more convinced than ever that God honors those who follow His directions—even though some will misread, misapply, and take His counsel to an extreme. Please understand that I have never and would never advocate any action that would be unfair or abusive to children. How could I, in light of what you just read in the last chapter? Children are originated and "woven together" by the Creator, remember? Each one is a precious, unique God-given gift with divinely prescribed abilities. It's a small wonder Jesus taught,

> But whoever causes one of these little ones who believe in
> Me to stumble, it is better for him that a heavy millstone be

*hung around his neck, and that he be drowned in the depth
of the sea (Matthew 18:6).*

But that statement was never meant to imply that a child
should be given unhindered and unchecked freedom. Look again
at the title I have given this chapter. Thank goodness, I have
learned a few things since God gave us our four. Thirty years ago
I would probably have entitled the chapter "Shape Up or Ship
Out," and I would've offered five or six precise steps guaranteed
to result in successful parenting. Not now . . . not on your life! I'll
leave those ideals to speakers and authors who don't have a
houseful of kids. And with years of hard-knocks-and-sleepless-
nights experience as a dad behind me, I want to return to
Proverbs, the ancient book of wisdom, and allow some of those
time-tested principles to emerge in all their glory.

A Statement Worth Remembering

Just before reading Solomon's counsel, take time to ponder
a thought worth remembering: Rather than causing your child
to question your love, discipline *confirms* your love. A child
who lives with consistent, fair correction learns that you value
him or her. When you care enough to set healthy limits, take
the time to enforce the rules, and model the things you expect,
children grow up much happier and more secure than those
who are given virtually free rein. Numerous tests have proven
that well-loved yet justly disciplined children are healthier, and
mature to be more productive, secure adults than those raised
in ultra-permissive environments.

Return with me to an old statement from Scripture you
may have forgotten was in the Book:

*He who spares his rod hates his son, but he who loves him
disciplines him diligently (Proverbs 13:24).*

It was insightful of Solomon to link love with discipline. Those
who truly love their children realize the importance of consistent

discipline. A child senses that parents care when they stand their ground and maintain established parameters. This provides an emotional undergirding essential for mature adulthood.

Three Important Distinctions

Since ours is a day of extremism, it is necessary to clarify a few distinctions for there to be complete understanding. First, *there is a distinction between abuse and discipline.* Even though I have already attempted to remove all doubt about this, I want to make myself painfully clear. Invariably, when someone desires to find fault with a person who believes in the disciplining of children, the most effective way to do so is to claim *abuse.* Let's contrast the two:

Abuse	**Discipline**
Unfair and unexpected	Fair and expected
Degrading and demoralizing	Upholds dignity
Extreme—too harsh, brutal	Balanced—within limits
Torturous—leaves scars	Painful—but leaves no scars
Results from hatred and resentment	Prompted by love and concern
Creates terror, emotional damage, and resentment of authority	Leads to healthy respect of and for authority
Destroys self-esteem; leads to horrifying, permanent damage and the inability, later in life, to maintain responsibilities	Strengthens self-esteem; leads to the individual's ability to later discipline himself

Some homes are houses of horror. Sick and sinful parents (who themselves were often victims of child abuse) lack sufficient inner strength to control themselves when they administer discipline. Some, because of drugs or alcohol, do not even realize when they are operating out of control.

I live in the sprawling Los Angeles metropolis, an enormous jungle of human needs. Hardly a day passes that I do not see, hear, or read of children being abused. I vividly remember when a small child was left inside a locked car, windows closed, on a day so hot the child perished. The heartbreaking stories are endless.

Sexual abuse is another facet of this tragic scene, more prevalent than any of us wants to admit. Some of the accounts of child abuse I come across bring tears to my eyes. Perhaps that is why I've gone overboard to make sure no one even implies I advocate a discipline that comes anywhere near abuse.

Second, *there is a distinction between crushing the spirit and shaping the will.* In another proverb we read about a "broken spirit."

A joyful heart makes a cheerful face, but when the heart is sad, the spirit is broken (Proverbs 15:13).

Consider another one; same idea but different words.

A joyful heart is good medicine, but a broken spirit dries up the bones (Proverbs 17:22).

It would be safe to substitute the word *crushed* for *broken*. Let it never be forgotten that one of the ultimate goals of discipline is to build up a child's inner strength, to give him or her the security and the self-confidence that will provide inner assistance throughout the remaining years of life . . . to help cultivate a submissive spirit, a servant's heart. But when the spirit is crushed within a child, the light goes out deep down inside. The "drive" needed for reaching goals and accomplishing objectives grinds to a halt, leaving him or her awash and adrift. Wise is the parent who keeps a protective watch over the child's fragile spirit while attempting to shape that stubborn will.

Third, *there is a distinction between normal childishness and willful defiance.* Every growing youngster needs space in which to discover, learn, make mistakes, and experience all the other things involved in growing toward maturity. Children naturally forget to do a chore every now and then. They spill their milk and water . . . and juice . . . and Coke . . . and cereal . . . EVERYTHING! They stumble and fall. They break things. They forget and leave stuff like rocks and snails and frogs in their pockets. They slip in the bathtub and crack their noggins. They get clean clothes soiled seconds after they go outside. They forget you told them to stay clean.

That's all part of being a child. They're not trying to be malicious or defiant, they're just learning the ropes. To come down hard on a little one for such actions is unfair. Discipline is inappropriate on those occasions.

Principles For Dealing With Defiance

Willful defiance is another matter. Here I have in mind a child's deliberate disobedience. I doubt such behavior needs a great deal of explanation. Teachers see it in today's classrooms. Merchants face it in their shops. Cops encounter it on the streets. Youth workers in churches across America are forever forced to deal with it. Why? *Because parents won't.* The permissiveness found in homes today is downright disgusting. It is not uncommon to find child-centered homes where children intimidate their parents. Afraid to be strong, hesitant to stand firm against the determined will of their youngster, parents create a domestic setting that becomes unbearable.

Author and speaker Dennis Waitley describes an unforgettable encounter he had with a little rebel he tagged, "Bradford the Barbarian."

> In my parenting and leadership seminars, I tell a true story about a young couple who invited me to their home for dinner some time ago after an all-day program at a university. This man and woman, both highly intelligent, with advanced degrees, had opted for a "child-centered" home so their five-year-old son Bradford would have everything at his disposal to become a winner out there in the competitive world.

When I arrived at their driveway in front of a fashionable two-story Tudor home at the end of a cul-de-sac, I should have known what was in store for me. I stepped on his E. T. doll getting out of the car and was greeted by, "Watch where you're walking or you'll have to buy me a new one!"

Entering the front door, I instantly discovered that this was Bradford's place, not his parents'. The furnishings, it appeared, were originally of fine quality. I thought I recognized an Ethan Allen piece that had suffered "the wrath of Khan." We attempted to have a cup of hot cider in the family room, but Bradford was busy running his new Intellivision controls. Trying to find a place to sit down was like hopping on one foot through a mine field, blindfolded.

Bradford got to eat first, in the living room, so he wouldn't be lonely. I nearly dropped my hot cup in my lap in surprise when they brought out a high chair that was designed like an aircraft ejection seat with four legs and straps . . . He was five years old, and had to be strapped in a high chair to get through one meal!

As we started our salads in the dining room, which was an open alcove adjoining the living room, young Bradford dumped his dinner on the carpet and proceeded to pour his milk on top of it to ensure that the peas and carrots would go deep into the shag fibers. His mother entreated, "Brad, honey, don't do that. Mommy wants you to grow up strong and healthy like Daddy. I'll get you some more dinner while Daddy cleans it up."

While they were occupied with their chores, Bradford had unfastened his seat belts, scrambled down from his perch, and joined me in the dining room, helping himself to my olives. "I think you should wait for your own dinner," I said politely, removing his hand from my salad bowl. He swung his leg up, to kick me in the knee, but my old ex-pilot reflexes didn't fail me and I crossed my legs so quickly that he missed, came off his feet, and came down hard on the floor on the seat of his pants. You'd have thought he was at the dentist's office! He screamed and ran to his mother, sobbing, "He hit me!" When his parents asked what happened, I calmly informed them that he had fallen accidentally and that, besides, "I'd never hit the head of a household!"

I knew it was time to be on my way when they put Prince Valiant to bed by placing granola cookies on the stairs as enticers. He ate his way up to bed! "How are you ever going to motivate him to go to school?" I asked quietly. "Oh, I'm sure we'll come up with something," they laughed. "Yes, but what if the neighborhood dogs eat what you put out? He'll lose his way just like Hansel and Gretel!" (I asked the Lord for forgiveness for not remaining silent, as I drove back to the airport.)[25]

How can we keep that kind of thing from occurring in our own home? It isn't enough to think positive and pray a lot. Nor will the job get done by dropping your youngster off at the church a couple times a week. Trust me, it will require hands-on discipline. *Your* hands, parents. Let's consider four two-word suggestions that worked in the Swindoll home.

Start Early

Contrary to popular belief, waiting until your children are in school won't help. Instead of getting easier the longer you wait, discipline gets increasingly more difficult. Look closely at two proverbs:

> *He who spares the rod hates his son, but he who loves him disciplines him diligently (Proverbs 13:24).*

> *Foolishness is bound up in the heart of a child; the rod of discipline will remove it far from him (Proverbs 22:15).*

In the first proverb, the term *diligently* is worth serious study. Originally, it meant "dawn, early in the day." The term took on more meaning as time passed. It came to mean pursuing something early on . . . early in life. Adding that meaning, the statement could be rendered: "He who spares the rod hates his son, but he who loves him seeks him early in life with discipline."

Why start early? Why not wait until the teen years when you can dialogue more intelligently? Because "foolishness" is bound tightly in your child's inner being. Remember the "bad bents" presented toward the end of the previous chapter? Same thought here.

"Foolishness" sounds rather mischievous and impish . . . somewhat lighthearted and fun-loving. But the Hebrews saw it as far more serious. "The fool has said in his heart, 'There is no God'" (Psalm 14:1). The "foolish" possess a God-mocking, instruction-hating nature. "Fools," therefore, despise discipline. Foolishness has a disrespect for authority. Determined to go its own way, it resists all reproof. And remember, all this "is bound up in the heart of a child"—*your* child. Starting early to shape that foolish will is wise. A child given to foolish ways only accelerates in defiance as time passes.

Parents, don't delay the discipline process. God will give you wisdom as you present to Him your desire for a child whose heart is tender and under control. Of course, parents must adapt their disciplining procedure according to each child's age. Older children can (and should) be reasoned with . . . but if you wait to start, it will only get harder.

Stay Balanced

Look again at Proverbs 22:15:

Foolishness is bound up in the heart of a child; the rod of discipline will remove it far from him.

Obviously, the Lord has corporeal punishment in mind. Discipline here is the idea of inflicting pain in order to associate pain with wrong. The child learns two simple yet essential facts: wrong brings pain, right brings pleasure.

The spanking communicates a firm, painful message. I am not referring to a slap on the face. Neither the face nor the upper part of the body are designed to handle such a blow. God has provided a perfect place on the body for pain. He has even supplied that area with some extra padding! And when the rod of discipline is administered His way with the right motive, firmly and briefly, no permanent damage will remain. According to God's promise, it will drive foolishness from him.

To keep you from smiling about foolishness—ignoring the severity of it—think of foolishness as ugly and devastating as a demon. Such potential danger must be dealt with! You owe it to your neighborhood, the teacher at school, to society in general to drive foolishness from your child. If you do not, you will live to regret it.

Keeping a proper balance in mind, there is yet another passage you should consider:

> *Do not hold back discipline from the child, although you beat him with the rod, he will not die. You shall beat him with the rod, and deliver his soul from Sheol (Proverbs 23:13–14).*

It may surprise you to know that as I read that, I am relieved. If discipline is administered correctly, no parent should ever fear that death will result. When I hear of a child being abused so severely that he died, I know it was *not* biblical discipline that was used; it was an extreme, uncontrolled action of human insanity. God promises parents that death will not occur when they discipline His way. In fact, proper discipline will preserve your child from additional heartache! "Even though you smite him with the rod, you will deliver his soul from Sheol (or the place of death, the grave)." Discipline provides deliverance.

Rather than giving license to treat a child with brutality, this guards us against it. This says, in effect, "Firmly punish when there has been willful defiance, and you have the assurance from God that your offspring will not die." Such discipline won't kill.

The Hebrew word *yah-saar,* translated "rod," troubled me when I first undertook this study years ago. I was bothered because it sounded harsh. And then I was relieved to know it is translated *rod,* because the Hebrew word means "club." (I suddenly became grateful my father did not know Hebrew in those days.) Don't overlook this: *yah-saar* calls for an implement when disciplining one's children. Perhaps we should think about that for a few moments.

During part of my growing-up years, my dad was a machinist. He had strong arms. When he spanked me, it was not with a switch or paddle, but with his hand. Perhaps that's the reason

I lived much of my younger years in fear of my father—I identified my father with the pain of his punishment.

As we began to rear our children (and we *so* wanted to do it God's way), Cynthia and I decided we would always use a little paddle whenever we disciplined our children. The paddle we employed was connected to a little fly-back ball about the size of a ping-pong paddle. We'd remove the rubber tether and ball and then use only the paddle. We had several of them located in various spots in the house. For some strange reason they kept disappearing so we wound up having to hide them. That way they would always be in a safe place out of sight.

We followed a particular process, which I'll explain a little later. I am pleased to report that it worked: our children connected the pain *to the paddle* and not to us.

One time after I had spanked our younger daughter and we had worked through the whole thing, she was in her room getting ready to go to bed. Suddenly, she blurted out: "Daddy, come here!" I thought, *What in the world's wrong? What's she done . . . licked her night light?* I rushed into her room to find out the problem. Glaring at the paddle I had inadvertently left on her dresser, she cried; "Get that thing out of here!" Interestingly, she wanted me near, but not "that thing."

Maybe that's the reason God suggests the "rod" when disciplining. But you may still be unconvinced. You may still feel it unfair or somehow brutal to even strike your child or use any implement. You may fear that your youngster may question your love if you bring pain.

Stop and think for a moment of God's dealing with you and me. I remind you that God says He loves us, and whom He loves He *scourges* (Hebrews 12:6). Now *there* is a severe word! It could mean "takes the hide off." I know my heavenly Father loves me and cares for me. How do I know? When I act up, He gets me alone and skins my behind. Believe me, I never forget His thrashings. I need those times. If I were allowed to run roughshod over His prescribed will for me and He let me get away with it, I would wonder if He really cared.

But to stay balanced, we must remember there should be verbal correction along with physical pain. It is necessary to add our words of reproof. Why would I suggest such a combination? Look at Proverbs 3:11–12:

> *My son, do not reject the discipline of the LORD, or loathe His reproof, for whom the LORD loves He reproves, even as a father, the son in whom he delights.*

What does all that mean? When you balance your discipline principles, you maintain not only a firm rod, but a faithful tongue. The two go together.

Periodically, I have heard people say, "There were times as a child when I got a spanking but didn't know why." That means the discipline lacked balance . . . a no-no! A child needs to be dealt with firmly when he has done wrong, but he always—yes, *always*—needs to know why. It is incorrect and unfair discipline when a child has no idea why he got a spanking.

It is extremely important for parents to remember that as the child grows older, there should be less and less physical punishment and more and more verbal correction. Once he reaches a level of maturity, there is no more paddling . . . only discussion. Your counsel changes from physical to verbal as your child matures. I should add this: There is no special age for all kids when this time comes. Some children have moved beyond the spanking phase when they reach the age of nine or ten. (I haven't met many, but there are some like that.) By the time the teen years arrive, you have gotten dangerously close to that fragile self-will where a paddle will do more harm than good. There are rare exceptions, of course.

Let's also understand that verbal correction is not a tongue-lashing. The Hebrew term means "to prove, to convince." We convince our child verbally that wrong is bad and cannot be tolerated. Remember, the statement in Proverbs concluded:

> *For whom the LORD loves He reproves, even as a father, the son in whom he delights (v. 12).*

That's helpful. The word *delight* means "to approve of someone, to respect." It even means "to admire, to affirm."

Does your child know you admire him or her? Your admiration helps them admire themselves. Affirmation works wonders!

Your child not only needs the periodic pop of the paddle on the right place and at the right time, he also needs the wise correction of your tongue. This helps him (or her) reason through the whole issue of defiance and its consequence. Sometimes children realize that certain folks in authority over them cannot lay a hand on them, so they take advantage of that by intensifying their rebellion. It can become a pretty defiant standoff. At those times all that can be done is verbal . . . but don't think for a moment that all is in vain!

My longtime friend, Dr. James Dobson, writes of one of the funniest (and I might add effective) examples of this I have ever read.

In the absence of parental leadership, some children become extremely obnoxious and defiant, especially in public places. Perhaps the best example was a ten-year-old boy named Robert, who was a patient of my good friend Dr. William Slonecker. Dr. Slonecker said his pediatric staff dreaded the days when Robert was scheduled for an office visit. He literally attacked the clinic, grabbing instruments and files and telephones. His passive mother could do little more than shake her head in bewilderment.

During one physical examination, Dr. Slonecker observed severe cavities in Robert's teeth and knew that the boy must be referred to a local dentist. But who would be given the honor? A referral like Robert could mean the end of a professional friendship. Dr. Slonecker eventually decided to send him to an older dentist who reportedly understood children. The confrontation that followed now stands as one of the classic moments in the history of human conflict.

Robert arrived in the dental office, prepared for battle.

"Get in the chair, young man," said the doctor. "No chance!" replied the boy.

"Son, I told you to climb onto the chair, and that's what I intend for you to do," said the dentist.

Robert stared at his opponent for a moment and then replied, "If you make me get in that chair, I will take off all my clothes."

The dentist calmly said, "Son, take 'em off." The boy forthwith removed his shirt, undershirt, shoes and socks, and then looked up in defiance.

"All right, son," said the dentist. "Now get on the chair."

"You didn't hear me," sputtered Robert. "I said if you make me get on that chair, I will take off all my clothes."

"Son, take 'em off," replied the man. Robert proceeded to remove his pants and shorts, finally standing totally naked before the dentist and his assistant.

"Now, son, get in the chair," said the doctor. Robert did as he was told, and sat cooperatively through the entire procedure. When the cavities were drilled and filled, he was instructed to step down from the chair.

"Give me my clothes now," said the boy.

"I'm sorry," replied the dentist. "Tell your mother that we're going to keep your clothes tonight. She can pick them up tomorrow."

Can you comprehend the shock Robert's mother received when the door to the waiting room opened, and there stood her pink son, as naked as the day he was born? The room was filled with patients, but Robert and his mom walked past them and into the hall. They went down a public elevator and into the parking lot, ignoring the snickers of onlookers.

The next day, Robert's mother returned to retrieve his clothes, and asked to have a word with the dentist. However, she did not come to protest. These were her sentiments: "You don't know how much I appreciate what happened here yesterday. You see, Robert has been blackmailing me about his clothes for years. Whenever we are in a public place, such as a grocery store, he makes unreasonable demands of me. If I don't immediately buy him what he wants, he threatens to take off all his clothes. You are the first person who has called his bluff, doctor, and the impact on Robert has been incredible!"[26]

One more verse on this, and then we'll move to the third principle. I love Proverbs 29:15 because it gives the balance:

The rod and reproof give wisdom, but a child who gets his own way brings shame to his mother.

The rod (that's corporeal punishment) and reproof (that's verbal instruction) give wisdom. We build a strong family, parents, as we start early and stay balanced in this business of discipline.

Be Consistent

We have now come to one of my toughest struggles as a parent. Quite possibly it is yours, too. At times I knew in my heart that my child had been willfully defiant and ought to be spanked, but I didn't follow through. At other times I *knew* something had gone on, but didn't probe any deeper because I lacked the energy to hassle with it. But that didn't help my children. They carry with them that same tendency, I'm sure. The problem, plain and simple, is inconsistency.

Although we haven't always been consistent, when we did follow through, here is the way we did it. I pass the procedure on to you with the hope it will give you a guideline to follow. First, we established the rules firmly so the children understood what was expected, what was right and what was wrong. Before they could talk—when they were too young for us to communicate together—a single swat on the bottom was sufficient. They learned to connect their pain with our displeasure and pain. Disobedience brought about a painful experience! From the beginning, however, we did our best to make sure the rules were known. No child should be surprised by a spanking.

Second, whenever we disciplined for breaking the rules, we did it privately. (God disciplines us in private.) If at all possible, we tried not to have anyone else witness the spanking. That is most humiliating for a child to endure in front of others. Not even our children watched as another sibling got spanked. Why add embarrassment to the pain of being disciplined? Just as we didn't display and compare report cards in front of one another, we didn't spank in the presence of other family members or friends of the family. Remember what I wrote earlier? Discipline should uphold the dignity of a child; it should not humiliate him.

More than a few times we have been shopping, and I have had to leave the grocery store to spank a child—*my* child, you understand. (There were times I'd like to have left a grocery store to spank *another* child, but it wasn't my right.) The most private place available was the car. So we would get in the car, and I would deal with the defiance. Normally, of course, this would be done in the child's own room, door closed.

Third, after the reason was clearly and briefly explained and the spanking was firmly administered, we held and consoled the child. Sometimes we sobbed with our son or daughter. I don't write that to make points, I write it simply because it is true. I can hardly remember a time when spankings occurred that I didn't feel like weeping with my child. It always hurt me to hurt my child. We held the child closely and talked quietly to him or her—sometimes as long as thirty minutes—and then we'd leave the room together. We wouldn't exile our kids to cry alone in their rooms. If ever a child needs the tenderness and presence of a parent, it is after the administration of discipline.

We found with our youngest child that he would reach up for us to hold him. He would automatically reach up, expecting our affirmation and compassion. Then we would talk through what had happened and how it must never happen again—how it grieved his daddy or mother and brought unhappiness into our home and family.

A couple of very important specifics should be mentioned. First, sibling rivalry simply would not be tolerated. In our home, a brother or a sister would not be allowed to attack the other, physically or verbally. We required that disagreements be talked out. Yes, it took time. Yes, it often required Mom or Dad to sit in and "umpire." But we refused to "let 'em fight it out" as we looked the other way. The scourge of sibling rivalry, in my opinion, is more damaging to domestic harmony than perhaps any other single conflict a family must face. Please hear me: Your children *must* learn how to solve their differences in a calm, intelligent, controlled manner or they will carry a rival spirit with them into adulthood.

Second, we did our best to deal as severely with bad *attitudes* as we did with wrong actions. As with sibling rivalry, that's not easy to do. Now that they are grown, we notice that our grown children will observe a bad attitude in another child, or even at times in one another, and comment, "He needs an attitude adjustment . . . somebody ought to get his attention." They have really learned the importance of a positive, cooperative attitude.

Start early. Stay balanced. Be consistent.

We need one more guideline to wrap up this chapter. In all honesty, it is one I probably would not have mentioned thirty years ago.

Be Reasonable

In it all you must be reasonable.

Perfect children do not live in your home or mine. Neither do perfect parents. Understand, there will be times when you will break your own rules. To live under the assault of constant guilt will do neither you nor your family any good. For lack of a better way to put it, leave a little "wobble room." Try very hard not to demand perfection or to bring up past-and-forgiven wrongs or to set your expectation level too high. A family must remain a team. That means you must pull together . . . flex, adjust, give, take. When children grow up in a "reasonable" environment, they feel the freedom to fail without a ton of guilt falling all over them. They also grow up with better memories of how things were in their younger years.

Major Goals and Objectives

Let me help you with a couple of major objectives and goals that relate to discipline. Here's the first—a realistic goal for parents: *Model God's role until your child reaches the place where the role of authority shifts*. We are to model God's place of authority until our children are sufficiently mature to shift the authority from us to their heavenly Parent. Beyond that transitional time, parents, take your hands off! You are dealing with an adult at that point, not a child, so don't treat him like a child. Release him.

If it's off to college, release your grip. If it's marriage, release him to marriage. If it's his own career, fine; let him pursue that career. Respect his God-appointed right to grow up. Model God's role of authority until the children reach the place where there is a natural shift of authority, then let 'em go!

A second and final goal for our parenting is this: *Cultivate within your children a healthy respect for themselves and others, so they will perform well regardless of the odds against them.* While shaping your children's lives, work hard to cultivate such a healthy respect for themselves and others that they can adapt and go far beyond what others may envision. Cynthia and I tried to make that a major objective as we invested hours with our children. After all, the parents' ultimate goal is to build determination, hope, resiliency, and fiber into each child's inner being. That takes years!

The following true account is not only a fine story of one family, it is a perfect example of my concluding principle.

Michael Elmore is a gastroenterologist. That's a four-bit word meaning a physician who specializes in diseases of the digestive tract. While in medical school he took an IQ test and scored 126, which is considered a "superior" rating. Who would ever have guessed that more than thirty-five years ago his principal told Michael's mother her boy was "nearly retarded"? Charlotte Elmore handled it wisely . . . she simply refused to believe what she was told. Furthermore, she never told Michael until the day he graduated from medical school. Let's read Charlotte's story, which begins in the principal's office when Michael was six years old:

> In desperation, I asked if he could be retested. She shook her head and said no. In an attempt to show her just how "normal" Michael really was, I began telling her about all the things that Michael did well. But she brushed my comments aside and stood up, dismissing me. "Michael will be all right," she said.

Later that evening, after Michael and his three-year-old sister, Linda, were in bed, I tearfully told Frank what I had learned that day. After talking it over, we agreed that we knew our son much better than the principal did or than an IQ test did. We decided that Michael's low test score must have been a mistake.

Like me, Frank could not believe that our son was "nearly retarded." Instead, he told me about some of the things Michael recently had done that he felt proved Michael was intelligent. . . . He said that one night Michael showed an interest in the blueprint sketches he was working on, so he found Michael's set of odd-shaped blocks and quickly sketched two-dimensional drawings of each of them. Frank then asked Michael to match each block with its corresponding drawing. Frank said he was pleased at how well Michael did. Frank also told me how easily Michael made things with his toy construction sets from the diagrams that came with the toys.

We moved to Fort Wayne, Indiana, in 1962, and Michael entered Concordia Lutheran High School. His grades warranted his selecting college preparatory courses, including biology, Latin, and algebra—the subjects we had been told, when he was back in first grade, he would never be able to handle. Biology soon became his favorite subject. He started telling everyone he was going to be a doctor.

Michael entered Indiana University at Bloomington in 1965 as a premedical student. By midyear, with a 3.47 grade point average, he had made the dean's list, and his faculty counselor gave him special permission to take more than the recommended number of course hours. He earned enough credits to be accepted into the Indiana University School of Medicine in Indianapolis at the end of his junior year in college.

During his first year at medical school, Michael took another IQ test and scored 126, an increase of 36 points. According to his elementary school principal, an increase like that was impossible.

On graduation day, May 21, 1972, Frank, Linda, and I attended the ceremony and hugged our Dr. Mike! After the ceremony, we told Michael and Linda about the low IQ test score Michael had received when he was six as we had planned to do all along. At first, both of them thought we were joking. Since that day, Michael sometimes will look at us and say with a big grin, "My parents never told me that I couldn't be a doctor—that is, not until *after* I graduated from medical school!" It's his way of thanking us for the faith we had in him.

It has been said that children often live up to what adults expect of them—tell a child he is "dumb" and he may play the part. We often wonder what would have happened if we had treated Michael as "nearly retarded" and imposed a limit on his dreams.[27]

Do your children know how much you believe in them? Are they aware of how highly you value them? Would you be as determined as the Elmores to reject some IQ score? Do you protect your children from uncertain information that could damage their self-esteem? There'll never be a better time to answer those questions than today. You may want to start by reaching your arms around your children, not assuming they know it, and telling them what a delight they are in your life. Assure each of them of your confidence, your belief in them. You may have another Michael on your hands who has the potential of achieving far more than some test score would suggest.

It has been a long, long time since some kids have heard those words. Don't assume they know it. Parents who hope to shape their children's wills with wisdom need to blend a lot of love and affirmation into their discipline . . . which is what my next chapter is all about.

Enhancing Esteem

"You get the Red Plate!"

I cannot recall how many times those five words have bounced off the walls in the Swindoll home. Perhaps hundreds! It is one of the many ways we have found to bring a fresh burst of affirmation and encouragement to different members of our family.

Let me explain. The Red Plate is just that—a bright red plate with white hand-painted lettering along the edge that reads, "You Are Special Today." When we first got our Red Plate (they can be purchased at most gift stores), a small explanatory brochure was in the box:

> The Red Plate is the perfect way to acknowledge a family member's special triumphs, to celebrate a birthday or praise a job well done, reward a goal achieved, or simply to say, YOU ARE SPECIAL TODAY. When the Red Plate is used, any meal becomes a celebration honoring a special person, event, or deed. It is a visible reminder of love and esteem.
> The Red Plate—make it a tradition in your family, symboliz-

ing the good and happy times. It will speak volumes of love
when words just aren't enough.[28]

Every family has times when words aren't enough, our family included. One of the members of our family suffered a deep disappointment a number of years ago. No one outside our family knew how much it hurt, because no one else knew how much our family had dreamed of that moment. But it fizzled. At that particular time, we surprised the person in our family by serving her supper on the Red Plate—along with hugs and kisses of understanding.

When a birthday rolls around, the Red Plate appears on the table in honor of that birth. If it's Mother's Day or Father's Day, we underscore the occasion by pulling out the ol' Red Plate. When our Colleen finished running the Los Angeles marathon in March of 1988, she ate supper—a first-class feast Cynthia prepared for her, our family, and a couple of her close friends to enjoy—on the Red Plate. As she sat down with a broad smile, everyone applauded our runner. Curt had run off a big banner on his computer which read in bold letters, COLS, WE ARE PROUD OF YOU! It was taped on the wall near the table where we ate. It hung there for weeks.

We have celebrated being elected as a high school cheerleader, making the football team, graduating, or even passing a tough course(!). You'll smile, but the Swindolls have hauled the thing into a restaurant (hidden from view) and surprised the one we were celebrating that evening by having our waiter place it in front of the "honored guest" . . . as we all applauded. Cynthia and I love doing stuff like that!

Let's face it: self-esteem will not be cultivated from classmates at school, or from folks in the neighborhood, or fellow employees at work. The guys in the back office aren't sitting around looking for ways to affirm. Even friends frequently fail to dispense needed encouragement. *Enhancing esteem is pretty much a family matter, and if it doesn't happen there, it's doubtful it will happen anywhere.*

My point, I hope, is clear. If parents are going to discipline their young with the kind of consistency and determination I pressed for in the previous chapter, then we would do well to balance all that with an equally strong commitment to enhancing the esteem of our children. Believe me, they need all we can give!

In her excellent book, *Your Child's Self-Esteem,* Dorothy Briggs writes words of wisdom:

> If you are like most parents, your hopes for your children are based on more than their avoiding nervous breakdowns, alcoholism, or delinquency. You want life's positives for them: inner confidence; a sense of purpose and involvement; meaningful, constructive relationships with others; success at school and in work. Most of all—happiness. *What* you want is clear. Your uncertainties are more often wrapped around *how* to help them to these goals. We parents hunger for a basic rule of thumb as a guide—particularly during moments of stress and confusion.
>
> Today, enough evidence has accumulated to give you just such a formula: if your child has *high self-esteem,* he has it made. Mounting research shows that the fully functioning child (or adult) is different from the person who flounders through life.
>
> The difference lies in his attitude toward himself, his degree of self-esteem.
>
> What is self-esteem? It is how a person feels about himself. It is his over-all judgment of himself—how much he likes his particular person.
>
> *High self-esteem is not a noisy conceit.* It is a quiet sense of self-respect, a feeling of self-worth. When you have it deep inside, you're glad you're you. Conceit is but whitewash to cover low self-esteem. With high self-esteem you don't waste time and energy impressing others; you already know you have value.
>
> Your child's judgment of himself influences the kinds of friends he chooses, how he gets along with others, the kind of person he marries, and how productive he will be. It affects his creativity, integrity, stability, and even whether he will be a leader or a follower. His feelings of self-worth form the core of his personality and determine the use he makes of his apti-

tudes and abilities. His attitude toward himself has a direct
bearing on how he lives all parts of his life. *In fact, self-esteem
is the mainspring that slates every child for success or failure as a
human being.*

    The importance of self-esteem in your child's life can
hardly be over-emphasized.[29]

Enhancing your child's self-esteem is next to the greatest contribution you can make in your child's life. The greatest, of course
is helping him cultivate a meaningful, lasting relationship with
the living God. Let me put it straight and simple: If your child is
launched from your nest secure in Christ and confident he has
been designed by God to fulfill a special calling, equipped with
the tools to handle the demands of everyday life, you've done
your job. If you accomplish that, my fellow parent, you deserve
to eat off the Red Plate for the rest of your life!

Essential Value of Self-esteem

I could write paragraph after paragraph about the importance
of a personal sense of esteem, telling one story after another . . .
but there are already numerous books that do that. What turns
my crank is to see what the Bible has to say about self-esteem. If
God's Book promotes it—and indeed it does—then we know it is
a pursuit well worth our time and effort.

The last part of Ephesians 5 is dedicated to the home in
general and to marriage in particular. Wives are given wise
counsel in verses 22–24, and husbands are addressed in verses
25–29. Let's look at that latter section.

*Husbands, love your wives, just as Christ also loved the
church and gave Himself up for her; that He might sanctify
her, having cleansed her by the washing of water with the
word, that He might present to Himself the church in all her
glory, having no spot or wrinkle or any such thing; but that
she should be holy and blameless. So husbands ought also
to love their own wives as their own bodies (vv. 25–28).*

Let that sink in, men. The love we are to demonstrate on behalf of our wives is in direct proportion to the love we have for ourselves—not a noisy conceit, as Briggs wrote, but a quiet and deep sense of self-worth. Show me a wife who feels loved and appreciated by her husband and I'll guarantee she is married to a man who properly loves himself. But if she's a wife who sighs and says, "Couldn't somebody teach my husband how to love me?" I can assure you she has a man whose self-esteem is lagging.

Until you have a proper sense of self-love, a healthy and wholesome self-esteem, you are not able freely and fully to love someone else. You don't give yourself to others or consider them valuable if you don't first of all consider yourself worthy. Your own insecurities cause you to be constantly preoccupied with yourself. Love draws upon the resourcefulness of one's own esteem in order to have a sufficient supply to release it to someone else. It takes personal security to do that.

So husbands ought also to love their own wives as their own bodies. He who loves his own wife loves himself; for no one ever hated his own flesh . . . (vv. 28–29).

No one (in his right mind) ever hated himself! I add that because I'm writing to some people today who do hate themselves. It may be the best-kept secret in the home where you live or in the place where you work, but the truth is that some of you dislike (dare I say despise?) yourself. You've never loved yourself. You don't see your value or worth. You feel useless, not needed, and simply tolerated by others. You feel out of step and out of place. You feel you have little to contribute to society. At times you even wonder why in the world God brought you into existence or kept you on this earth for all these years. Yes, there are some who are so emotionally damaged they literally hate themselves. But the fact is, none *in their right minds* hate themselves, certainly those who think as God designed them to think do not hate themselves.

But what can we do? How can self-esteem begin to emerge? Look at the contrast that follows:

For no one ever hated his own flesh, but nourishes and cherishes it, just as Christ also does the church (v. 29).

Take a few moments to meditate on those two words: *nourish* and *cherish*. The first word is a Greek term that simply means "to bring." But that Greek term has a prefix which causes the words to mean "to bring out." If I were to reach into a beautiful arrangement of flowers and pluck one of the blossoms, I would "pull out" the blossom from the arrangement. I would "bring it out from among" the other flowers. That is the original meaning behind this word translated *nourish*. No one in his right mind hates himself, but he has the ability to bring out what is deep within and let it emerge.

That same Greek term appears in Ephesians 6:4, only there it is used with regard to *children*.

And, fathers, do not provoke your children to anger; but bring them up in the discipline and instruction of the Lord.

In other words, bring out from within your children a respect for authority. It is the parents' task to discipline their children so that they bring out from within them a desire to follow careful instructions from those in authority. The ultimate objective in this is that they someday can handle authority completely on their own, with no need for someone to prompt such submission.

Returning to Ephesians 5:29, we observe the importance of nourishing oneself . . . of "drawing out from within" oneself certain qualities. And then what do we do with what we draw out? Scripture says we then *cherish* what is there. I find it very interesting that this original term is used only twice in the New Testament—here and in 1 Thessalonians 2:7, where we read of a mother who "tenderly cares" for her nursing infant. This word literally means "to warm, to heat." It is used in the Book of Deuteronomy in the Septuagint (the ancient translation of the Hebrew Old Testament into Greek). It is a colorful term that represents a mother hen sitting on her eggs or hovering over her brood of little chicks. She warms them, she protects and cares for them. Realizing the value of each, she "nourishes" them.

Let me put it this way. People who reach adulthood with a good self-image have the ability to draw out from within themselves the things that are worthwhile, to focus clearly on them. Such individuals are secure, resourceful, and competent to handle what life throws at them. When a man really loves himself, he knows what is within him and brings it out. No matter how strong the peer pressure around him may be, he refuses to fold and fade. He brings out and protects what is valuable.

So it must be in a family. A mother who sees talent and abilities in her child, regardless of the mess that's being made, nourishes those things. She "warms" and protects them so her child can discover, "I have talent . . . I have ability."

Benjamin West, a British artist, tells how he first became aware of his artistic skills. One day his mother went out, leaving him in charge of his little sister, Sally. In his mother's absence, he discovered some bottles of colored ink and to amuse her, he began to paint Sally's portrait. In doing so, he made quite a mess of things . . . spilled numerous ink splotches here and there. When his mother returned, she saw the mess, but said nothing about it. She deliberately looked beyond all that as she picked up the piece of paper. Smiling, she exclaimed, "Why, it's Sally!" She then stooped and kissed her son. From that time on, Benjamin West would say, "My mother's kiss made me a painter."[30] God gave the talent, but a very secure and wise mother gave the gift wings.

In the hassled, harried world in which we live, parents, it is easy to focus on the mess instead of the gift . . . to miss the beauty of a hidden talent. The primary secret of enhancing esteem? Nourish and cherish. By cultivating what God has placed into our children's lives, we bring out those capabilities and we "kiss" them into reality. Affectionately hovering over our brood, we hatch those eggs, and each child grows up trusting in God, yes, but also believing in himself . . . which causes him to think, *I am valuable.*

When Self-esteem Is Lacking

A question that comes to anyone's mind who thinks serious-ly about all this is, "What are some signs of a poor self-esteem?"

I do not pretend to be a psychologist or psychiatrist, but I am a fairly good student of human nature and have several observa-tions. We stop at nothing to hide the awful truth from others.

To begin with, *we erect defenses*. The tough guy on the block has a self-esteem problem. So does the bully at school. The superstrong, always-have-to-be-in-charge mentality is a dead giveaway. Show me an individual who aggressively fights to be first, to look good, to rationalize around his one-upmanship, and I'll show you a frightened little boy who struggles with an unhealthy, inadequate self-esteem.

We also tend to wear masks when we lack a good self-esteem. Often the mask is frowning. It shouts, "I'll FIGHT my way through life! My fists will do my talking!" It's a pathetic sight to see adults who try to hide their low self-esteem in that manner. Another mask says, "I'll withdraw" or, "I'll conform. Whatever the crowd wants to do, I'll do it and please everybody."

Another mask commonly seen in our day is smiling. It says, "I'll be a clown. I'll make everybody laugh so the attention will turn from me to the funny stuff I say." This is especially effec-tive in our American culture. Clowning is used to mask a phys-ical imperfection or an extremely painful past. Who hasn't split his sides laughing as Bill Cosby describes his family roots that were deep in poverty? Many of today's comedians use their humor as a defense against childhood hurts. One of my favorites, Jonathan Winters, has unveiled his personal heartaches. His parents were divorced when he was only seven. Unknown to many who enjoy his creative routines, he used to cry when he was alone. Cruelly, other children said he had no father. Winters now uses humor to make the pain bearable.

Then there's Rodney Dangerfield. An absolutely hilarious guy who shakes his head, rolls his eyes, loosens his tie, and mutters his favorite line, "I'll tell ya, I don't get no respect." It makes everybody laugh. How revealing! We laugh at the very things the man would find unendurably painful were they not cloaked in humor. Whether it is Joan Rivers, Woody Allen, Johnny Carson, Bob Hope, or George Burns, if we looked deep enough, long enough, we would find pain in their past . . . lots of it. Laughter helps us overlook the comedian's actual and very real pain. As Solomon insightfully wrote:

> *Even in laughter the heart may ache, and joy may end in grief (Proverbs 14:13, NIV).*

The Living Bible renders that same verse:

> *Laughter cannot mask a heavy heart. When the laughter ends, the grief remains.*

How perfectly that verse applies to the comedian backstage after the performance has ended and the laughing crowd has gone home. "When the laughter ends, the grief remains." Please don't misunderstand. Not every jokester is struggling with a painful past. Let's not think that all laughter is a cover-up. Every family needs a good sense of humor. And, dads, we need to encourage it! That's one of the secrets of rearing happy teenagers . . . but more on that later!

Let me conclude this section by saying your child needs help in this area more than any other. It is the key that unlocks the door to happiness and wholeness. Children and teens everywhere are sending out signals, crying, "Help!" You may not be the parent but rather a teacher, uncle, aunt, coach, pastor, or friend. Whatever you can do to slide through the defenses and get beneath the masks (which are nothing more than scar tissue surrounding a deep, painful wound), do it! Don't wait until later. Step in and help.

When Self-esteem is Strong

What a difference the presence of esteem makes! Look again at the scripture we've been studying.

*Even so husbands should love their wives as [being in a
sense] their own bodies. He who loves his own wife loves
himself. For no man ever hated his own flesh, but nourishes
and carefully protects and cherishes it, as Christ does the
church, because we are members (parts) of His body
(Ephesians 5:28–30, TAB).*

*Children, obey your parents in the Lord [as His representa-
tives], for this is just and right. Honor (esteem and value as
precious) your father and your mother; this is the first com-
mandment with a promise: [Exodus 20:12.] That all may be
well with you and that you may live long on the earth.
Fathers, do not irritate and provoke your children to
anger—do not exasperate them to resentment—but rear
them [tenderly] in the training and discipline and the counsel and admonition of the LORD (Ephesians 6:1–4, TAB).*

When you have a wholesome, confident self-esteem,
you're able to love. You're able to give yourself. You're able to
pull out what is best in the other person, including your children. You're actually able to focus on what is best for them . . .
to bring it out, instead of nagging or harassing them. I have
also observed that a sense of security is passed on to our
young. It's beautiful to see such qualities emerging—even in a
young child.

Cynthia and I have spent a great deal of energy and attention on building a good self-image in each of our four. We
deliberately verbalize our approval, our confidence, our trust.
Year after year and in different ways, we have conveyed our
affirmation. Hopefully, our efforts are paying off. On occasion,
we are encouraged to see the signs of inner strength emerging.

Several years ago I was invited to speak at one of the
chapels for a professional football team. The team happened to
be playing the San Diego Chargers on a Monday night at Jack
Murphy Stadium in San Diego. I decided to invite our younger
son and one of his friends to join me. We had a terrific time
together, lots of laughs and fun. I was curious to see how my
son would respond in a situation where he was in the midst of

several world-class athletes and renowned coaches and announcers. What I observed was most interesting.

His friend was delirious with excitement. As we sat in the hotel coffee shop eating our hamburgers before the chapel and game, Chuck's buddy could not get over seeing, "actually *seeing*," this famous guy and that well-known ball player. Our friend was tooling around the restaurant stealing a glance here and there, hoping for a smile or an autograph. Not Chuck. He seemed more concerned about not wanting onions on his hamburger and wondering what time the game started than the fact that he was within arms reach of a nationally known all-pro quarterback or a 270-pound defensive end.

I must confess . . . I was pleased. My son was secure enough to keep a calm equilibrium in a setting where many other kids his age would have been blown away. And not just kids! To be honest, I found myself wishing someone would introduce me to a couple of those guys. But not Chuck. He was too busy finishing his Coke.

If you are overly impressed while in the presence of celebrities, it may be because you worship stardom and those individuals who've reached it. If you're not careful, you will erect secret idols in your mind. A low self-esteem causes you to have a fixation on someone other than yourself as you live out your frustrations and fantasies through their "success." But let the television get turned off, let the ball player fade, let the stars fall, and you're back inside your fragile shell struggling for existence. Some of the loneliest people I know are those who no longer believe in themselves and try to find their security in others.

Notice in Ephesians 5:28 the theological basis for a healthy self-esteem:

> *So husbands ought also to love their own wives as their own bodies. He who loves his own wife loves himself.*

He doesn't say, "Shame on you for loving yourself!" On the contrary, the statement implies that this is a sign of good mental health. As we just observed . . .

BUILDING THE STRUCTURE

No one ever hated his own flesh, but nourishes and cherishes it, just as Christ also does the church (v. 29).

Frankly, I think we evangelicals have done more damage than good with "worm" theology! I'm getting weary of being told (and having people encourage me to emphasize) how wrong and filthy and unrighteous and godless we are. I realize we all have bents toward evil, as I have already stated. Certainly, until we understand we're depraved sinners, we will never see our need for a Savior. But surely that is not all there is to the message of Christianity! In some circles, however, that seems to be the only message.

A person in Jesus Christ can *and ought to be* the most ful- filled, confident, satisfied person in all this world. But more often than not, he isn't. Many have become so convinced of their depravity, they are now all worm and no butterfly. The best they expect is to struggle and spin inside the cocoon. If you fly free, you're most unusual. Worms aren't supposed to fly, you know. You're supposed to struggle. You're supposed to hurt. In fact, if you're really spiritual, you continue to say only bad things about yourself and to look humble (whatever that means) and to walk with a stoop, giving the appearance that you're down on your luck. For sure, you ought to be dignified and straight-faced. You're not supposed to feel good about yourself or give any hint of self-confidence. Certainly, you should not appear relaxed or laugh out loud!

I love what was said of Charles Haddon Spurgeon, the famous London preacher known for his unintimidated confi- dence. Boy, did he keep 'em guessing! On occasion in the pul- pit, he would lean back and absolutely roar with laughter in front of all those proper British. Finally, a few frowning critics pulled him aside and began to confront him about his "frivoli- ty." He listened as long as he could stand it, then responded with something like, "Oh, gentlemen, if you only knew how much I *hold back,* you would commend me."[31]

People with a healthy self-esteem feel the freedom to laugh a lot! I've received letters from people who listen to my program, "Insight for Living," saying, "Chuck, I often tune in to listen to your program. Listen, man . . . you can stop preaching, but don't ever stop laughing!" I've even had a few add, "Yours is the only laughter that comes into our home."

I am saddened that we don't promote a joyful faith. We have become a frowning, demanding, exacting body of people who look more like grim undertakers than joyful children of the living God. Let me encourage you to help change all that! Cultivate laughter at home.

It is clear that the one who loves himself is better able to love others and relax in their presence. The philosophical framework of all this is rather simple to uncover. Why is it important to love yourself? Because only then are you equipped to love others (v. 25). Only then can you bring out the best in the other person (v. 27).

Are you committed to your child's good? What words do you want to ring in your child's ears and memory as he or she finally leaves home and launches out? Words such as, "Good job, Son" and, "Nice work, young lady, we're proud of you." Or statements like, "It could have been done better," "You could have done it faster," "You really could work harder, you know!"

I heard of a father who was teaching his son how to mow the grass. The little fella did a pretty fair job for a rookie. Naturally, he missed a couple of patches. Instead of the father's bragging on how well the boy did, he focused only on those two places his son had missed. That is so easy to do!

One painful memory comes to mind as I write these words. I recall having been away on a trip for several days. As soon as I drove the car in our driveway, I realized the trash had been picked up during my absence. Wouldn't you know it, the first words out of my mouth as soon as I walked in the door were, "Hey, Chuck!" He answered from his room, "Oh, hi, Dad . . . *welcome home.*" To which I replied, "Did you remember to put

the trash cans out front, Son?" Those were my very first words
. . . immediately following his warm welcome home.

He had forgotten. Crestfallen, he walked to the top of the
stairs, looked down at me and admitted it had slipped his
mind. He said he was sorry two or three times as I delivered
lecture number forty-nine . . . or was it ninety-four?

That evening I realized how negative and petty my perspective had been. I admitted it to him. I asked him to please forgive me. He graciously forgave me for the forty-ninth time . . .
or was it the ninety-fourth?

You know by now that I firmly believe in teaching responsibility. It is important, no question, but is it so important as to
occupy the first moments inside the house after being away for
six days? Hardly. Sadness grips me as I reflect on various occasions when I could have strengthened my wife's and children's
esteem . . . but didn't. I am grateful for a family that has been
willing to forgive this father again and again for the same mistakes. That's grace!

Three Very Practical Yet Powerful Suggestions

Most of us know what we ought to do. What we really
need is help in how to do it. To give substance to my suggestions, let's return to the great book of Proverbs. In it, I find several suggestions that will help us enhance another's esteem.

A Commitment to Discover

> A plan in the heart of a man is like deep water, but a man
> of understanding draws it out (Proverbs 20:5).

Focus on the word *plan*. To make it even more practical, let's
think of this "plan" in these terms: "A plan in the heart of a *child*
is like deep water, but a parent of understanding draws it out."

What plan does Solomon have in mind? I think we could
call it the basic principles of life; the building blocks of
thoughts and desires. A person's deepest inner thoughts. They

are like sunken treasure on the ocean floor. They are covered over with all kinds of debris that keep them secret, which is why they are said to be in "deep water." The writer has in mind the feelings in the nucleus of the soul. They may be hidden, but a parent, friend, mate, or anyone who is a person "of understanding" is able to draw them out.

Families who enhance each other's esteem are families committed to discovering and understanding one another. We consciously work at it. Some days we fail. Other times we accomplish the goal, and the rewards are so satisfying. We are learning to work at finding the good, the strength, the benefit, the hidden counsel, the "plan" in the heart of one another, then drawing it out and valuing it.

Do you have a child who is mechanically inclined? He needs to know you notice. Make comments about it. Brag on his ability. Do you have a child who is athletic, well coordinated? He needs to know you believe he is well coordinated. You say, "That's obvious." But perhaps he hasn't heard it directly from you. He wants to hear you *say* it. You have a child who is intellectually gifted? You sense that she would be good at research, probing deeply into various subjects? *Tell her.* Mention the future possibilities. Help her find the right university. Rather than hammering away on petty stuff that doesn't matter, spend more time discovering how your children's interests can be channeled. Building a strong self-esteem takes a commitment to discover.

A Willingness to Get Involved

Another proverb deserves our attention. It is Proverbs 27:17:

Iron sharpens iron, so one man sharpens another.

This beautiful word picture out of the Old Testament is the idea of a whetstone on a dull ax that needs to be sharpened. If you go into the butcher shop and ask the butcher to slice off several steaks from a large side of beef, he will first put the knife to the sharpening iron and quickly scrape it to a razor's edge. The point can't be missed: What is true of iron-on-iron is true of person-with-person. We sharpen each other to a keen edge.

Let's apply it to parent and child. "As iron sharpens iron, so the parent sharpens the child."

This represents a willingness to touch . . . to get involved. If the discovery process is to happen, the parent must willingly commit the time and energy to make it occur. Yes, it is costly. It may cost you extra money for music lessons. It may cost you time as you go to the ball field and watch them play or to the rink and watch them skate.

My family and I watched a brother and sister skating duo as they represented the U.S.A. in the 1988 Winter Olympics in Calgary. Their mom and dad were in the stands cheering them on with tear-stained faces. The media did a quick flashback and described the sacrifices the couple had made to make this magical moment happen. The family had chosen to continue living in a modest mobile home . . . to pass up various enjoyments so that their son and daughter could continue to develop their skills as ice skaters. The father had recently gone through a period of illness, but there they were, both mom and dad, waving Old Glory and encouraging their kids on.

"Was it worth it? Was all that sacrifice worth it?" asked the reporter. Both answered in unison, "Every minute of it . . . we'd do it again without hesitation." Those parents are involved, sharpening their children's esteem, and loving "every minute of it!"

It will take time for you to spend an evening at a school theater and watch your children perform in drama. It will take an extensive commitment of time. Patience will be a virtue as you witness the slow progress, the struggle to perfect something they have made or built, something they have drawn or accomplished. But never forget, you "sharpen iron" by getting involved.

I can still remember teaching our four children how to ride a bike. Most parents feel uneasy when they teach a child how to keep his balance. You have a panic attack the first time your children commit their lives to two wheels rather than three or four. (Later, when they graduate to four, the panic returns!) At first they don't understand how they could ever stay up on two little tires. And the father or mother is there, saying, "You can do it. Come on, you can do it!"

You did not teach your child to ride a bike while you sat inside the house, sipped a cup of coffee, and read a magazine. You didn't yell out a window, "That's it, Son, now lean to the left next time (yawn). Yeah, now you're doin' better. Oops, too bad. Well, hop up and try again!" No, not on your life. When it comes to riding a bike, you're out there coaching, running alongside, panting, sweating, encouraging, praying, shouting suggestions . . . always affirming. You give a little shove, then as they start falling, you run like mad and grab 'em before they hit the gravel and take the hide off their hands and knees.

We were in our first pastorate in Waltham, Massachusetts, when I taught our oldest how to ride a bike. He learned by riding around the church grounds. Around and around he rode as I trotted alongside. I began to let go and let him pedal a few feet, then grabbed hold. Finally, I watched as he faded out of sight. My heart skipped a beat. He was alone. Then I saw him coming around the other side. "Curt! You *did* it! All the way!" He was grinning from ear to ear as I was screaming. Confidently, he peddled up next to me. I hugged him tightly. Man, was I involved! Wise, affirming parenting includes a willingness to be involved.

An Ability to Reflect

> As in water face reflects face, so the heart of man reflects man (Proverbs 27:19).

You'll notice, if you check that verse in your Bible, the word *reflect* is in italics, which means that particular term is not in the Hebrew. Literally, it reads, "As in water, face—a face, so the heart of man, a man." Because "reflects" is somewhat obvious, the editors have helped us understand its implication by putting it in the text. Here is the general idea: "Just as by looking on the surface of a quiet pool of water you are able to see your face; so the heart reflects itself with the help of another."

A reliable German Old Testament scholar, Franz Delitzsch, writes:

> As in the water-mirror each one beholds his own face, so out of the heart of another each sees his own heart, i.e., he finds in another the dispositions and feelings of his own heart—the face finds in water its reflection, and the heart of a man finds in (another) man its echo.[32]

Solomon seems to be saying we cannot, on our own, fully know ourselves. We need insight and help from another source. As water is needed to provide a mirror-reflection of our external face, another individual is needed to help us mirror our inner being. Ideally, we get this "reflection" first from our parents. As we grow up, we learn who we are and hopefully (though their approval and affirmation) we learn to *like* who we are. As we learn and mature and our parents "reflect" what they see, we feel affirmed and increasingly more secure. Actually, we discover ourselves. When parents mirror life for their children, the children learn what life is about. And as that "reflection" gets fine-tuned, the growing child discovers that he or she is accepted, worthwhile, and a significant person. On the other hand, if the parent lacks the ability to reflect, the child lives in obscurity and begins to feel ignored, lacking in value, and insecure. I can hardly overestimate the value of parental reflection.

I appreciate what one writer asks: "Have you ever thought of yourself as a mirror? You are one—a psychological mirror your child uses to build his identity. And his whole life is affected by the conclusions he draws."

> Every infant is born without a sense of self. Each one must *learn* to be human in the sense that you and I use this word. Once in a while a child has been found who has managed to survive in complete isolation from other people. With no language, no conscience, no need for others, no sense of identity, the "wolf-child" is human only in appearance. Such cases teach that the

sense of selfhood or personhood is not instinctual. It is a social achievement, learned from living with others.[33]

How do I, as a parent, discover? How do I get involved? How do I reflect?

First, I develop good, open communication. As I have mentioned over and over, I listen. I provide an acceptable and permissible setting where it is okay for any family member to say what he or she really feels. I develop that freedom to say it like it really is. It's a real world out there, so there has to be plenty of room for real talk. No religious mumbo-jumbo. No expected cliches or empty "God talk" that sounds pious but says little.

Second, I help each child compensate. By compensation I have in mind assisting them to achieve what they're able to do, helping them overcome the things they're not able to do. A child who doesn't make high grades can still have self-esteem in an academically challenging school. He compensates for his lack by excelling in another field, like music or drama or photography or athletics. In doing so, he learns to love himself properly by achieving in that realm rather than with grades.

There will be parents who will read this chapter on enhancing esteem and still not be convinced of its importance. The truth remains, however, that this sensitive area is one of the major causes of family conflicts and parental heartaches.

A child *must* develop a good, strong self-esteem!

Nothing can substitute for it.

It is never automatic.

The secret rests with parents who are committed to doing everything possible to make it happen.

Are you willing to make such a commitment to your family's self-esteem . . . beginning today? Bravo! You have my sincere applause. In fact, you deserve the Red Plate for supper tonight.

Be my guest.

7

Challenging Years of Adolescence

My wife and I have a bone to pick with several prophets of doom. False prophets, that is.

Years ago when our children were small and life was rather simple, Cynthia and I were enjoying our little kids to the hilt. Problem was, we kept getting pulled aside by grim-faced folks who warned us to "enjoy it while you can . . . it won't last."

With deep frowns and tight lips, these mournful souls would roll their eyes and caution us about the awful days ahead. They shook their heads and wagged their index fingers as they shared their war stories. Since they had survived "the plague," they felt it was their duty to inform us of what we had to dread.

And what was this awful pestilence on the horizon? *Adolescence!*

We may have endured "the terrible twos" (which really wasn't all that terrible) but, they predicted, "You ain't seen nothin' yet—just you wait!" I can still see their faces and hear their groans.

I'm happy to report they were wrong. One-hundred-eighty degrees off. Totally out to lunch.

We were told we would lose touch. We never did.

We were warned that our fun as a family would diminish and finally end. It only increased.

We were instructed on how to survive the ugly years of rebellion and resentment. They never came.

I do not write this out of pride or with an unsympathetic attitude toward some who have gone through tough times with their teenagers. I am simply testifying that in our case, we were badly misinformed. Never (yes, that is the correct word to use) were we embarrassed by our growing-up kids . . . or turned off . . . or physically threatened . . . or verbally stiff-armed. So, just in case you have a child or two who may be on the verge of adolescence, do not be afraid. And, for sure, don't think the fun is over. Here is one man's family (there are many others, believe me) for whom the teen years spelled neither disappointment nor disaster. The principles I have been underscoring throughout this book continued to work and, to this day, pay wonderful dividends.

A Secret Some Parents Forget

Bear in mind I am *not* saying the adolescent years are just like the early childhood years. Whoever thinks that is in for an enormous shock. In order for families to stay close and enjoy a fairly consistent level of harmony and unity through adolescence, you must be willing to change. Let me say it even stronger: When it comes to rearing teenagers, *rigidity is lethal.* Parents who refuse to flex, who insist on everything remaining exactly as it was in earlier years can expect their kids to rebel. But parents who are secure and mature enough to give ground, provide space, allow room, listen more than lecture, release tight control, maintain a calm and affirming attitude and a good sense of humor can look forward to some of the most invigorating and adventuresome years in all of life. At least, that has been our experience.

Cynthia and I have determined that we are going to remain not only parents in the home—but our children's best friends, as well. We have refused to allow anything to drive a wedge in our relationship or break down the lifeline of open and honest communication within our family. We have said that ever since we held each infant in our arms, and we kept repeating it year after year as each grew up.

Pulling that off, however, has required changes in our household. If we expected to maintain our children's respect and sustain that close level of mutual commitment, not only would they need to adjust and cooperate, we would, too.

Has it always been smooth? No. Were there times when we weren't sure how things would turn out? Yes. Was there some source we could turn to for insight and encouragement? Usually, we gleaned most of the help we needed from the Scripture and prayer. But that didn't work like stroking a rabbit's foot. Sometimes, even when we sought the Lord's direction, we weren't absolutely positive about the next step. Perhaps our Lord came to our rescue because He knew we were open and willing to change in whatever way He led us. And perhaps our teenagers remained cooperative with us and compatible with one another because they knew we always wanted to be fair—even if it meant giving up our way for what we discovered to be the right way.

Was it worth it? I mean, really worth all the talking and listening and learning and changing . . . worth all the times when we refused to turn and walk away? A thousand times, *yes!* Nothing on earth, parents, is worth more effort or offers greater rewards. To quote an ancient sage:

> Could I climb the highest place in Athens, I would lift my voice and proclaim: "Fellow citizens, why do you turn and scrape every stone to gather wealth, and take so little care of your children, to whom one day you must relinquish it all?"[34]

Four Questions Adolescents are Asking

Parents need to be willing to change because the period of time between the ages of twelve and twenty represents nothing but change.

The little boy who once hung around mom and dad operated within a fairly close and predictable circle of events. He had no list of expectations in himself or others. Within a few months he finds all that changing. As he enters adolescence, he begins an incredible, often painful, process of change. He wants to be a man, but can't pull it off. He wants his independence, but can't afford it. He discovers that the world of possibilities is bigger than his home, school, church, and a baseball diamond. Furthermore, his body starts doing weird things it has never done before. To add to his confusion, that little girl he and his buddies would never have thought of allowing to join their club suddenly begins to interest him.

Speaking of girls, they have their own stuff to worry about. *And do they worry!* In younger years life was fun 'n' games. Dolls, a friend or two to spend the night, giggles at the table, summer vacations, birthday parties, Christmas holidays, and a new dress for Easter or the piano recital. No big deal . . . except for having to take turns doing the dishes and cleaning her room every once in a while. So simple. So easy. Then almost overnight she becomes extremely conscious. Back then she couldn't care less if her hair cooperated; now every strand is of mammoth concern. Her favorite place in the home is in front of a mirror—any mirror. Each tiny zit assures her that leprosy is just around the corner. And clothes? We're talking daily nervous breakdown. And she's got this body that won't make up its mind . . . plus the kids at school and the commercials on the tube and the magazines in the rack all team up in some kind of secret conspiracy that convinces your once easygoing little lass she is horribly overweight, ugly beyond belief, and hopelessly condemned to a life of embarrassment.

Peer pressure, that ever-present, never-resting beast who arrives uninvited and makes endless demands at that time of life can no longer be ignored. It is there and it is not silent! If anyone reading my words is beginning to think I am exaggerating, just answer one basic question: Have you ever met somebody who would like to go through their adolescent years again? I've asked that question in audiences all across America and have yet to see the first hand raised. The changes, the pressures, the adjustments, the pain, the confusion—yes, even for the Christian teenager—are mind-boggling. When asked that question, most folks sigh and groan aloud!

Having reared our own houseful of teens and having pastored churches where teenagers (by the hundreds) have felt free to express their frustrations, I have boiled down their most essential questions to four.

- **Who am I?**
- **What attitudes will I choose?**
- **Whose rules will I respect?**
- **Which lifestyle will I adopt?**

Understand, they may never verbalize those things or ask them in the precise words I've used. And, for sure, their questions are not limited to these four. Yet these four issues are at the root of most of their struggles. Before we analyze them in greater detail, let's go back and discover in each one the fundamental realm of concern.

First: WHO AM I? This is a struggle with *identity*.

Adolescents know who their parents are, who their teachers are, and who their friends are much better than they know who *they* are. During these transitional years they are questioning, observing, rejecting, imagining, trying out ideas, and playing various roles. Is it their attempt to make the family miserable? No. It's the only way they know to discover who they are.

Second: WHAT ATTITUDES WILL I CHOOSE? This is a struggle with *responsibility*.

In their heads, adolescents think, *I want my freedom . . . but I'm not sure I'm willing to pay the price.* They vote a loud "Yes!" to privileges, but those responsibilities that come in the same package get either a resounding "No!" or "Hold on . . . it may not be worth it." Teens like cars, but not monthly payments or repair bills. They want supper ready, but they don't want to help fix it. They enjoy parties, but not the clean-up. You've got the idea.

Third: WHOSE RULES WILL I RESPECT? Obviously, this represents a struggle with *authority.*

In a day of the diminishing hero, this is especially difficult. Though they may not announce it, adolescents are watching, evaluating, and deciding. They have a penchant for fairness. Furthermore, they will expect much more of others than they can produce themselves. If, for example, they've been burned by a parent who was brutal or walked out, or a teacher or coach who was unfair, their struggle with authority can be exceedingly complicated.

Fourth: WHICH LIFESTYLE WILL I ADOPT? Here is the very common struggle with *conformity.*

During childhood, life boiled down to emulating parents. Mom and dad don't drink or use drugs? No problem; neither does the child. Parents don't allow vulgar jokes or cursing? The child adjusts accordingly. Church every Sunday? Same for the kid. Folks appreciate higher education? Dropping out of high school is out of the question. But let those teenage years roll in and listen to the *why* questions. Other kids at school, stuff on display in the movies, and the whole mind-set of the secular world bombard the adolescent. He struggles to find his way through the maze. If parents are unwilling to flex, to reason, to acknowledge life's numerous tensions, to answer *why* again and again, the kid will drive 'em nuts!

A Brief Word of Caution

We are back to that favorite word of mine when I think of the family . . . *wisdom*. How we need it! When questions are asked that cannot be answered with a simple yes or no, when issues arise and there is no clearly defined manner in which to deal with them, wisdom must emerge. Wisdom makes parents more patient and tolerant with a rash teenager who is struggling to find his way. Wisdom keeps our mouths shut at times when any verbal response would only lead to an argument. Wisdom helps us know when it is time to act or talk, listen or affirm, confront or embrace. As we dig deeper into each of these four struggles and as you sift through the particular situation in your family, ask God for the wisdom you need to respond as you should . . . or perhaps to back off and let Him take charge.

Please let me caution you: Unique struggles require unique solutions. Beware of the "formula approach" as you look for resources to help you in family life. Watch out for those who promise quick solutions or "Seven Easy Steps to Family Harmony." You must always take care, lest you overreact and force something to fit exactly into a setting that needs a more custom-made approach.

Wisdom keeps things sensible and reasonable, guarding us against generalizations. Parents who refuse to adjust, who won't put on the brakes as they plow full bore into the adolescent years, who spit out rules and enforce tighter regulations (while quoting lots of scriptures in defense of their actions) can expect immediate resistance and rebellion. Furthermore, they will create some dreadful memories that neither they nor their kids will be able to erase. Domestic scars are painful . . . many of them permanent. Therefore, please read *the need for wisdom* into each page of this book, into each principle I present.

Four Scriptural Examples of Changing Adolescents

Four Old Testament characters represent the four struggles I've mentioned. The first is a fella named Jephthah.

The Struggle with Identity: Jephthah

Now Jephthah the Gileadite was a valiant warrior, but he was the son of a harlot (Judges 11:1).

What an opening line! "Jephthah the Gileadite was a valiant warrior." Our tendency when we read that is to think, "Man, the guy must have had a fantastic, secure home life." Wrong. All we have to do is read the rest of the sentence and the whole picture comes into better focus: " . . . but he was the son of a harlot." Immediately we get the picture of Jephthah's roots. Rejection. Embarrassment. Neglect. Anger.

The writer informs us of his father's name, but never tells us the mother's. She was a woman of the street. The Living Bible tells the sad story rather bluntly.

Now Jephthah was a great warrior from the land of Gilead, but his mother was a prostitute. His father (whose name was Gilead) had several other sons by his legitimate wife, and when these half brothers grew up, they chased Jephthah out of the country.

"You son of a whore!" they said. "You'll not get any of our father's estate."

So Jephthah fled from his father's home . . .
(Judges 11:1–3, TLB).

Did Jephthah struggle with his identity? You had better believe it. That home was too full of tension. He needed friends to help him survive.

So Jephthah fled from his brothers and lived in the land of Tob; and worthless fellows gathered themselves about Jephthah, and they went out with him (v. 3).

That gang of thugs gave the lad a sense of security . . . a new identity. You see, if a boy doesn't find a secure place in his home, he will find it with his friends. And almost without exception, the friends who will be attracted to a kid like that will be a lower class bunch, called here "worthless." It doesn't mean they had no worth at all, it means they had no sense of respectability. Sort of the original Hell's Angels type. They lived on the street, hung around low-life joints, and slept under some bridge. It should surprise nobody that this gang gave Jephthah a reason to keep existing.

I suppose if they had driven motorcycles in those days, the gang would have been called the "Tob Mob" or something like that. The guys were bad news, Jephthah included. He was the classic example of a guy you never want your daughter to date. What he lacked at home he found on the street.

What's happening? What's he doing? He's trying to find his identity, a reason to go on living. He doesn't know who his mom is. His brothers (another possible source of security) say, "We don't want you around." His dad tosses him out. So Jephthah winds up on the street. That's where a lot of kids are growing up today—on the streets. They look tough. They look self-assured. What they lack, however, is *individual* identity. The group gives them their identity. They look alike, dress alike, act alike. Most gangs have the same identifying mark. On the surface, other teens are tempted to think, *Wow, have they got it together!* Wrong again. There's not a secure one in the bunch. Their uniqueness is the group, being in with friends.

That's all Jephthah had.

When you follow the account into the next phase, you see a lot of resentment coming out of the young man.

> *And it came about after a while that the sons of Ammon fought against Israel. And it happened when the sons of Ammon fought against Israel that the elders of Gilead went to get Jephthah from the land of Tob; and they said to Jephthah, "Come and be our chief that we may fight against the sons of Ammon." Then Jephthah said, to the elders of Gilead, "Did you not hate me and drive me from my father's house? So why have you come to me now when you are in trouble?" And the*

elders of Gilead said to Jephthah, "For this reason we have now returned to you, that you may go with us and fight with the sons of Ammon" (Judges 11:4–8).

They came to him and asked, "Can you fight?" That's like asking A.J. Foyt if he could drive you around the block. Or Al Hirt if he could blow jazz. *Could he fight?* His middle name was Fight!

They said, "We need a guy who knows how to battle and brawl. We need somebody to overthrow the Ammonites. Could you do it? Get those guys off our backs and you'll become our leader."

What a strange turn of events. With a sneer Jephthah responded, "Me? Where were you when I needed you? Where were you when my dad said, 'Jephthah, who?' And my brothers said, 'Get lost!'" He had deep feelings of resentment.

He did take the job, however, and became Israel's judge. Except for a couple of rash decisions in his later life, he managed fairly well. But what I want you to notice in this account is that Jephthah found his security and identity in his friendships. Even though his friends were crummy, they were available and accepting.

This is a perfect place to pause and ask parents several questions. Here's one to chew on: *Are you actively involved in helping your children choose their friends?* If you're not, you may be sorry. They are going to choose some companions as they get older. It sure helps if they are taught early some of the qualities of a friend.

This leads to another question: *Have you ever sat down and talked through the qualities of a good friend?* You say, "What's this big thing about friends? I'm the parent." Believe me, for adolescents, friends are virtually everything. When they turn twelve, thirteen, and older, their friends' counsel will often seem more reliable to them than yours. Kids find an enormous amount of their identity among their peers. As they turn us off, temporarily feeling independent, they listen to the gang.

Another question: *Have you ever talked with your child about how to keep from looking foolish in the eyes of his friends?* Our adolescents feel terribly self-conscious. Whatever we can do to soften the blows of others' stares and comments, we should do it.

A final question: *Are you helping your child stand alone on tough issues so that others will want to follow him or her rather than vice versa?*

It dawned on me several years ago that alcohol is commonly provided almost every place I travel. Airlines always make it available. Business-sponsored banquets usually offer a cocktail hour. Hotel rooms provide it. I was suddenly seized with the thought: Do my children know how to say no to it? How will my children know how to handle it? When the majority is experimenting with drugs or sex and my kid is the only one (or one of the few) saying "Naw, I don't need that," how can he maintain that stance? That prompted me to begin a training program for my family. We began to discuss the secrets of standing alone.

You may think, "Well, if he's a Christian kid coming from our home, he just oughta know how to do it." Trust me, he doesn't. Furthermore, he probably won't feel comfortable walking up to you and asking, "How do you do it? Help me out." Take the initiative! Don't kid yourself for a minute. Your ninth-graders-to-be wonder all summer long, "How in the world am I gonna handle it when I walk into that huge high school?" Scariest place in the world. Do you think for a moment they're going to *say* they're scared? Only in the most protected environments and probably only to their closest friend. Parents, this is a beautiful opportunity for us to get involved, to help them know who they are.

The Struggle with Responsibility: Absalom

I mentioned earlier that a second trouble spot for teens is *responsibility*. To help us come to terms with this one, we need to glance at the life of Absalom in 2 Samuel 13.

Do you remember the story? His dad, David, blew it. Yes, David, as in *King* David. It may surprise you to learn he not only had numerous wives, he also had a bunch of kids. On top of that, the man had several concubines through whom more children were born. In the midst of all that domestic confusion, a little boy named Absalom was born. Right about that time, during the boy's impressionable childhood years, David, the hero of Absalom's life, compromised with Bathsheba. Absalom's model collapsed. That once respected father failed his son deeply.

That was bad enough . . . but later Absalom has to face the horrible news that Amnon, his half-brother, has sexually violated Absalom's lovely, precious sister, Tamar. He is enraged! Absalom waits for his father to step in and do something about what happened. David does virtually nothing. I can't help but wonder if David's passivity wasn't spawned in the backwash of his own adultery. How could the king discipline one of his boys for lack of control in the same area (sexual lust) he failed to conquer?

All hell breaks loose. Frustrated by his dad's apathy, Absalom has Amnon killed. Being indirectly responsible for the murder of his half brother, he runs for his life.

> Now Absalom fled and went to Talmai the son of
> Ammihud, the king of Geshur. And David mourned for his
> son every day. So Absalom had fled and gone to Geshur, and
> was there three years. And the heart of King David longed to
> go out to Absalom (13:37–39).

The boy was confused and resentful. He didn't know how to handle the pressure. What was he wrestling with? Responsibility . . . which evidenced itself in a bad attitude which led him to act irresponsibly.

David was passive, which confused Absalom. Unwisely, Absalom took the issue in his own hands—he had Amnon killed. Now the frightened teenager doesn't know what to do. He's suddenly forced to face the consequences of his own wrong. To make matters worse, instead of staying, he escapes "to Talmai, the son of Ammihud, the king of Geshur." If you take the time to check 2 Samuel 3:3, you will discover that

Talmai is his maternal grandfather. Isn't it interesting that the boy, under intense pressure—the most pressure he has felt in his entire life—runs to his granddaddy? It's the one place he felt secure, safe, understood.

If there are grandparents reading these words, there's one ingredient you have that busy dads and moms seldom have . . . time. Take time for your grandchildren. They need it. Time to listen. Time to affirm, to caution, to love . . . yes, even time to counsel.

I'm intrigued that David mourned every day for his son. Why didn't he just swallow his pride and go get him? Why did David let his boy stay away so long? Ultimately, he knew where he was. "He longed to go out to Absalom." Why didn't he do it? Maybe there were a dozen reasons, but he failed to reach out, to heal the emotional wound. And "Absalom . . . was there three years." Without his father . . . only Granddad Talmai.

Finally, David could handle it no longer.

Then the king said to Joab, "Behold now, I will surely do this thing: go therefore, bring back the young man Absalom. . . . So Joab arose and went to Geshur, and brought Absalom to Jerusalem. However the king said, "Let him turn to his own house, and let him not see my face." So Absalom turned to his own house and did not see the king's face (2 Samuel 14:21, 23–24).

Interestingly, it doesn't say his "father's face," it says "the king's face." Perhaps that suggests the two of them had a king-subject relationship, rather than a father-son relationship.

And to Absalom there were born three sons, and one daughter whose name was Tamar; she was a woman of beautiful appearance (v. 27).

I find it revealing that he named his daughter Tamar. Why, of course! Tamar remained the fairest of his dreams. The young man is living with an unresolved conflict. There was that rape years ago, still fresh on his mind. Next, a father who refused to step in and deal with the offender . . . which resulted in a murder . . . which led to his escaping and staying away for three years. And when he had his own family, Tamar was the name he chose for his daughter. He still mourned the abuse his sister suffered, which his dad failed to deal with.

According to the biblical record, Absalom lived two full years in Jerusalem and never once saw his dad. Even though he was just across the city, really not that far, it seemed as though they were half a world removed. What does he do, now that he's back in town? Read for yourself:

> Now it came about after this that Absalom provided for himself a chariot and horses, and fifty men as runners before him. And Absalom used to rise early and stand beside the way to the gate; and it happened that when any man had a suit to come to the king for judgment, Absalom would call to him and say, "From what city are you?" And he would say, "Your servant is from one of the tribes of Israel." Then Absalom would say to him, "See, your claims are good and right, but no man listens to you on the part of the king." Moreover, Absalom would say, "Oh that one would appoint me judge in the land, then every man who has any suit or cause could come to me, and I would give him justice." And it happened that when a man came near to prostrate himself before him, he would put out his hand and take hold of him and kiss him. And in this manner Absalom dealt with all Israel who came to the king for judgment; so Absalom stole away the hearts of the men of Israel (2 Samuel 15:1–6).

Did he ever! The story reads like a modern-day version of a troubled adolescent in the streets of Hollywood. "If I can't get the satisfaction I need at home, if I can't come to terms with my dad, if I can't solve my problem with responsibility, then I'll take life into my own hands." Which is exactly what he does. He leads an insurrection. And guess what? Do you think David confronts him man to man? No, he runs. He gathers all the stuff from the throne and takes off. Absalom later mocks his dad. Ultimately, he is murdered and David is overwhelmed with grief. We'll look at that in greater depth in chapter 11.

This is no imaginary drama in Jerusalem dreamed up in the mind of some Jewish playwright. This is inspired Scripture from God that can help parents with their adolescents today. It is saying much to us. Things like: Listen, affirm, deal with wrong, communicate, feel, hear the unspoken messages, realize the struggle, stand for truth, be available, hold firm to integrity, talk, solve the conflicts. But don't sit passively by and hope the troubles will somehow fly away.

I feel as strongly about this as anything I've written in years. How easy it is, parents, to slough off our responsibility! Every time we do, our kids resent it. We're hoping somehow something magical will happen between the ages of twelve and twenty. The church, we tell ourselves, will do its thing with our kids and they'll turn out okay. Don't get me wrong; helpful, important things can be provided by a caring church family and by a pastoral staff and a good youth ministry. But, never doubt it, it's what happens in the home that has the greater impact.

The Struggle with Authority: Josiah

When he was only eight years old, Josiah was placed on the throne of Judah. Remarkable! Only a third grader, yet appointed king. Young . . . but amazingly sensitive to God.

> Josiah was eight years old when he became king, and he reigned thirty-one years in Jerusalem. And he did right in the sight of the LORD, and walked in the ways of his father David and did not turn aside to the right or to the left (2 Chronicles 34:1–2).

Can you imagine? Obviously, he needed to turn somewhere for authority. No one would believe the words of this primary school lad, which meant he had to listen to the counsel of someone. Who became Josiah's authority?

Look at verse 3:

> For in the eighth year of his reign while he was still a youth . . .

Some scholars suggest that between the ages of eight and sixteen he was given counsel, so that by this sixteenth year he made some proclamations. He declared the game plan that would be necessary to clean up the country. At age sixteen! Notice what it says,

. . . he began to seek the God of his father David (v. 3).

Darash is the Hebrew verb. It means "to seek with care, to inquire, to search out." So, while an adolescent (age sixteen), Josiah began to make a diligent search into the person of Jehovah. Faced with a series of incredible decisions, the youthful king had enough sense to turn his attention to the Lord God. In his search for Jehovah and in his serious, diligent inquiry into the Torah (God's Word—the books of the law) he became aware of a path that would not fail. As a result, he pointed his people toward righteousness.

This is a good time to state the other side of an issue. I have written a lot about the value of a godly home—the importance of sensitive, wise parents. There are times, however, when certain kids do well later on in life *in spite of* their heritage. Josiah is an example. He didn't get any counsel from his dad (if I read 2 Chronicles 33 correctly). He certainly didn't find an exemplary model in his grandfather Manasseh. For almost six decades, that old reprobate was known for nothing but wickedness. The nation became a cesspool. Yet almost overnight this tiny flower, Josiah, grows like a fragrant rose over a septic tank. And he makes decisions absolutely crossgrained from his recent heritage.

This is real encouragement for those of you whose background was less than loving, stable, or godly. Unloved, unappreciated, unwanted, and untrained, you've sort of brought yourself up. I want to assure you, there is hope. You can be a Josiah. And to any of you adults who rub shoulders with struggling teenage guys and gals: Be aware of any opportunity to point them toward the Bible and your Lord. Someone in Josiah's inner circle must have nudged him to open the long-neglected scrolls. Someone must have said, "Son, if you want to make sense of this poor, troubled world, here's where you need to start looking." If you love teens and you're sensitive to the Spirit's voice, you could be that individual to a searching young life.

Josiah, we're told, began to make a diligent search. *He was pursuing a trustworthy authority.* He said to himself, "It is Jehovah who will be my authority. I will listen to and honor His counsel. All the other counsel will bow to His counsel."

So for four years, as the youthful king sought the Lord with his whole heart, he established a process of cleaning up his nation. By the twelfth year, strong-worded edicts began flowing from the royal palace.

> *For in the eighth year of his reign while he was still a youth, he began to seek the God of his father David; and in the twelfth year he began to purge Judah and Jerusalem of the high places, the Asherim, the carved images, and the molten images. And they tore down the altars of the Baals in his presence, and the incense altars that were high above them he chopped down; also the Asherim, the carved images, and the molten images he broke in pieces and ground to powder and scattered it on the graves of those who had sacrificed to them. Then he burned the bones of the priests on their altars, and purged Judah and Jerusalem. And in the cities of Manasseh, Ephraim, Simeon even as far as Naphtali, in their surrounding ruins, he also tore down the altars and beat the Asherim and the carved images into powder, and chopped down all the incense altars throughout the land of Israel. Then he returned to Jerusalem (vv. 3–7).*

That was King Josiah, fresh out of puberty! He was only an adolescent, making decisions that would rock a nation like ours today, to say nothing of Judah after fifty-seven consecutive years of wickedness.

What a remarkable story! Do you want to know what influenced Josiah to be such a contrast to his times? It was the Word of God which Josiah found and followed, and it was a tender heart which the young man nourished. The verses that follow the ones we've looked at in 2 Chronicles bear out these two observations. He embraced Scripture without reservation, and he cultivated a heart for God. When those two issues are in place, the struggle with authority virtually solves itself.

The Struggle with Conformity: Daniel

I've saved one of my all-time favorite stories until last. Chapter 1 of Daniel records a marvelous example of an adolescent whose battle with conformity was won in a most unusual setting.

Judah, the nation over which Josiah had reigned, refused to maintain the young monarch's reforms. After he died, they fell back into their old ways and were finally conquered by the Chaldeans (or Babylonians).

The king of Babylon, Nebuchadnezzar, decided there were some bright young Jewish men he wanted in his court. They could become bilingual and be a great help to him. And he would be a wiser, certainly a more diplomatic king, if he had some of those guys around him who were from the Jewish culture.

So, Nebuchadnezzar, rather than killing everybody, said something like this to Ashpenaz, his right-hand man: "Hand pick some choice young men who've got their act together. No losers! Locate all the sharp young minds you can find, and bring 'em in. We're going to put them through a three-year, postgraduate (brain-washing) crash course in Chaldean culture." His plan was to hand-tool a small group of bright young Jews.

That's exactly what happened. He threw the book at them. He gave them everything he could dig up in his Chaldean culture during a three-year course.

> Then the king ordered Ashpenaz, the chief of his officials, to bring in some of the sons of Israel, including some of the royal family and of the nobles, youths in whom was no defect, who were good-looking, showing intelligence in every branch of wisdom, endowed with understanding, and discerning knowledge, and who had ability for serving in the

king's court; and he ordered him to teach them the literature and language of the Chaldeans (Daniel 1:3–4).

It says, "youths in whom was no defect." The word youth is used broadly in the Old Testament. We have every reason to believe here it has reference to those formative years of adolescence, perhaps fourteen to sixteen years old.

None in the group had any physical disability. They were gifted, handsome, and demonstrated intelligence in every realm of knowledge. I don't know how they tested them or even how they interviewed them. All I know is they pulled a group together, all endowed with understanding and discerning knowledge. They were the bright guys on the campus in the days of Judah, "the sharp ones from the student body," we would say today. They were the leaders, because the king wanted them to be influential in his Chaldean court.

The Chaldean plan was to change their thinking. Talk about conformity! Talk about peer pressure! Here are these monotheistic, rigid, straitlaced, Jewish young men moving into the liberal court of Babylon. That would be like leaving an ultra-fundamentalistic, dogmatic college in Shelter Cave, Pennsyltucky, for Cal Berkeley. It was a deliberate plan to break down their narrow theology and philosophy of life and broaden their horizons with any number of tempting things. Their diet was also to change:

And the king appointed for them a daily ration from the king's choice food and from the wine which he drank, and appointed that they should be educated three years, at the end of which they were to enter the king's personal service (v. 5).

We can hardly imagine the pressure on those young men. They gave them new names to change their sense of identity and changed their whole pursuit in life. Now this isn't just casual peer pressure from a few kids in the back row at Gunney Sack High School. This is a definite, well-defined Babylonian plan carried out by professionals to make Jews into Chaldean thinkers. Got it? The whole culture was to be adopted, including a new diet. And it was at that very point Daniel put on the brakes.

> *But Daniel made up his mind that he would not defile himself with the king's choice food or with the wine which he drank; so he sought permission from the commander of the officials that he might not defile himself (v. 8).*

That is a very carefully chosen set of words. Daniel's approach here is extremely important. I would imagine with Daniel's wisdom and understanding, mentioned in verses 3 and 4, that he tactfully went to this commander and offered an alternate plan—a "ten-day, money back guarantee." And the result? He was "granted favor" and allowed to do it.

Daniel had said to him, "Please test your servants for ten days, and let us be given some vegetables to eat and water to drink" (v. 12). That's all he asked.

As I read this I get the distinct feeling that Daniel didn't make a fool of himself. He did not fight it; he simply made a request. He said, in effect, "Give us grits and cornbread; you guys can have all those steaks and pork chops you want. All we need are the basics: whole-grain cereal, a few vegetables, and water."

> *Then let our appearance be observed in your presence, and the appearance of the youths who are eating the king's choice food; and deal with your servants according to what you see (v. 13).*

I have purposely not emphasized the most vital part until now. It is the reason Daniel would not cooperate with the plan. He *"made up his mind."*

Let me write to the teenager for a few moments. You may be going through a struggle. You may not have had the most ideal home life or background. Even now, you know you don't have it all put together. You may not even know what your career's going to be. (I'd be surprised if you did.) You may not have all of your convictions worked through. But I'll tell you what you do have. You have the ability to *make up your mind.* Illustration? Daniel! He made up his mind *before* the plan was put into operation. Before the pressure mounted.

The summer before school started he determined in his mind, "I'm not going to do this. I'm not going to do that. I'm going to work out a way that will keep me from having to fall in line with the group around me." And he determined, through a very wise plan, a special way to be distinctive. To stand alone. His secret was no superhuman achievement; he simply made up his mind.

Now, I'm not able to guarantee that if you make up your mind about God you'll be the valedictorian of your high school graduating class. But I'll guarantee you this, God will come to your aid. You will be unique. You will become the focal point of another kind of leadership on your campus. You will become an impact on your team, your club, or your youth group. They will see the difference.

Notice Daniel's parents are never mentioned here or anywhere. They don't make Daniel's mind up for him. The young man makes up his own mind. All this verifies that a teenager has all the mental and emotional apparatus necessary to choose for righteousness, for what is best before God. Daniel certainly did. He determined before God that he would follow a precise plan when school started. If he could do that, so can any other adolescent. *That includes you.*

He was so convincing that the authorities agreed with him—even at great personal risk. They tested him and his buddies after ten days.

> *And at the end of ten days their appearance seemed better and they were fatter than all the youths who had been eating the king's choice food (v. 15).*

It seemed incredible. There had been no T-bones . . . no after-dinner drinks . . . no malts, no sundaes, no special little tidbits, nothing. Just cereal, vegetables, and water. (Sounds dreadful, but it worked wonders.)

So the overseer continued to withhold their choice food and the wine they were to drink, and kept giving them vegetables. And as for these four youths, God gave them knowledge and intelligence in every branch of literature and wisdom; Daniel even understood all kinds of visions and dreams (vv. 16–17).

How in the world could it have happened? God honored their convictions. This reminds me of a proverb:

When a man's ways are pleasing to the LORD, he makes even his enemies to be at peace with him (Proverbs 16:7).

When commencement time arrived, the four graduated at the top of their class!

Then at the end of the days which the king had specified for presenting them, the commander of the officials presented them before Nebuchadnezzar. And the king talked with them, and out of them all not one was found like Daniel, Hananiah, Mishael and Azariah; so they entered the king's personal service. And as for every matter of wisdom and understanding about which the king consulted them, he found them ten times better than all the magicians and conjurers who were in all his realm (vv. 18–20).

Do you know where making up one's mind works? You name it. It works at conventions where businessmen have to spend a week. It works on the road where traveling salesmen have to spend a lot of their spare time. It works in the military, when you're stuck in a situation and there is nobody around to encourage you or hold you accountable. It works on a campus: in the dorm, fraternity, or sorority; in class. It works in a family, especially within the heart of every teenager. Making up one's mind is the answer to the struggle with conformity. Cynthia and I have seen it work time and again as our four were growing up.

A Broad Application

I want to close this chapter by offering two practical suggestions: First, *an adolescent must be given room to make up his mind.* Flex is essential. We must give our teens room. That includes the room to fail. We need to cut the cord slowly. It's like letting a kite climb further and further into the wild blue while you reel out the string. Are there dangers from trees and power lines? Sure there are. But you're still holding that string until the moment arrives (God will give you the wisdom to know when) to hand it over to the divine Parent. Your counsel is valuable. Your support is valuable. But one day you must let go.

Parents provide a family with a bedrock foundation; however, without flexibility, disaster can occur. My thoughts turn to an analogy that illustrates this rather clearly: the Golden Gate Bridge in San Francisco. That bridge is the city's boldest structure in that its great south pier rests directly upon the San Andreas Fault. It is an amazing study in contrasts between flexibility and strength. Here is the way one man describes that unique combination:

> It is built to sway some twenty feet at the center of its one-mile suspension span. The secret to its durability is its flexibility that enables this sway, but that is not all. By design, every part of the bridge—its concrete roadway, its steel railings, its cross beams—is inevitably related from one welded joint to the other up through the vast cable system to two great towers and two great land anchor piers. The towers bear most of the weight, and they are deeply embedded into the rock foundation beneath the sea. In other words, the bridge is totally preoccupied with its foundation. This is its secret! Flexibility and foundation.[35]

Mom and Dad, twin towers of strength, provide the family with its rock-like foundation. But in order for there to be a continual flow of communication and understanding, the bridge must flex!

Finally: *Personal convictions stand the test much better than forced convictions.* It is more powerful to make up *your own* mind to do something, rather than respond to what someone else tells you to do. Illustration: dieting. A doctor can mention all kinds of eating behavior changes, but not until we decide to do something will things change. And it won't take $120 jogging suits or $90 athletic shoes or an elaborate program somebody promotes. The secret is what happens in the mind. You simply determine it is going to occur. And it happens. Just like that. It isn't easy, but starting is crucial.

So it is in the battle with adolescence. And parents, especially you who really want the best for your children (I know exactly how you feel), you have to give them room to make up their minds. Have a talk with them. Work it through, okay? Please, please do that.

If you will . . . if you are just as willing to change as you expect your teenagers to be, the challenging years of adolescence will be just that.

Challenging, not impossible.

8

Having Fun with Your Family

A hurry-up lifestyle results in a throw-away culture. Things that should be lasting and meaningful are sacrificed on the altar of the temporary and superficial.

The major fallout in such a setting is the habit of viewing relationships casually. This cavalier attitude cripples society in various ways:

- **Friends walk away instead of work through.**
- **Partnerships dissolve rather than solve.**
- **Neighbors no longer visit and relax together. They erect stone walls and exist on isolated islands.**
- **The aged are resented, not honored.**
- **Husbands and wives divorce rather than persevere.**
- **Children are brushed aside rather than nourished; used and abused rather than cherished and cultivaed.**

Caught in the vortex of all this, the most common response is to become negative and pessimistic. Everything begins to look dark. We start anticipating failure, impossibilities, and inevitable doom. We become rigid, much too serious. We start focusing on what *isn't* going well and our whole frame of reference, to use Bunyan's vivid analogy, takes on the likeness of the "Slough of Despond." Indifference pokes a slow leak in our boat as Intensity and Anxiety climb aboard. How difficult it is to remain positive and encouraged in such a dismal context . . . yet how essential!

I heard recently about a man who was driving through North Carolina. As he approached one of the little towns nestled in the mountains, he noticed a large sign near the city limits marker. It read:

WE UNDERSTAND THAT A SERIOUS RECESSION IS SUPPOSED TO HAPPEN THIS YEAR, BUT WE'VE DECIDED NOT TO PARTICIPATE.

I love it! With an attitude like that, the place becomes an oasis of hope and joy in a desert of depression.

Let me encourage you to adopt a similar mindset in your family. Let's stop taking our cues from the morning paper and the evening news. Let's decide not to be influenced by those grim statistics! I'm tired of the pessimism that dominates even the weather report. How about a switch? Instead of remembering that tomorrow will have a 20 percent chance of rain, what's wrong with thinking about the 80 percent chance of sunshine?

Call me crazy if you like (you won't be the first), but I am more convinced than ever that attitudes shape just about everything we do. Not facts, not a group of so-called authorities. Not some big, thick book spelling the demise of civilization . . . but *attitudes*. When those attitudes get refocused on God's power and His incredible purposes for living, hang on to your socks! Instead of running from each other in our relationships, we would be running toward one another. Before we realized it, people would become more important to us than status, fame, or fortune.

BUILDING THE STRUCTURE

I believe it was the writer Christopher Morely who said that if everybody had only five minutes to live, every phone booth in the world would be occupied by someone. Each would be sending out final words of affection and affirmation.

I may have questioned that before I endured an earthquake. Living here in southern California, you never know when "the big one" will hit. Little tremors and rock 'n' rollers keep us wondering. Early one October morning several years ago I was enjoying some quiet study in my office. Suddenly, the floor began to move. Doors started to bump and windows rattled. Within seconds I was partially covered with books from the shelves above my head. My desk lamp rocked back and forth. I stumbled across the room to stand in a doorway as the thought flashed through my mind, *If this isn't "The Big One," I can't imagine what IT will be like!*

As you know, it wasn't. We still have it to look forward to. It's supposed to happen each year, but I've decided not to participate!

Guess the very first thing I did when the shaking calmed down. Right. I picked up the phone and called home. First, I checked to see if Cynthia, Cols, and Chuck were okay. I then made two more calls . . . one to our son and his wife, Curt and Deb, and the other to our daughter and her husband, Charissa and Byron (mainly to check on the grandkids).

Relationships! When the quake hit, I never once thought, *I wonder who the church will get as my replacement.* Or, *Did we pick up the dry cleaning yesterday?* Or, *We probably ought to cancel our subscription to* Newsweek. Or, *Shoot! I forgot to get the car washed.* No way! My entire focus was on those people who bear my name, who complete the loop in my family circle.

Relationships! Never sell them short. If we'll slow down the hurry-up lifestyle for a moment and pause to catch our breath, we'll realize the need to call a halt to our throw-away culture.

Flexibility: It Is Essential

Uptight families cease to function properly. When dad is tense and mom is irritable, the kids have no trouble deciphering the message: Shut up and don't mess around. Feelings start getting internalized and confused. Negotiations are strained. Fear builds up as tension mounts. Communication is finally reduced to looks, frowns, shrugs, sarcastic jabs, and put-downs. Cooperation and teamwork fall by the wayside. Extremes emerge—long periods of silence periodically interrupted by shouting matches. Far from a haven of rest, such a home becomes a hell on earth.

In the previous chapter, I underlined the value of flexibility. Because my emphasis was on adolescence, I applied most of my comments to that changing period of life. In this chapter, I want to broaden the base of my application and address the essential need for flexibility in the whole family scene.

Remember, I'm not writing of some sterile, theoretical technique, but rather of a relational attitude. I offer no "series of steps" that will ultimately lead to a flexible family. Wisdom, remember, must be given room to flow. It cannot be reduced to analytical formulas or computer programs. As I have emphasized throughout these pages, building a strong family is a daily process, a trial-and-error, learn-as-you-go series of discoveries that has little to do with rigid rules and regulations . . . and everything to do with attitudes and actions.

My message in this particular chapter is this: In order to grow, mature, and flourish, everyone needs room; let's provide plenty of it.

Watching other families over the years has confirmed what I've discovered in my own: The two entrenched enemies of flexibility are Hurry and Rigidity. Each results in family tension. Each, therefore, must be exposed.

What's the Hurry?

The older I get the more I appreciate the benefits of taking time. Woodwork done slowly and meticulously by a craftsman is beautiful, and able to endure the test of the elements. Art—whether musical compositions, needlework, sculpture, or painting—requires time and attention to detail. Even the cultivation of our walk with God or some ministry skill requires a great deal of time to develop.

The psalmist realized this when he wrote, "Be still, and know that I am God" (Psalm 46:10, NIV). The Hebrew does not suggest standing around and letting your mind wander—not that kind of being still. Rather, it means "Let go, relax." The New American Standard renders this, "Cease striving." What a timely admonition!

If all this is true of other realms and responsibilities, it is certainly applicable to the home and family. Children were not created to be "jerked up" (as my mother used to put it), but to be cared for with gentleness and attention to detail. They require time . . . lots of it. Not all of it needs to be supervised, however.

Perhaps the best way to describe my early childhood world of play is with the word *relaxed*. Lots of friends in the neighborhood. Sandlot football down at the end of Quince Street in East Houston on an open field adjacent to St. Andrews Methodist Church. Endless and exhausting hours of one-on-one or "horse" over at Eugene's house—with Freddie and Bruce—as the four of us shot hoops against the garage backboard. Then there was always "Hide 'n' Seek" and "Kick the Can"—until suppertime. Weekends found me playing Cowboys and Indians, making scooters out of beat-up roller skates, running races and relays down the street, shooting my BB gun in the woods down by the creek, and messing around with crawdads after a rain.

Plenty of time to grow up . . . easygoing, relaxing hours.

In the summer, there were family reunions down below Palacios at my granddaddy's little bay cabin, plus fishing, floundering, crabbing, swimming, driving the tractor, making rafts out of toesacks and old inner tubes, seining for bait, and eating. My—*did we eat!* Fresh shrimp, crab gumbo, fried gulf trout, barbecued beef cooked on chicken wire stretched over an open pit of hickory coals, freshly plucked watermelon, big brown eggs (laid that very morning), thick slab bacon, home-made biscuits, gravy, hand-cranked ice cream . . . *I gotta stop!*

Best of all, my brother, sister, and I were given room to be kids. Just kids. I went to school barefoot until the fourth grade (when Wanda Ragland and I fell madly in love), and I was still playing cops and robbers in junior high. Nobody hurried me to grow up. I suppose everybody figured it would just happen. I can still remember one hot summer afternoon sitting on the curb in torn blue jeans, licking a Popsicle and thinking, *This is the life!* I had finished mowing the grass, putting out the trash, mopping the bathroom floor, and throwing my paper route (my major chores), and was about to head down to the church with my well-worn football to play until my daddy whistled, signaling supper.

I was just a kid. No big expectations drove me to excel or achieve. Life was allowed to run its own course back then, like a lazy river working its way down from the slopes to the sea. No big deal, no adult pressure to perform, just downhome, easy livin', fun, growin' up stuff. And plenty of time. A lingering, relaxed childhood was mine to enjoy.

No longer, it seems. Forty-plus years removed from my laid-back lifestyle, there is a new youngster in our city streets. Have you noticed? Perhaps I'm overly sensitive because I've read David Elkind's splendid book *The Hurried Child,* with the provocative subtitle, *Growing Up Too Fast Too Soon.*[36] On the cover is a little girl, not more than eleven or twelve . . . with earrings (pierced ears, of course), plucked eyebrows, carefully applied cosmetics, teased and feathered hair, and exquisite jewelry. I've looked at that picture dozens of times, and on each occasion I see more. She bears the look of bewildered innocence—almost like a helpless calf being pushed to slaughter.

She's afraid, but can't say so; it wouldn't be chic. She's into a role that deprives her the freedom to be simply a child. The problem? She is being hurried—like so many children and adolescents today. The luxury of childhood is no longer an option.

She reminds me of the seven-year-old whom Susan Ferraro mentioned in an article titled "Hotsy Totsy." It was the little girl's birthday party: ice cream and cake, a donkey poster with twelve tails waiting to be pinned, a door prize, the works.

> "Ooh," sighed seven-year-old Melissa as she opened her first present. It was Calvin Klein jeans. "Aah," she gasped as the second box revealed a bright new top from Gloria Vanderbilt. There were Christian Dior undies from grandma—a satiny little chemise and matching bloomer bottoms—and mother herself had fallen for a marvelous party outfit from Yves St. Laurent. Melissa's best friend gave her an Izod sports shirt, complete with alligator emblem.[37]

It's not the clothes. It's not those silly brand names that bug me. It's the message they announce. It's the hurry-up woven through those thread and styles. It's the subliminal strokes and sensations a child in the second grade can wear but isn't equipped to handle.

The media isn't going to be outdone, either. Music, books, films, and of course, television increasingly portray the young as precocious and seductive. Kids are given scripts and scenes that present them in more or less explicit sexual and manipulative situations. "Such portrayals," writes Elkind, "force children to think they should act grown up before they are ready." This is certainly true in movies like *Little Darlings* where the two principals—teenaged girls—are in competition as to who will lose her virginity first. And I think I'll gag if I hear any more songs like "Take Your Time (Do it Right)" or "Do That to Me One More Time."

I'm no expert, understand, just a father and a concerned observer. From what I've read and heard on the subject, I understand that emotions and feelings are the most complex and intricate part of development. They have their own timing and rhythm and cannot be hurried. Children can grow up fast in some ways, but not in others. It is tough enough with nobody pushing, but I'm convinced it's bewildering, even confusing, when children's behavior and appearance are hurried to speak "adult" while their insides cry "child." It simply isn't fair!

America's most outstanding high school quarterback was written up in *Sports Illustrated* several years ago. His name is Todd Marinovich. His record of passing yardage (9,914) is all-time tops. His senior year in high school he threw for more yards than Jim Kelly or Dan Marino or John Elway did in theirs. Of 104 Division I-A colleges and universities, no less than 100 of them were jumping through the hoop to have this young phenom. The pros must already be salivating. We're talking franchise.

But before we get too impressed, let's back away a few feet, step into the time tunnel, and relive how this young man arrived at this so-called enviable moment. It is a mouth-opening, mind-boggling account of parental fanaticism. Todd's dad, Marv, has been the primary force behind his son's life. Trudi, his mother, has also cooperated. The article from which I quote has a telling title, "Bred to Be a Superstar."

> What's fascinating about Marinovich, a 6'4–$\frac{1}{2}$", 212 pound lefthanded redhead, is that he is, in a real sense, America's first test-tube athlete. He has never eaten a Big Mac or an Oreo or a Ding Dong. When he went to birthday parties as a kid, he would take his own cake and ice cream to avoid sugar and refined white flour. He would eat homemade catsup, prepared with honey. He did consume beef but not the kind injected with hormones. He ate only unprocessed dairy products. He teethed on frozen kidney. When Todd was one month old, Marv was already working on his physical conditioning. He stretched his hamstrings. Pushups were next. Marv invented a game in which Todd would try to lift a medicine ball onto a kitchen counter. Marv also put him on a balance beam. Both activities grew easier when Todd learned to walk. There was a football in Todd's crib from day one. . . .
> Eventually Marv started gathering experts to work on every aspect of Todd's physical condition—speed, agility,

strength, flexibility, quickness, body control, endurance, nutrition. He found one to improve Todd's peripheral vision. He enlisted a throwing coach and a motion coach and a psychologist. These days 13 different experts are donating their time in the name of science.

Tom House, the pitching coach for the Texas Rangers and a computer whiz, has analyzed Todd's form and found that while his balance is perfect, his arm is 4.53 inches too low throughout his delivery. Todd, who listens to everyone, is working on it. This Team Marinovich is the creation of Marv, who was a two-way lineman and a captain at USC in 1962, a marginal pro in the AFL with the Raiders and a sometime assistant coach for the Raiders, the Rams, the Cardinals, and the Hawaiians of the defunct WFL.

Though Marv owns an athletic research center—a sort of high-tech gym—his true occupation has been the development of his son, an enterprise that has yet to produce a monetary dividend. And the Marinovich marriage ended last year after 24 years. "All Marv has done," says a friend, "is give up his entire life for Todd."

Which is fine with Marv. Father and son now live in a one-bedroom apartment. Todd has the bedroom, and Marv sleeps on the sofa in the living room. On weekends Todd visits Trudi, who has moved back in with her parents in Newport Beach.

"I think I'm a tyrant," says Marv. "But I think you have to be to succeed. The best thing about it is my relationship with my son. We wanted to have the healthiest possible mom and the healthiest possible child. It's fanatical, but I don't know if you can be a great success without being fanatic." He pauses and then continues, "I suppose it was a little overdone."[38]

That, ladies and gents, is classic understatement! I cannot help but wonder if Todd will someday miss having been a child.

Scripture clearly states, "There is an appointed time for everything" (Ecclesiastes 3:1). *How about time to be a child?* How about time to grow up slowly, carefully, yes, even protected, and dare I add, a little naive? How about time to "speak as a child, think as a child, reason as a child" (1 Corinthians 13:11)? It will take a lot of effort to make that happen. For a few, it is too big a hassle. Maybe it's because we're too busy being what we're not and pushing our kids to do the same. Let's back off and start having fun again! Let's return to the psalmist's counsel to relax . . . to cease struggling.

Flexibility, folks, doesn't come easy! You and I are surrounded by peers who tend to pressure us by making what I call hurry-up comments. We hear them every day. They're about as subtle as a Mac truck.

"Our son is only seven, but you ought to see him on his PC. Wow! The kid's a whiz."

"We've decided that our preschooler needs to get serious about the future, so we've got her into dance and modeling classes. After all, the possibilities are endless once she gets into making commercials."

"We think Timmy has real athletic ability. We've talked him into that basketball clinic for nine-year-olds. The pros will want the kid before long!"

Don't get me wrong. I have already written on the importance of parents' seeing potential and being there as an encouragement . . . but to push for too much, too fast, too early takes away the fun of growing up . . . of being just a relaxed, tightly knit family with well-developed, close relationships.

Take it easy! Much of what parents push for will naturally flow in time. Put your energy into cultivating close relationships. Those high-powered goals have a way of emerging at the right time.

Why the Rigidity?

There is an equally disturbing concern of mine that is robbing fun from families—rigidity. What makes this one especially subtle is that it is present in homes of well-meaning Christian parents. Wanting to guard their children from the pitfalls of a permissive, godless society, they push the pendulum to the opposite extreme. For all the right reasons, these parents decide to put the clamps on all liberty. A willingness to listen, to reason, to give a little, to shrug and pass certain things off as part of growing up is considered too permissive. In place of all that is the erection of a brick fortress, where unbending rules are adhered to and nonnegotiables are regularly spelled out by super-intense parents.

At the risk of sounding repetitive, I must state again that a major reason our family has remained close through each state, and to this day continues to grow together and have fun together, has been our commitment to staying flexible. I hesitate to speak of this lest it all suddenly screech to a halt. I'm reminded of what one whale said to his mate, "Better watch it; when you get to the top and start to blow, that's when you get harpooned!"

My desire is neither to "blow" as if we've arrived, nor to shame those who are struggling through times of family turmoil. The only reason I return to the familiar song of the Swindolls' close-knit family is to encourage you with the thought, "It can work! These things he is writing about have been proven over the years in their lives." Trust me, we have made numerous mistakes and have frequently failed to carry out what we knew was best. Somehow we have survived, still walking in harmony. The grace of God is the main reason—plus children who have continued to forgive us, partly because they never had reasons to doubt their value in our eyes.

Let me return to this issue of domestic rigidity. Frankly, it cuts cross-grain with the magnificent grace and liberty of the gospel. Christ's death and resurrection provide the basis of the gospel. That "good news" has to do with our being liberated from bondage by His provision . . . bondage to the law (which condemned us) and bondage to the power of sin (which intensified our guilt before God). Freed, we are now able to call our God *Father,* and our Savior *Friend.* What joy, what refreshing space this provides! It is like being set free from prison. Spiritually, we have moved into a realm of such ecstatic delight, the mere thought of being enslaved again is repulsive.

To quote Jesus Himself: "If therefore the Son shall make you free, you shall be free indeed" (John 8:36).

Think of it! Free *indeed*. Totally and completely free in Him. At last, free to love, to serve, to laugh, to relax in His presence. Free to be all we were designed to be. Free to share openly . . . free to think, to create, to call Him our Friend!

My question is obvious. If that is true of our condition in God's heavenly family, why shouldn't it be true in our earthly family? What keeps us from that level of spontaneity, closeness, and hilarious joy? Who came along and stole the joy from the family . . . especially the Christian family? Who had the audacity to shove us back behind the bars of a relational prison? I say, *out* with such enemies of freedom!

If you know your Bible, you know which New Testament letter I have on my mind right now: Galatians. It is only six chapters long—less than 150 verses—but it packs a wallop. Paul wrote it because a group of Judaistic legalists had moved in on this congregation and stolen their liberty. He decided to expose the false teachers and exhort the Galatian Christians to break the bonds that were slowly but surely enslaving them.

Rather than my quoting passage after passage, I encourage you to take the time to read the Galatian letter in one sitting. You'll get the picture. My purpose in mentioning it is that there are several analogies between living in God's family strictly by tight rules and rigid regulations and living in our earthly family the same way. My observation is that neither works. The joy, the spontaneity, and the creativity dry up. So does the fun. In either place people exist in fear, realizing the hammer may fall at any moment. Furthermore, in the loss of liberty there is also the loss of motivation. Worst of all, life gets reduced to nothing more than a grim existence, best described by Ray Stedman who pictured our hurry-up lifestyle in these vivid words:

> *This is the age of the half-read page,*
> *The quick hash and the mad dash,*
> *The bright night with the nerves tight,*

The plane hop with the brief stop;
The lamp tan in a short span,
The big shot in a good spot,
The brain strain and the heart pain,
The catnaps until the spring snaps;
And the fun is gone.

Children are a lot like chickens . . . they need room to squawk, lay a few eggs, flap their wings, even to fly the coop. Otherwise, let me warn you, all that lid-sitting will one day explode and you'll wish you had not taken such a protective stance.

How to Keep the Fun in the Family

Some of you are sincerely interested in changing. You see that what you have been doing isn't working. You want to lighten up and let the pressure off. You've had enough of protectionism and legalism. Good for you! You're well on your way to happiness at home if that is your attitude. Let me suggest several guidelines which will help make it happen.

First, *try to be absolutely authentic.* I know that seems like a threatening thought, but it is a giant step toward open communication.

How does authenticity reveal itself? It isn't that difficult.

If you aren't sure of yourself, admit it.

If you're afraid of the risk, say so.

If you don't know the answer to a question your teenager asks you, use those wonderfully relieving words, "I don't know."

If you were wrong, confess it.

If you feel under pressure from others, own up to it.

If your kids ask why, refuse to dodge behind that favorite of all parental cliches, "Because I said so." Be painfully honest with yourself. If you cannot think of a reason, maybe that's God's way of saying you need to bend and even give in. Our youngsters (and oldsters) deserve to know the truth . . . even if *we* were not raised in such a vulnerable environment. One father describes it this way:

The speech was finished and the audience had been generous with its applause, and in the car on the way home my fourteen-year-old son turned to me and said: "I really admire you, Dad, being able to get up there and give a speech like that. You always know what to say to people. You always seem to know what you're doing."

I smiled when he said that. I may even have blushed modestly. But, at that moment, I didn't know what to say at all. After a while I thanked him and assured him that some day he would be comfortable speaking in front of an audience, that he would always know what to say to people, that he would always know what he was doing. But what I really wanted to say to my son was that his father was not at all what he appeared to be and that being a man is frequently a facade.

It has taken me a long time to admit that—even to myself. Especially to myself. *My* father, after all, really *had* always known what *he* was doing. He was strong and confident and he never felt pain, never knew fear. There wasn't a leaky faucet he couldn't fix or an engine he couldn't manage to get running again. Mechanics never fooled him, salesmen never conned him. He was always calm in emergencies, always cool under fire. He never cried.

For a long time I wondered how such a man could have produced such a weakling for a son. I wondered where the self-doubts and the fears I felt all the time had come from. I wondered why the faucets I fixed always dripped twice as fast after I got finished with them, why engines that sputtered before I started to work on them went stone-dead under my wrench. I dreaded the thought that some day my father would see me cry. I didn't realize that fathers are not always everything they seem to be.

It's different for fathers than it is for mothers. Motherhood is honest, close to the surface. Mothers don't have to hide what they feel. They don't have to pretend.

When there are sounds downstairs in the middle of the night, a mother is allowed to pull the covers over her head and hope that they will go away. A father is supposed to put on his slippers and robe and march boldly down the stairs, even if he's pretty sure that it's the Manson family waiting for him in the kitchen.

When the road signs are confusing and the scenery is starting to look awfully unfamiliar, it's perfectly natural for a mother to pull over to the side of the road and ask for directions from the first person who comes along. A father is supposed to know exactly where he's going, even if he has to drive two hundred miles out of the way to prove it. . . .

Mothers can bang a new jar of peanut butter on the floor until the lid is loose enough to turn. Fathers are supposed to twist it off with their bare hands—without getting red in the face.

Mothers who lose their jobs are unfortunate. Fathers who lose their jobs are failures. When a mother gets hurt she may want to swear, but she is only allowed to cry. When a father gets hurt he may want to cry, but he is only allowed to swear. . . .

I should have told him that the only reason his father, like lots of fathers, doesn't admit his weaknesses is because he is afraid that someone will think he is not a real man.

More important, what I should have said to my fourteen-year-old son in the car that night is that someday, when he's a father, he'll feel fear and self-doubt and pain, and that it's all right. But my father never told me, and I haven't told my son.[39]

Second, *keep the rules and policies to a bare minimum.* This is especially true as the children get older. Younger children need the security of knowing where the boundaries are. That's the basis of discipline, as I explained in chapter 5. But as little ones grow and begin to show healthy signs of exerting their independence, let it happen. Add more flex. Keep an open mind. I am not suggesting that you compromise on issues of integrity or purity. Of course not! There are limits.

Giving room to grow is one thing. Giving up all moral restrictions and personal convictions for the sake of "peace at any price" is another thing entirely. More on this in chapter 10 on dealing with the older rebel.

My point here has to do with adding the oil of wisdom to the gears of relationships. As children grow older and begin to think for themselves, wise parents realize that more rules and longer lists of policies only antagonize. Kids lose respect for parents who refuse to discuss reasons and never negotiate the rules.

As our children began to date, we found it necessary to establish times and places. They were expected to tell us where they were going and when they would be returning. We made it clear that if something kept them from getting to the previously stated place or being home by the agreed-upon time, a phone call was expected—even if it meant pulling off the freeway on the way home and finding a public phone to call us. Only on the rarest occasions was that simple policy unworkable. As they grew older, a later time to return home was permitted, but the phone call remained firm. We explained it was a matter of courtesy, not distrust. When two of our children married, we found it interesting that they were so accustomed to that communication accountability they continued the habit. They now call their mates when they are going to be later than expected. The "rule" has become a way of life, which is the mark of a workable rule.

Third, *unless it is absolutely impossible to do so, say yes*. That may sound like a funny statement until you think it through. The average parental reaction is no. Regardless of the question kids ask, most parents think *no* more often than *yes*. So Cynthia and I developed a policy early on that we'd think yes ... and only when we found ourselves absolutely unable to say yes would we be forced to say no.

It is amazing how much of a positive influence that simple guideline provided for our home. I can testify that it revolutionized my attitude. Let me give you some examples.

"Can we sleep outside tonight?" Normally, like all dads, I would think and say, "No." In my mind would be all kinds of airtight reasons: "The mosquitoes" or "You'll need to go to the bathroom and the door will be locked" or "What if it rains?" You know, dumb stuff. No longer. Sleeping outside became fine and dandy. I got to where I *preferred* 'em out there!

Another was "Can we sleep in our clothes?" Why not? (Who really cares *what* kids sleep in?) As my wife finally observed, once you have four you're so grateful they're in bed, what they wear is of absolutely no consequence.

"Can we have a party?" Sure. "How about a two-day party?" Have at it! We taught them that the privilege of having a party included the responsibility of cleaning up after it . . . which was perfectly okay with them. The atmosphere became more and more fun, which is what family living is all about, right?

Say yes just as often as you can.

Fourth, *a failure is not the end of the world.* When relationships are valued, when having fun is important, when saying yes is emphasized, there is risk involved. There will be times when a rule is inadvertently broken—a failure in the system occurs. So it goes. If it was accidental, welcome to the human race. Forgiveness follows confession. No grudges. Hopefully (if dad stays quiet like he should), no lectures. If the rule was broken on purpose, that is another matter and is dealt with (privately) in a much more serious manner. Nevertheless, any home that is run on the grace principle must have what our family calls "wobble room." Things don't always run to perfection, but the main issue is the attitude. A submissive, absolutely honest admission with a repentant spirit earns a lot of points in the Swindoll abode.

All of us mean well at the start of any plan, but the human element, being what it is, can't help but slip in occasionally. It's like the following diet plan someone passed on to me last year.

The Stress Diet

Breakfast
$1/2$ grapefruit
1 piece whole-wheat toast
8 oz. skim milk

Lunch
4 oz. lean broiled chicken breast
1 cup steamed zucchini
1 Oreo cookie
Herb tea

Mid-afternoon snack
Rest of the package of Oreo cookies
1 qt. rocky road ice cream
1 jar hot fudge

Dinner
2 loaves garlic bread
large mushroom and pepperoni pizza
large pitcher root beer
3 Milky Ways
Entire frozen cheesecake, eaten directly from the freezer

That smile looks good on your face. Your family needs to see it more often!

Flex Those Fun Muscles!

If you have stayed with me until now, you are to be commended. Ultra-rigid parents have probably stopped reading and have started writing me a letter of disagreement!

Would you like two or three ideas for developing your "flex" muscles? If so, here they are.

1. *When the family is young, balance the tighter rules with a strong emphasis on trust.* Our kids need to know we trust them, want only the best for them, believe in them. Rather than viewing them with suspicion and sneaking around like a CIA spy, we need to convey our confidence in their loyalty. That's what grace is all about. Furthermore, children flourish in such a setting. This is a good time to add that the difference between "principles" and "rules" is radical. Rules can be made and therefore reshaped or broken. Principles cannot be arbitrarily made; they must never be broken. Rules are temporal; principles are eternal. Rules are helpful; principles are essential. Wise are the parents who understand those distinctions.

2. *As time passes, deliberately relax more and release the controls.* Yes, that's a risk. Yes, it's hard to do. But it won't get easier if you wait until they turn twenty! I think it would be great if parents would actually write out a "declaration of indepen-

dence" for each one of the kids and hand it to them at a time when they reach a level of maturity and can handle it, like at graduation from high school or some such event.

3. *Throughout the process, cultivate and value the importance of close relationships.* Nothing, absolutely nothing on this earth is more important to us when the chips are down than the members of our family. Do everything possible to cultivate those relationships.

Author J. Allan Petersen, writing on this very subject, tells of a traumatic experience he endured that drilled this fact home. It happened on an airplane.

> Every nook and cranny of the big 747 was crowded. It took off in the middle of the night in Brazil where I'd been speaking. As it moved into the night I began to doze. I don't know how long I slept, but I was starting to wake when I heard a strong voice announcing, "We have a very serious emergency." Three engines had gone because of fuel contamination, and the other engine would go any second.
>
> The steward said in English, "Now you must do exactly as we tell you. Don't anyone think of doing anything we do not suggest. Your life depends on us. We are trained for your safety, so you must do exactly as we tell you."
>
> Then he rattled this off in Portuguese. Everybody looked soberly at one another.
>
> The steward said, "Now pull down the curtains, in a few minutes we are going to turn off all the lights."
>
> My thought exclaimed, "Lord."
>
> The plane veered and banked, as the crew tried to get it back to the airport. The steward ran up and down the aisle and barked out orders, "Now take that card out of the seat pocket, and I want you to look at this diagram." You know, I've flown millions of miles over the world and here I thought I had the card memorized, but I panicked because I couldn't find the crazy card. Everybody looked stunned as we felt the plane plunge down.
>
> Finally, the steward said, "Now tighten the seat belts as tight as you can, and pull up your legs and bury your head in your lap." We couldn't look out to see where we were—high or low.
>
> I peeked around—the Portuguese were crossing themselves, and I thought, "This is it. This is serious. I can't believe

this. I didn't know this was going to happen tonight. I guess this is it." And I had a crazy sensation.

Then the steward's voice broke into my consciousness, barking out in this machine-gun fashion, "Prepare for impact." Frankly, I wasn't thinking about the photocopier. I wasn't worried about the oil in my car. At times like that, involuntarily, from deep inside of us, something comes out that's never structured, planned or rehearsed. And all I could do was pray. Everybody started to pray. I found myself praying in a way I never thought of doing. As I buried my head in my lap and pulled my knees up, as I was convinced it was over I said, "Oh, God, thank You. Thank You for the incredible privilege of knowing You. Life has been wonderful." And as the plane was going down my last thought, my last cry, "Oh, God, my wife! My children!"

Now I should say for the sake of you, the reader, that I survived! As I wandered about in the middle of the night in the airport with a knot in my stomach and cotton in my mouth, I couldn't speak. I ached all over.

I thought, "What did I do? What did I say? What were my last thoughts? Why did I think that?" I wondered, "What was the bottom line?"

Here's the bottom line: *relationship.*

When I . . . saw my wife at the airport, I looked at her and rushed to hold her hand. I just looked at her a moment then threw my arms around her and said, "Oh, I appreciate you." And then with tears in my eyes, I looked at her again, and said, "I appreciate you so much. I didn't know if I'd ever see you again; oh, I appreciate you."

When I arrived home, I found my three sons and said, "I appreciate you. Boy, I'm glad you're in this house and I'm a part of you."

I am only one, you are only one. But because we are in a family we hold a piece of the puzzle in our own power. And what we can do, we should do. I trust that you will say with me, "And by the grace of God, I will do what I can do in my home."[40]

If you are getting caught in the squirrel cage of a hurry-up lifestyle, let me urge you to slow it down and get off. Your family deserves more than the leftovers of your time. By the grace of God do what you can do.

Start today. Please.

PART THREE

WEATHERING

THE

STORM

9

Warning the Uninvolved

Right about now I sense some of you are beginning to think "this book is just too ideal . . . where are the *struggles* of family life?"

Perhaps the absence of "realism" within these pages thus far leaves you feeling overlooked and alone. Rather than dwelling at length on family crises, I have spent eight chapters telling you that my wife and I have enjoyed each stage of parenting. I have not sprinkled in stories where we helped one of our kids work through drug addiction or an alcohol habit. Nor have I told you about bailing one of our sons out of jail, or talking another out of suicide, or wrenching a son out of the clutches of a cult, or helping a daughter through an illegitimate pregnancy.

To top things off, I really lost you when I said we have *enjoyed* our teenagers! Yes, I'd imagine right about now you may be thinking this volume belongs in Fantasyland rather than your hands. You may be interested to know that these final six chapters turn the corner. If, indeed, you anticipated reading more in this book about how to cope with the difficulties of family life, these chapters are for you.

Actually, I have some good news and some bad news. The good news is that the rest of this volume is committed to real-world stuff. The bad news is that I don't have a magic wand to wave over any of these more somber family struggles. I am anxious to help any way I can, but I cannot promise you a quick and easy solution. I refuse to promise you a neat rose garden if you will only take these four steps, memorize a half dozen verses of Scripture, or employ this or that formula. Solving problems is not that simple. We are people seeking a strong family, not super saints dodging the struggles in today's society.

For the final six chapters, therefore, I want to focus on some of the darker slices of life many families are forced to endure. I may not touch on your particular area of need, but perhaps you'll find fresh help and encouragement that will give you sufficient strength to go on. I hope so.

The Facts Don't Lie

In a report to our nation's president, entitled *The Family: Preserving America's Future,* these serious statements appear:

> The statistics on the pathology affecting many American families are overwhelming. Consider the following statistical portrait of the 3.6 million children who began their formal schooling in the United States in September of 1986:
> — 14 percent were children of unmarried parents.
> — 40 percent will live in a broken home before they reach 18.
> — Between one-quarter and one-third are latchkey children with no one to greet them when they come home from school.

Other trends are equally disturbing, for example:

> — In 1960, there were 393,000 divorces in America; by 1985, that number had increased more than threefold to 1,187,000.

— Births out of wedlock, as a percentage of all births, increased more than 450 percent in just 30 years.[41]

The family needs help!

Indeed it does. When you add to those grim facts the realities of daily abortions, wife battering, and child abuse (every two minutes in America a child is being attacked by one or both parents), incest, kidnapping, the accelerating suicide rate among the young, neglect, kiddie porn, juvenile crime, and the epidemic of sexually transmitted diseases—many of them new and virulent—you realize that the report to our president was not exaggerated.

None of these facts seem all that gripping as long as we can keep the disintegrating family at arm's distance. We don't feel the sting while they remain safe, clinical statistics for our president to worry over. But once one of these tragedies touches us personally, our cool, smug indifference changes to acute concern.

Child abuse, for example, may be little more than another news item in a long list of sad accounts reported on the evening news. We shake our heads and passively think *What a shame!* as we finish our supper in a hurry. But when one of our own grandchildren turns up abused, the pain suddenly becomes real. Or when we hear that another family split up, it's easy to cluck our tongues and whine about "the signs of the times" . . . until it happens to one of our closest friends or a neighbor across the street. At that moment, the reality of domestic disintegration seems especially personal and terribly tragic. Even optimists like me can no longer smile and look the other way. Something must be done—*now.*

Urgency replaces passivity once reality strikes home.

During my fifty-plus years on this old earth, I have been allowed to witness firsthand the disintegration of several families. Most of the collapses have occurred in neighborhoods where I have lived either as a child or as a husband and father with a family of my own. All of the homes involved were once what you and I would call fairly strong—meaning both parents were originally in love with each other, and the children were wanted, loved, and seemed well-adjusted. From all outward appearance, there were healthy and agreeable relationships among the family members. In none of the homes was there any sign of poverty, abuse, physical affliction, or mental disorder. Each of these families seemed outwardly harmonious and relationally close. Each home seemed a happy place to be. But each eroded so drastically that the hope of recovery and rehabilitation faded from view.

To this day the memory of watching those families crumble haunts and saddens me. Without trying to sound dramatic, I still remember the faces of those family members, and I still ache for them.

No doubt you too have witnessed similar scenes. Perhaps you identify with all this. It may have happened in your home . . . it may be happening right now.

If your family is still intact, if you're still very much in love, if you're still communicating, still supportive, still laughing and playing together, you're an exception rather than the rule. And rather than feeling proud, I would encourage you to be deeply grateful. Our tired, tragic society needs you.

Some of you have been stripped of some of the things that would have made a solid family easier to pull off. Death has taken a mate or a child, or an illness has come in—uninvited and unexpected—and drained your energy. But you're still standing tall. Perhaps a divorce against your wishes has stolen some of the fun from your life. But God has graciously brought you into another relationship and you're able to go on from there, because you're working hard at it and want it to be different than before. Good for you. Please, don't ever quit! We don't have enough models like you.

A Disintegrating Family Way Back When

I would like to take a few moments to visit a troubled home that existed centuries ago. But I should warn you, I want us to do more than just sit back and frown. We need to locate and linger over some of the danger signals that ultimately spelled the disintegration of one man's family. My hope is that we might learn some never-to-be-forgotten lessons from what we observe.

The Bible records the scene quite graphically in the ancient Book of 1 Samuel. First off, let's meet the family.

A Father Named Eli

The dad, Eli, is mentioned frequently in chapter 1 of this account. We are told that he held a very responsible position. In fact, he wore two hats that required a lot of time; he was both priest and judge in the community. In those days it was not uncommon for a priest to also serve as a judge.

My maternal grandfather fulfilled a similar dual role in the little Texas town of El Campo where I was born. For many years L. O. Lundy was both a religious leader (not a pastor, but a greatly respected adult Sunday school teacher in a local church) and also Justice of the Peace. And all through my growing-up years—in fact, until my granddad's death—I recall that my own father never called him Dad, but rather "Judge Lundy." He was well known in the county as a religious leader and public figure.

That's precisely the way it was with "Judge Eli." Publicly, Eli was a household name. The last sentence in 1 Samuel 4:18 reads, "He judged Israel forty years." Remember that. He held down a responsible position. He was not only a busy man, he was highly respected. Almost without exception, when Eli is referred to in the Bible, he's called Eli the priest or Eli the judge.

Eli was also a believer. For him to represent God to the people he had to be a man of God in the truest sense of the title. Chapter 2, verse 11, refers to him as "Eli the priest." That name, Eli, by the way, means either "Jehovah is high" or simply "Jehovah, my God." Most likely the latter, which assures us that this religious public figure was a man of faith.

Next, we learn that Eli was a father. Professionally, he was both priest and judge. Personally, he was a believer. Domestically, he was the father of two sons. They are named for us in 1 Samuel 1:3—Hophni and Phinehas.

God's Word tells us four other details about Eli. First, he was very old, so we understand that his boys were young men, not small children. Chapter 3, verse 2, adds this comment:

> ". . . his eyesight had begun to grow dim and he could not see well."

And when we come to the end of his life, we notice that his eyesight is so bad he is almost blind. First Samuel 4:15 states his age at death—ninety-eight years old.

Second, Eli was spiritually sensitive. When God was speaking to young Samuel, Eli sensed it was the Lord. He even told the boy what to do.

> So the LORD called Samuel again for the third time. And he arose and went to Eli, and said, "Here I am, for you called me." Then Eli discerned that the LORD was calling the boy. And Eli said to Samuel, "Go lie down, and it shall be if He calls you, that you shall say, 'Speak, LORD, for Thy servant is listening.'" So Samuel went and lay down in his place (1 Samuel 3:8–9).

Eli discerned God's presence that night. He knew what it meant to contact God. I don't want you to have the idea that Eli was some kind of renegade dad, running wild in an ego-centered pursuit of notoriety. That's an inaccurate picture. I don't see him going through the motions of his religious life as a phony.

Third, Eli was out of shape. To put it bluntly, the man was fat. Unfair of me to say that? You decide after reading the following.

> And it came about when he mentioned the ark of God that Eli fell off the seat backward beside the gate, and his neck was broken and he died, for he was old and heavy. Thus he judged Israel forty years (1 Samuel 4:18).

We can't appreciate the significance of that until we tie it into the whole story, which I will do in a few moments. But suffice to say, the man was not only old, he was quite overweight.

While we're in verse 18, the fourth observation I would make about Eli is that he stuck to his job. He wasn't a restless drifter, a fly-by-night preacher who stayed on the move. The man remained in Shiloh, his home base, and faithfully ministered there for forty years. You've got to respect Eli for not shifting from this position to that or from one place to another. So much for the father.

Two Natural Sons, Hophni and Phinehas

". . . And the two sons of Eli, Hophni and Phinehas were priests to the LORD there" (1 Samuel 1:3).

In Scripture, a father's profession frequently became a son's. In this case, like father, like sons, . . . but how different in character! Professionally, they were priests. But before you entertain respect for their ministry, better turn to chapter 2, verse 12 . . . and hold on tight. Eli's two sons were absolutely profane men—unbelieving and rebellious.

"Now the sons of Eli were worthless men; they did not know the LORD."

The men may have been priests by profession, but in their hearts they were far from God. That's nothing unique. For centuries there have been false prophets, false teachers, worthless pastors, unbelieving preachers. There always will be. Eli's sons may have worn the garb and gone through the motions of the priesthood, but their lifestyle reflected anything but devotion to Jehovah. They lived scandalous lives.

"Now the sons of Eli were worthless men; they did not know the LORD and the custom of the priests with the people. When any man was offering a sacrifice, the priest's servant would come while the meat was boiling, with a three-pronged fork in his hand. Then he would thrust it into the pan, or kettle, or caldron, or pot; all that the fork brought up

*the priest would take for himself. Thus they did in Shiloh to
all the Israelites who came there. Also, before they burned
the fat, the priest's servant would come and say to the man
who was sacrificing, "Give the priest meat for roasting, as
he will not take boiled meat from you, only raw." And if the
man said to him, "They must surely burn the fat first, and
then take as much as you desire," then he would say, "No,
but you shall give it to me now; and if not, I will take it by
force." Thus the sin of the young men was very great before
the LORD, for the men despised the offering to the LORD" (1
Samuel 2:12–17).*

Don't miss that last statement. There's brash impudence in the
tone of those words. They were guilty of going through meaningless motions of the priesthood to satisfy their own appetites.
They had no reverence for God in their hearts, no sensitivity
for the significance of the offering. To those fellas, religious
responsibilities were nothing more than ritualistic public tasks
in order to put food in their bellies.

On top of all that, the two brothers lived immoral lives.

*"Now Eli was very old; and he heard all that his sons were
doing to all Israel, and how they lay with the women who
served at the doorway of the tent of meeting"
(1 Samuel 2:22).*

Their reputation became notorious. Even when the news of
their immorality spread, they didn't try to hide it. A little later
in this story we read they were also rebellious and stubborn.
They refused to listen to the counsel of others.

Amazing! With a father who, as a priest and judge, had
given his whole life to the things of God, those two grown
sons became cynical. Unlike their dad, they cared nothing for
the things of God. Eli had a couple of boys whose hearts were
darkened and whose wills were calloused. To them, God was a
distant Deity; the ministry, a boring joke.

It is nothing new that PKs and MKs (preachers' kids, mis-
sionaries' kids) can often live notorious lives. A friend in Texas

once told me with a smile, "The reason preachers' kids are so bad is because they hang around all those deacons' kids!"

Perhaps that's more rationalization than truth, but it is easy for preachers' kids to suffer from what I call the "hothouse syndrome." All their lives, all they hear, all they're in touch with is biblical stuff, spiritual stuff, churchy stuff, God talk, lots of prayers, lots of meetings, lots of church people, until they're up to their eyebrows with it. If we preachers and pastors aren't careful, we can think that our children are walking in line with the Lord, loving Him as much as we do, when, in fact, they're turned off. Even worse, they can develop a cynicism toward spiritual things, just as we see right here in the lives of Hophni and Phinehas.

An Adopted Son Named Samuel

Eli had one more son . . . a boy named Samuel, whom he adopted after his own sons reached adulthood. Samuel's mother and father were Hannah and Elkanah. The boy's conception was a gift from God. His birth thrilled his parents' hearts. Hannah had promised, "Lord, if You give me a son, I will give him back to You." And that's exactly what she did.

> Now when she had weaned him, she took him up with her, with a three-year-old bull and one ephah of flour and a jug of wine, and brought him to the house of the LORD in Shiloh, although the child was young. . . . "For this boy I prayed, and the LORD has given me my petition which I asked of Him. So I have also dedicated him to the LORD; as long as he lives he is dedicated to the LORD." And he worshiped the LORD there (1 Samuel 1:24, 27–28).

The scene isn't peaceful—a little boy placed into a home occupied by two older rebellious brothers and a passive foster father who is aging, overweight, and rapidly losing touch. Operation disintegration.

And yet we read:

> . . . But the boy ministered to the LORD before Eli the priest (2:11).

I take it Eli worked hard, helping his adopted son learn the process and responsibilities of worship in the house of God.

Chapter 3, verse 19, offers us one more observation.

> *Thus Samuel grew and the LORD was with him and let none of his words fail.*

It seems as though the Lord wrapped a beautiful, protective bubble around Samuel. It is wonderful to imagine.

Observing the Scene from a Distance

Now that we've met a family, let's try to think what it would be like if they lived next door to us, or perhaps on the same block. I'm certain we would have noticed the rebellious lives of Eli's two sons.

The Sins of the Sons

If I correctly analyze the family of Eli, the most disturbing and obvious fact is the sinfulness of Hophni and Phinehas. We are told they despised the offering of the Lord, We are also told they were engaged in illicit and unashamed immorality right out in the open . . . *at the doorway of the tent of meeting.* In fact, the Lord's people knew it. We're not surprised to read they circulated the stories among themselves about the two priests living ungodly lifestyles. We would have heard such stories if we had lived near them back then.

An interesting statement in verse 13 of chapter 3 is that they brought a curse on themselves. I take this to mean that after spending sufficient time in this calloused condition, things became so bad their depraved actions became irreversible. An irrevocable judgment came into the mind of God for these boys. Their lifestyle was so continually godless there was no way out but death. Perhaps an ancient "sin unto death" would be another way of putting it.

The Warnings of Others

If we had been bugs on the wall in the rooms of Eli's home, we would have heard four reports coming to the ears of Eli. The first warning came from *the public* in general.

> *[Eli] heard all that his sons were doing to all Israel . . . And he said to them, "Why do you do such things, the evil things that I hear from all these people? No, my sons; for the report is not good which I hear the LORD's people circulating" (1 Samuel 2:22–24).*

So it was common knowledge. The public didn't keep the news from the judge they loved. The old priest was being told by the Lord's people, "What your sons are doing is wrong. It's hurting the cause. It is a slanderous, scandalous thing. You're being injured. More importantly, the work of God is being hurt."

No question, Eli heard the warnings . . . not just from the people of the community but also from *an unnamed prophet.* He's simply called "a man of God." Look at his sober words of warning:

> *Then a man of God came to Eli and said to him, "Thus says the LORD, 'Did I not indeed reveal Myself to the house of your father when they were in Egypt in bondage to Pharaoh's house? And did I not choose them from all the tribes of Israel to be My priests, to go up to My altar, to burn incense, to carry an ephod before Me; and did I not give to the house of your father all the fire offerings of the sons of Israel? Why do you kick at My sacrifice and at My offering which I have commanded in my dwelling, and honor your sons above Me, by making yourselves fat with the choicest of every offering of My people Israel?' Therefore the LORD God of Israel declares, 'I did indeed say that your house and the house of your father should walk before Me forever;' but now the LORD declares, 'Far be it from Me—for those who honor Me I will honor, and those who despise Me will be lightly esteemed. Behold, the days are coming when I will break your strength and the strength of your father's house so that there will not be an old man in your house. And you*

will see the distress of My dwelling, in spite of all that I do good for Israel; and an old man will not be in your house forever. Yet I will not cut off every man of yours from My altar that your eyes may fail from weeping and your soul grieve, and all the increase of your house will die in the prime of life. And this will be the sign to you which shall come concerning your two sons, Hophni and Phinehas: on the same day both of them shall die'" (1 Samuel 2:27–34).

I'd call that the straight scoop! He not only heard from the people and a prophet, he also heard from *God Himself.*

And the LORD said to Samuel, "Behold, I am about to do a thing in Israel at which both ears of everyone who hears it will tingle. In that day I will carry out against Eli all that I have spoken concerning his house, from beginning to end (1 Samuel 3:11–12).

Serious Words of Warning!

In God's evaluation, the acid test of a father's leadership is not in the realm of his social skills, his public relations, his managerial abilities at the office, or how well he handles himself before the public. It is in the home. This is especially true for a minister of a church. Remember those immortal words of Paul to Timothy—indirectly to all of us holding positions of leadership in a local church?

It is a trustworthy statement: if any man aspires to the office of overseer, it is a fine work he desires to do. An overseer, then, must be above reproach, the husband of one wife, temperate, prudent, respectable, hospitable, able to teach, not addicted to wine or pugnacious, but gentle, uncontentious, free from the love of money. He must be one who manages his own household well, keeping his children under control with all dignity (but if a man does not know how to manage his own household, how will he take care of the church of God?) (1 Timothy 3:1–5).

Look again at what is written in those final lines. Leaders of flocks *must* be good managers at home.

I'm not only surprised, at times I'm appalled that some churches looking for pastoral leadership will not even meet the family members of the potential minister. They come along as a "surprise package" when he steps on the scene. The church may know the new minister, but it has hardly met and probably hasn't even interviewed the mate or talked with the children. And yet it is there—in *that* realm—the man must prove himself qualified or unqualified as a leader of the flock.

The Father's Response

How then, did Eli respond to those numerous warnings? His first response was an incomplete reproof.

> *He said to them, "Why do you do such things, the evil things that I hear from all these people? No, my sons; for the report is not good which I hear the LORD's people circulating" (2:23–24).*

Sounds pretty wimpy, doesn't it? "Say, fellas, been hearing a few comments about you two. You know, what I'm hearing isn't very good." That's about all he says. And do they listen to him? Why, of course not! They're adults. Remember? They're cynical . . . downright calloused. They're enjoying a freewheeling fun 'n' games lifestyle. Because Eli lacked authority, he failed to command their respect. Judge or not, priest or not, the man himself was part of the problem.

The second thing I notice is that he even indulged his sons. God pointed this out to the man.

> *Then a man of God came to Eli and said to him, "Thus says the LORD, 'Did I not indeed reveal Myself to the house of your father when they were in Egypt in bondage to Pharaoh's house? And did I not choose them from all the tribes of Israel to be My priests, to go up to My altar, to burn incense, to carry an ephod before Me; and did I not give to the house of your father all the fire offerings of the sons of Israel? Why do you kick at My sacrifice and at My offering which I have commanded in My dwelling, and honor your*

sons above Me, by making yourselves fat with the choicest of every offering of My people Israel?'" (2:27–29).

Eli honored his sons above the Lord by allowing them to take all those liberties with their priestly responsibilities. Eli may have stood back, arms folded, and frowned a bit, but that wasn't enough! He simply let it pass. In doing so, he implied tacit approval. The family was deteriorating before his very eyes!

I think I also detect a touch of passive fatalism along with Eli's indulgence and incomplete reproof. Do you feel the shrug of the old priest's shoulders when you read the following?

". . . It is the LORD; let Him do what seems good to Him" (3:18).

You may ask, "Well, what could Eli have done?" You may not want to know! Go back into the Law of Moses for the answer and be ready for a shocker.

"If any man has a stubborn and rebellious son who will not obey his father or his mother, and when they chastise him, he will not even listen to them, then his father and mother shall seize him, and bring him out to the elders of his city at the gateway of his home town. And they shall say to the elders of his city, 'This son of ours is stubborn and rebellious, he will not obey us, he is a glutton and a drunkard.' Then all the men of his city shall stone him to death; so you shall remove the evil from your midst, and all Israel shall hear of it and fear" (Deuteronomy 21:18–21).

Had Hophni or Phinehas been taken before the elders, and had the elders followed through God's way, I can assure you Eli would not have been a passive fatalist.

Signs of Domestic Disintegration

Enough of that ancient account. I find no less than four signs of family deterioration in this story.

First: *preoccupation with the father's profession to the exclusion of his family's needs.* The old fella was a busy priest and a respected judge. As a result, he became preoccupied with his public profession and failed to focus on his family's needs. Where had he been in their formative years? I seriously doubt the man was there to see his sons' slowly emerging cynicism. A child reveals his heart by his actions and by his words. It takes a discerning on-site parent to spot the danger signals. A father with a sensitive heart, or a mother who has her eyes open, will witness signs of deception—and deal with them early.

Alexander Whyte of yesteryear, one of Britain's best, points this out with these eloquent words:

> "Now the sons of Eli were sons of Belial; they knew not the Lord."
>
> Impossible! you would protest, if it were not in the Bible. But just because it is in the Bible, we are compelled to ask ourselves how it could possibly come about that the sons of such a sacred man as Eli was could ever become sons of Belial.
>
> What! not know the Lord, and they born and brought up within the very precincts of the Lord's house! Were not the first sounds they heard the praises of God in His sanctuary? Were not the first sights they saw their father in his robes beside the altar with all the tables, and the bread, and the sacrifices, and the incense round about him? And yet, there it is in black and white; there it is in blood and tears—"The sons of Eli were sons of Belial; they knew not the Lord."
>
> Let me think. Let me consider well how, conceivably, it could come about that Hophni and Phinehas could be born and brought up at Shiloh and not know the Lord. Well, for one thing, their father was never at home. What with judging all Israel, Eli never saw his children till they were in their beds. 'What mean ye by this ordinance?' all the other children in Israel asked their fathers as they came up to the temple. And all the way up and all the way down again those fathers took their inquiring children by the hand and told them all about Abraham, and Isaac, and Jacob, and Joseph, and Moses, and Aaron, and the exodus, and the wilderness, and the conquest, and the yearly passover. Hophni and

Phinehas were the only children in all Israel who saw the temple every day and paid no attention to it.

And, then, every father and mother knows this, how the years run away, and how their children grow up, till all of a sudden they are as tall as themselves. And very much faster than our tallest children did Eli's children grow up. All things, indeed, were banded against Eli; the very early ripeness of his sons was against Eli. He thought he would one day have time but it was his lifelong regret that he had never had time. And, what with one thing, and what with another; what with their father's preoccupation and their own evil hearts; the two young men were already sons of Belial when they should still have been little children.

"Why do ye do such things? For I fear of all your evil dealings by all this people. Nay, my sons, this is no good report that I hear." Like our own proverb, Eli is seen shutting the stable-door with many tears and sobs years and years after the steeds have been stolen.[42]

Second: *refusal to face the severity of the sons' lifestyle*. Eli was busy rationalizing all the pain away. He heard the report, and he may well have sighed and shook his gray head. But he didn't face the severity of it or its consequences sufficiently. God had stated:

> *I will carry out against Eli all that I have spoken concerning his house, from beginning to end. For I have told him that I am about to judge his house forever for the iniquity which he knew, because his sons brought a curse on themselves and he did not rebuke them (3:12–13).*

What an indictment! Eli knew, but, please note, Eli *did not act*. The *Living Bible* paraphrases Proverbs 19:18 like this:

> *Discipline your son in his early years while there is hope. If you don't you will ruin his life.*

In the Good News Bible, it reads:

> *Discipline your children while they are young enough to learn. If you don't, you are helping them destroy themselves.*

Third: *failure to respond correctly to the warnings of others*. God has ways of showing us. He uses people to let us see the truth. How important it is to hear those reproofs and respond correctly to the warnings of others!

When someone warns you about members in your family, how do you respond? A policeman calls you and tells you the truth about your rebellious child. Do you listen? The teacher at school mentions a persistent weakness. Do you heed the counsel and get involved? Do you thank that teacher? You have a few friends who are close enough and honest enough to tell you the truth. Do you hear their candid remarks? Do you respect their concern?

May I introduce another category? Grandparents. Grandparents sometimes have the unhappy task of saying, "Honey, come here. I want to tell you something about your snotty little kid." Well, maybe not that bluntly, but when they work up the courage to tell your straight, do you receive it or resist? We *must* respond correctly to the warnings of others.

Fourth: *Rationalization of wrong, thereby becoming a part of the problem.* I mentioned earlier that Eli was obese. Let me show what you may have missed in that story.

> *"Why do you kick at My sacrifice and at My offering which I have commanded in My dwelling, and honor your sons above Me, by making yourselves fat with the choicest of every offering of My people Israel?" (2:29).*

Notice, "yourselves" . . . plural! Meaning? Eli finally joined in and served himself from the meat his boys had taken. He bought into their lifestyle! That's why we read: "You have made yourselves fat." That's one of the reasons he died heavy. Some of his own weight had been picked up from adopting his sons' ways.

Centuries later as a prophet named Jeremiah walks through the ruins of his beloved Jerusalem, he laments:

> *"Our fathers sinned, and are no more; it is we who have borne their iniquities" (Lamentations 5:7).*

In today's terms, our fathers sinned, but we bought the farm. Our fathers ate the meal, and we have picked up the tab.

There's a lot of litter today, thanks to yesterday's trash. And the family is the place where all the garbage stacks up.

A Somber Yet Relevant Analysis

In an insightful volume written back in 1947, sociologist and historian Carle Zimmerman compared the deterioration and ultimate disintegration of various cultures with the parallel in the decline of the family unit in America. His study identified specific patterns of behavior that typified the final stages of the disintegration of each culture. Just before each culture fell into total disarray, certain conditions became prominent. Dr. Zimmerman traced those elements that led to the demise of the family unit. There were eleven in all . . . and among the eleven were:

— Increased and rapid, easy, "causeless" divorce. (Guilty and innocent party theory became a pure fiction.)
— Decreased number of children, population decay, and increased public disrespect for parents and parenthood.
— Elimination of the real meaning of the marriage ceremony.
— Popularity of pessimistic doctrines about the early heroes.
— Breaking down of most inhibitions against adultery.
— Revolts of youth against parents so that parenthood became more and more difficult for those who did try to raise children.
— Rapid rise and spread of juvenile delinquency.
— Common acceptance of all forms of sex perversions.[43]

All that sounds strangely familiar, doesn't it? And to think we are repeating history once again!

No need to restate the obvious. Domestic deterioration is happening. We must now focus not on how bad things have gotten, how weak and needy families are, but rather on how we can build strength back into the home. What specifically can be done to stop the cycle, to turn the tide, to get families—perhaps *your* family—back on course?

For starters, move right on to chapter ten. You'll get some specific help and encouragement for dealing with a most unpleasant domestic heartache—when a child grows up and becomes a rebel, or, as Jesus once described him, a prodigal.

Family Counsel

1. If your family is still intact, if you're still very much in love, if you're still communicating, still supportive, still laughing and playing together . . . I would encourage you to be deeply grateful. Don't take that family strength for granted! At an appropriate time, reflect as a couple or a family over the reasons for your happiness and harmony. Express appreciation to one another. Ask yourselves, "What are those things that could possibly threaten our family life over the next weeks and months—and how should we deal with them?" End your time together with prayer, asking the Lord's strength *and wisdom* to deal with the tests and crises which will invariably come your way.

2. First Samuel 3:19 tells us the Lord was with young Samuel and granted him spiritual success as he grew. Considering the type of domestic situation and environment the lad was nurtured in, this seems remarkable. Had the Lord really "wrapped a beautiful, protective bubble around him"? What effect do you think the influence and prayers of godly Hannah, his mother, might have had on his life as he grew up? What are the most powerful ways moms and dads can prepare their children for life in a disintegrating society?

10

Confronting the Unpleasant

One of the most appealing qualities of the Bible is its realism. Unlike many research volumes that are all theory, the Bible presents big doses of reality. It is not that there is no idealism in Scripture; there is. But invariably, where there is idealism, it is balanced well with realism.

For example, take the nation Israel—God's chosen people, the Jews. He originates them and calls them "Mine." He defends them. He sustains them. But, though He loves them, He doesn't hide the truth of their sinfulness. Their failures and rebellions are set forth realistically—in living color. The Bible also places on display certain men and women who were people of great courage—even heroism. God's Word presents these men and women standing alone, at times, against the current of wrong in their day. We are impressed by their uncompromising character. But never does the Bible shy away from revealing their scars, nor does it ignore their warts. Both appear without hesitation or apology.

We see Noah, for example, hammering away on the ark against incredible odds. Though it seemed it would never rain, we are impressed with Noah's persistence for over a century, a persistence which finally paid off. But in a brief matter of time after the flood, we see him in a shameful drunken stupor. God's Word shows us both sides.

We see Peter as he stands alone, ignoring the popular opinions of the people of his day, announcing to Jesus, "You are the Christ, the Son of the living God." But only a few weeks later, that same man is skulking around a fire denying he even knows the One on trial, about to be crucified. Such realism is woven throughout Scripture.

What is true of a nation and what is true of people in the Bible is also true of families. God invented the family. I've often said He holds the original patent on marriage. It was His idea. One man with one woman forever: conceiving, bearing, rearing, and releasing children. It is all His plan, and it is pictured for us in Scripture in an idealistic manner. However, there is a lot of realism about the family threaded through the fabric of Scripture.

The examples of family living we see in the Bible are not "idealistic." The families in the Bible are comprised of real, often struggling people. None of the parents in biblical days experienced perpetual harmony and perfect joy. As in our own times, some stood face to face with a stubborn and rebellious youngster. Confronting the unpleasant wasn't easy for them, either.

God and Rebellion

It may encourage you to know that God has never been pleased with rebellion. He takes a strong stand against it. If you are a parent living in the same home with an older child who is becoming increasingly more stubborn and rebellious, take heart. God stands with you in your determination to do what is right. He is grieved when He observes rebellion among the offspring of a home. He speaks sternly about it. Even in ancient days He refused to shrug His shoulders and look the other way.

On my mind is a scene out of the fifteenth chapter of 1 Samuel. Lest anyone be tempted to think rebellion is something only teenagers are guilty of, it is worth noting that the person on center stage in this chapter is not only a grown man, he is a *king* . . . the king of Israel. His name is Saul. To get to the point, Saul has acted impudently, maybe a better word is disobediently. He had been told to follow God's precise orders, but didn't. God viewed the king's disobedience as out-and-out rebellion. So the Lord dispatched Samuel to confront Saul. The rebuke is recorded in 1 Samuel 15:22–23:

> *And Samuel said,*
> *"Has the LORD as much delight in burnt offerings and sacrifices as in obeying the voice of the LORD? Behold, to obey is better than sacrifice, and to heed than the fat of rams. For rebellion is as the sin of divination, and insubordination is as iniquity and idolatry. Because you have rejected the word of the LORD, He has also rejected you from being king."*

Take time to analyze God's view of rebellion. He considers it in the same category as divination, which is demon worship. To God, a rebellious act is on the same level as *demonism*. And insubordination? Just read the verse. In God's eyes it is "as iniquity and idolatry." That's quite a statement, for God despises few things more than idolatry. Yet we read here "rebellion is as . . . divination, and insubordination is as . . . idolatry." Rebellion caused the king of Israel to be dethroned. Rebellion led, ultimately, to his removal from the highest office in the land.

When stubborn and persistent rebellion occurs, it is no idle matter. It is not humorous, cute, or "just a stage." Nor is it viewed as a little mischievous act in the eyes of God. Hard-core rebellion is a heinous sin, calling for the strongest resistance one can muster. If God doesn't ignore it, we can be sure it must not be overlooked by parents.

CONFRONTING THE UNPLEASANT

Let's be wise, however. Rebellion is not to be confused with the normal growing-up process, when our adolescents press for independence. Throughout the previous chapters I have been promoting the fact that a home ought to be the laboratory where parents help children become independent adults. As maturity develops, our young adults ultimately set their own curfew, handle their own finances, choose their own friends, and drive their own cars. They mature into self-government as they reach that level of responsibility. They come to the place where they can handle it. I remind you, there's no "magical age"—it comes earlier for some and later for others. This kind of healthy independence is not to be viewed by parents as a sign of rebellion. I think most of us would agree: Few things are more pitiful than to see an older adult inseparably linked to his or her parents . . . still dependent, still needing them to handle life's demands. On the other hand, older children who attempt to control the home by intimidating and bullying to get their own way must be dealt with. It is at that point parents must view rebellion with the same seriousness God does. It simply cannot be tolerated. Multiple authority figures in the same family spell chaos.

Without wishing to drift into a tirade of negative generalities, I want to state that we are rearing a generation of confused children. Many do not know who to respect because the standard at home keeps changing. They intimidate their parents without being confronted. That same intimidation is then shifted to their teachers at school, their youth leaders at church, and even the cop on the corner. If permitted, these indulged rebels will stop at nothing to get their way. I see it now more than ever in my twenty-five-plus years of ministry.

Let me give it to you straight: Parents, it is our mandate to deal firmly with rebellion. It will be unpleasant and difficult. It will always be heartrending, and on occasion you will think that you may lose your mind. But *you must stand firm.* Occasionally, it may get extremely volatile. It will be you against the rebel, with no easy way out. At such times, you either remain the authority or you relinquish that position and open the door to a miserable existence in which your entire family lives under siege. You may come to the place where you will wonder if you should call for professional help . . . or assistance from civil or police authorities. If it comes to that, you must act in the best interest of your family. You are the parent. You cannot afford to allow your authority in the home to be undermined.

I can name several families right now who spend their days under the threat of older, rebellious children still living at home. It is a tragic, pathetic sight. The parents do not know what they will face when they wake up in the morning. They do not know what to expect when the rebel comes home from school in the afternoon (if he even goes to school). They live in fear, constantly intimidated by a delinquent adolescent whose lifestyle is out of control. That situation didn't happen overnight. It was years in the making. God, who originated the family, never intended a home to be run like that.

Parable of a Rebellious Son

All this provides a perfect setting for the examination of a familiar story Jesus once told. The story of the prodigal son is being acted out in real life every day across America. I think the relevance of it will help us realize just how up to date Scripture really is. The story appears in Luke's Gospel, beginning with these simple words:

> *A certain man had two sons; and the younger of them said to his father, "Father, give me the share of the estate that falls to me." And he divided his wealth between them (15:11–12).*

The Setting

Jewish law stated that when a family had two sons, the older son would ultimately get two-thirds of the father's estate and the

younger son would get the remaining one-third. The financial
accounting would be settled at the father's retirement or death.
The younger son in this story demands with impatience: "I want
my share NOW." By implication: "I want to be rid of this place
and all its restrictions. I want to be out on my own." It is the philosophy most clearly stated in the pop tune of yesteryear, "I did it
my way." There is a tone of rebellion in the boy's voice. It's this
idea: "Give me my wealth. I have it coming."

The father does not argue or plead. Graciously, he releases
his son's portion and lets him leave. Not many days later, the
younger son gathers his belongings and splits. He journeys into
a distant country, probably thinking he would never return.

I find it interesting that the father released his boy without
a fight. We don't even read of a going-away lecture. Our admiration for that father is strong. It isn't easy to do what he did.
On the contrary, it is painful—and even a little frightening.

Ponder the wise, insightful words of Dr. John White:

> God's dealings with his people form a pattern for Christian
> parents. Like Him we may eventually have to allow our persis-
> tently rebellious children to harvest the consequences of their
> willfulness. The time can come when we have to withdraw all
> support from them and oblige them, because of their own
> decisions, to leave home. . . .
>
> There are times when an explosive situation demands fast
> action. Bitterness often rises in the "good children" whom the
> parents may neglect in their desire to restore their prodigal to
> his or her senses. And sometimes matters go so far that the
> parents are forced to choose whom they would rather have at
> home, the problem child or the nonproblem children. The
> squeaky wheel may get so much grease that the silent wheels
> disconnect themselves from the axle and roll away.
>
> Parents who are reluctant to take drastic steps should ask
> themselves. Are they too scared? There is every reason to be
> scared. What parent is not? The thought of exposing a child
> to physical hardship, to loneliness and to moral temptation
> flies in the face of every parental instinct. Or is it that parents
> fear public opinion? Are they still clinging to unrealistic
> hopes that matters will magically right themselves if only
> they hang on a little longer when it is plain they will not?

Parents who cling to their erring children must realize that by paying debts and legal expenses beyond clearly set guidelines, or even by offering continued shelter, food, and clothing, they can morally become a party to the delinquent behavior. Their actions can make it possible for rebellious children to continue to live as they have in the past. Home for them is merely a free hotel. Instead of helping them to follow godliness, parents are giving their children the message that there is no need for them to be godly since they, their parents, will always look after them and get them out of a hole.

The decision to dismiss children from home should not be made either because it will work or as a matter of expediency. It should be made on the basis of justice. And justice must consider every side of the problem. Is it morally just to keep children at home when other family members suffer deprivation in one form or another because of them? Are they old enough to care for themselves, that is, to hunt for work and provide themselves with food and shelter? Are they legally of age? Have they had plenty of warning about what will happen if they continue in the same way? Have the warnings been merely angry threats or serious talks explaining why such measures should be adopted? . . .

I do not have answers to all the questions I raise, but I must answer some.[44]

Dealing with rebellion is serious business. It is especially unpleasant because we're dealing with our own flesh and blood. There is actually no greater pain. I hardly need remind you there is no answer sheet in the back of some parenting textbook. There is no promise the delinquent will repent and come back. We can't even say for sure that he or she will be preserved from danger. Ours is an ugly, cold world. Things don't always work out well. None of these rebels "live happily ever after." Some, after they leave, dread the coming of every dawn.

Back to the story. The boy announces, "I'm leaving. Give me what's coming to me." Soon he is a mere speck on the horizon. I'm sure the father's heart was torn as he stood in the doorway, wondering if their eyes would ever meet again. Being a parent at such moments is the toughest task on earth.

The Lifestyle

*And not many days later, the younger son gathered every-
thing together and went on a journey into a distant country,
and there he squandered his estate with loose living. Now
when he had spent everything, a severe famine occurred in
that country, and he began to be in need (vv. 13–14).*

The boy burned his bridges behind him. Out of sight, out
of mind, he thought. He struck out for a freewheeling, no-has-
sle lifestyle. The right to call all his own shots. He'd had it up
to his earlobes with all those restrictions. Free at last! He began
to satisfy his desire to have all his inner itches scratched.

Who knows? Maybe he rented a little place near the beach
with a nice view and then established a circle of new friends.
For sure, he was able to enjoy a playboy lifestyle that never
could have been possible back home. His money bought him
plenty of booze, his friends (if you've got the money, they've
always got the time), and one chick after another. It was that
long-awaited no-holds-barred sexual fantasy he'd dreamed of
. . . operation gratification!

By and by his money ran out. At this point Scripture is very
eloquent in its brevity. Maybe a severe recession swept across
the country, and "he began to be in need." A growing panic
replaces his feeling of freedom. Welcome to real-world life on
the street. Finally, he was forced to search for work. Only problem was, he couldn't find any.

The young Jewish boy now had to dip to his lowest level.
He hired out in the shameful task of feeding swine.

*And he went and attached himself to one of the citizens of
that country, and he sent him into his fields to feed swine.
And he was longing to fill his stomach with the pods that
the swine were eating, and no one was giving anything to
him (vv. 15–16).*

Today's pigsty on city streets is worse than any of us can
imagine. I take a calculated risk in applying those first-century

words to the real world in this generation, but I opt to do so in hopes of stopping some young boy or girl who may be on the verge of running away. I'm aware that the next two paragraphs may be a bit too realistic for some, but maybe they will grab the attention of some young rebel and make him rethink the idea of walking away from the shelter and protection of home.

Boys are selling themselves not only on the streets of our high-density cities, but also in smaller towns across the country. In street jargon, the runaways are known as "chickens"— their customers, "chicken hawks." In the major cities, young male hookers wander through the streets in search of customers while callboy operations flourish. Pimps, skilled in initiating young runaways into the highly profitable, low-skilled trade, prowl bus depots and other transportation centers looking for incoming, unattached teenagers. On occasion, an unwilling boy is transformed into a male prostitute by drugs and brute force, kept as a prisoner until his usefulness has been exhausted and his body totally wasted. There are tightly run organizations in the United States and overseas geared to provide wealthy clients with both pornography and homosexual acts with boys. These highly paid entrepreneurs have higher standards than the street pimps. They use different procedures. Their boys will entertain movie stars, prominent athletes, politicians, and, in some cases, heads of state.

One young man trapped in this tragic vice phoned me anonymously not long ago. His shameful story, which I'll not repeat, was another horrible account of abuse. I've had that happen on various occasions when the runaway began to be in need. Totally confused, morally corrupted, and physically wasted, the boys remain scarred for life. Their voices reveal panic, confusion. They have trafficked in all the things that you and I would not discuss and could barely imagine. When they begin to be "in need," they don't know where to turn. Slowly but ever so surely, the anticipated delight of defiance begins to pay its wage, and they find themselves enslaved to a dreadful lifestyle. Their conscience, whatever is left of it, is like a fragile thread. All self-esteem has vanished. Suicide looms in their thoughts. There is nothing they haven't done. The fun of so-called freedom has long since passed. Addiction to drugs, alcohol, pornography, perversion, and a dozen more filthy unmentionables holds them in an inescapable grip.

The street may appear inviting. It may seem free and easygoing. But in truth it is a godless, shameless pigsty in the worst sense of the word. If you are thinking of running, better reevaluate that option!

This boy in the biblical account, realizing he was in need, suddenly realized that no one else around him cared like his dad once did back home. Did you notice the awful reality of his comment?

> *And he was longing to fill his stomach with the pods that the swine were eating, and no one was giving anything (v. 16).*

I call that life in the raw! Swine pods represent the backwash of ugly, raw, godless, debauched living. NOBODY gives a rip or offers a free lunch! And it gets worse . . . and worse . . . and worse. Finally, unable to find relief, depravity reaches full bloom: you submit to anyone; you eat anything; you sleep anywhere, with anyone, for any purpose. God's Book, like none other, tells us the truth. As I said at the beginning of this chapter, it doesn't fudge when it comes to reality.

The Return

The prodigal finally woke up and began to speak to God. The next statement is most significant: "he came to his senses." That suggests he was out of his senses—a temporary insanity—when he left. Perhaps that explains why parents cannot reason with rebels who resist all counsel.

Allow me to step in and remind all who are parents that you can rebuke a rebel. You can discipline him. You can warn him, try to correct him, and point him in the right direction. You can also stand your ground against his rebellion. But *you can't force him to change.* Some are so hellish in their rebellion they are absolutely unreasonable . . . I repeat, temporarily insane! At that point, you are at the mercy of time. Having released him, you must trust God to get his attention.

No one knows how long that boy was in the streets. I don't know how long he lived in the pigsty. But when he came to an end of himself, when he returned to his senses, he began to look up. For the first time in a long time, he thought straight.

> *He said, "How many of my father's hired men have more than enough bread, but I am dying here with hunger!" (v. 17).*

That tells us he was from a rather affluent home. Not only did the father have servants, not only did he have employees, but they were well fed.

Parents, at times it will take your child *years* of painful consequences to realize what he or she had back home. It may take failing at school or being expelled. It may take running away and being abused on the street. It may result in a prison sentence. Sometimes it will take literally years of loneliness, brokenness, and heartache. It may take the loss of a limb, the half-loss of their mind, or the infection of AIDS before they realize the consequences of rebellion. In most cases it will be a series of traumatic events that finally shake the prodigal awake.

This boy finally comes to his senses and says: "I will get up and go to my father, and will say to him, 'Father, I have sinned against heaven, and in your sight; I am no longer worthy to be called your son; make me as one of your hired men'" (v. 18–19).

In other words, "I expect nothing . . . I deserve zilch. I'll be satisfied to live in a lean-to out in the back yard. I am willing to work day and night. Dad, I just want to be back with you." Isn't it interesting he doesn't say, "I will go back to my neighborhood," or, "I want to go back to my room." He says, "I'll go to my *father*." Ponder that statement! Most of all, he missed a relationship.

Parents, the most significant thing in your home is *YOU*. It is not your things, your belongings, how many rooms you have in your house, or how many cars you park in your garage. It is you they remember when they come to an end of themselves.

"I'll go back to my daddy! I'll go back to the one who treated me right. I'll go back to the one who didn't budge, who stood firm on principle, who loved me enough to let me go. I'll go back to my father. And I'll just say, 'Make me as one of your servants.'" Those thoughts took a long, long time to surface. Rebellion dies hard, but when it dies, repentance emerges.

What an emotional reunion!

And he got up and came to his father. But while he was still a long way off, his father saw him, and felt compassion for him (v. 20).

Dad didn't come running toward him with his index finger pointing at him, blaming him and reprimanding him, "I told you so! I warned you!" No, he came with his arms outstretched, his heart full of compassion. The text says when the boy and father met, they "embraced." The Greek suggests they "kissed repeatedly." Dad kissed him again and again and again and again. What a scene! Words can't adequately describe the emotion of that epochal moment: A waiting dad arm in arm with a wayward lad, tears streaming down both faces.

Waiting for such a moment can seem like a lifetime. Sometimes you'll wait for months. Sometimes it will take years. Spring will come with its rains. And then the heat of summer. Still, no return. The rebel refuses to come home. The nostalgic winds of fall will blow in, bringing the chill of winter. Afterwards, the rains of another spring will return. Still, no sign of hope. No call. No son. The heat of another summer . . . the return of another fall will break your heart as you reflect on the peaceful, early days of childhood. "Where is my son? Where is my daughter?" Snows will fall, rains will come, summer will pass, and they still won't be home. Waiting seems eternal. I cannot adequately describe the agony some parents endure. The grief, at times, is beyond belief.

And, never forget, the misery of the runaway is equally painful. A man wrote to me recently. He described the consequences of carnality so vividly that I want to share with you a few excerpts from his letter.

> I'm sure most people don't realize the ultimate consequences of their deeds (I know I didn't). I feel sorrow for those who "fall" because I know what they have to look forward to. I don't doubt God's forgiveness and healing, but the scars go deep and the road back is so long and hard. He eventually will "restore the years the locusts have eaten" but it isn't an overnight transformation, and some losses you never regain. Whenever you have the opportunity, tell people that the time of pleasure doesn't even begin to offset the pain of the "whirlwind." The scars never leave and I'm convinced you never really attain the joy that God originally had planned for you. Maybe I'm wrong, but it's not worth the chance to experiment with. Regret is a gnawing destroyer of contentment.

When the short-lived fantasy in the fast lane has ended, scars linger. Now, back to our story.

At last, the boy shows up at home. Broken, bruised, ashamed, he searches for words. I can just hear the boy as he began to say his speech. He had practiced it: "Father, I have sinned against heaven and in your sight; I am no longer worthy to be called your son." Totally disregarding those words, the father shouted to his slaves, "Quickly, quickly, bring these things we need." (Notice, the son didn't even get a chance to finish his speech—never did get to "the hired man" part.) Dad yells through tears of joy, "This boy needs something to wear. Get rid of these street rags! Put a clean robe on him. He needs dignity. Put a ring on his finger—some new sandals on his feet."

The boy had been living like a slave. The dad looks down and says, "My boy deserves better than that! Put shoes on his feet. Kill Bruno! We'll have a feast like you can't imagine! Let's eat and be merry!" Can you imagine that table loaded with food? I smile as I visualize this lad, having so recently dined on pods in the swine's pen, now looking at more food than he has seen for months, maybe years.

But the best is yet to come.

For this son of mine was dead, and has come to life again (v. 24).

Isn't that *magnificent?* The dad says, "That boy who left home so long ago was virtually dead. He was like nothing I ever raised. He was not at all like us. He did not believe as we believed. He did not conduct himself as I had trained him. It was like he had died! But he has been raised. He was lost . . . totally out of it. No longer! He has been found." The boy's speech on how wrong he'd been, how undeserving he was, got submerged beneath the forgiveness and excitement of the father. Restored to a place of dignity and purpose, the prodigal must have felt completely overwhelmed . . . yes, even *needed.*

The final part of that episode is recorded in six wonderful words.

. . . and they began to be merry (v. 24).

What an understatement! Imagine the joy in the home at that reunion. It's a marvelous story! Alas, for some of you, it hasn't reached that joyful ending . . . not yet.

Confronting the Unpleasant in Your Family

Perhaps the best way to bring a chapter like this to a close is to summarize what we have seen in the story. Let me mention some helpful principles that will assist in our dealing with a rebel. I think they will affirm some parents. And for others of you, they will give you food for thought. Most of all I hope they speak to those of you who are seriously considering the possibility of running.

No rebellious child can be allowed to ruin a home.

I don't care how old or how gifted the child may be, no rebel is worth the destruction of a family unit. No matter the background, no matter how intimidating, no matter how violent, no matter how manipulative, or how much trouble it may be to confront the unpleasant, a rebel must not be allowed to ruin a home. I encourage you to read the book from which I quoted earlier, *Parents in Pain,* by Dr. John White. He presents quite a case for this principle.

If the level of rebellion necessitates a separation, you must choose principle over person.

If there is a principle at stake, no matter what the relationship, you stand on the principle, even if it is your child. Some will disagree with me on this, I realize, but I see it as an issue of justice. Part of the reason we have such a confused generation in our day is that the child doesn't know where the standard is. If it bends at home, then it will bend at school. And if it bends at school, then for him it bends in life . . . ultimately, everything bends. The lines of right and wrong get blurred. Kids who are permitted to take control don't know which way to go. Stand firm on this principle!

When true repentance occurs, forgiveness with a loving welcome is the response God honors.

I have a physician friend who lives in Texas. He has raised a family of boys. The boys were in their teens back in the wild 1960s—a decade of domestic and civil rebellion. It came time for the oldest son to go off to college. The young man was a gifted musician; he played beautiful violin. He chose a school on the West Coast and left home with his parents' blessing and approval. The affluent family provided for his every need that freshman year. But during that year away from home the boy bought into the whole nine yards of personal defiance. He got a full dose while on the West Coast and was enamored of it by the time he returned home that summer. I suppose we could say he went back home to "set the family straight." No chance.

What he didn't realize was that he was dealing with a father who had more grit and determination than he had given him credit for. Calmly, firmly, and through much prayer, that father realized early on what was happening and stood his ground.

Finally, as the boy was making all kinds of demands and creating havoc—denying any wrongdoing, the father sat him down for a talk, using words to this effect: "Son, if you wish to live like this, that is your prerogative. You are old enough to choose the lifestyle you prefer, but you can't do so under this roof. Your mother and I—and your brothers included—refuse to be intimidated. If you wish to leave, that is fine . . . but you need to remember that everything you have, I bought—and therefore own. I own that violin. I'd like you to leave it here in our home when you leave. I own your car. Don't plan to drive away in it. Leave it in the garage. You'll have to walk. I own your clothing. Leave your clothes in the closet when you walk out. I own everything that's on you, including your money. Please, empty your pockets before you go. I will let you keep the clothes on your back and the shoes you now have on your feet. There is the door; leave if you choose. We hope you'll decide to stay, but if not, leave now under those conditions."

It's amazing what an education that young collegian got all of a sudden as he sat in that beautiful living room facing his father, realizing he would have nothing if he left. He was bright enough to know he would be the loser if he walked out. The father concluded his talk with these words, "If you do go, don't return until you come back like you left a year ago, understanding how this home is run—fairly, lovingly, biblically, and—as always—under the authority of your mother and me."

They negotiated for just a few moments (it didn't take long!), and the boy saw the error of his way. I am pleased to report, his whole attitude changed. He has since become a mature, responsible, and secure young man.

There's an old gospel song that says,

> I've wandered far away from God,
> Now I'm coming home;
> The paths of sin too long I've trod,
> Lord, I'm coming home.

> I've tired of sin and straying, Lord,
> Now I'm coming home;
> I'll trust Thy love, believe Thy word,
> Lord, I'm coming home.[45]

The beautiful part of those lyrics is that the Father waits with His arms open, ready to say, "I forgive you; come on home."

A rebel is unpleasant to deal with, but not impossible. If you are in the midst of such a setting, believe me, you have my respect and my prayers. More importantly, you have God's strength on which to lean.

Allow me to close this chapter with a prayer.

Lord God, thank You for Your patience. Every one of us has known the horror of running, some farther than others. We've also known the joy of cleansing, some more than others. But right now, our hearts are moved for those who've wandered far away from You. How we wish they would begin to come to their senses. I pray You will bring them to full repentance. Neither I nor my reader can change anyone's heart, but You can do that. Use Your Word as a prod to push them back to obedience. Draw them to Yourself. Use whatever it takes to break that rebellious spirit. I pray for parents who live with the terror of their memories—the highest level of anxiety for a family to endure. I pray that You would sustain these fine parents who wait. Keep them going. Guard them from bitterness and resentment. Put Your arms around them and love them. Comfort them like a Shepherd during these days of waiting for their family member to return.

I pray as well for single parents today whose mates are runaways. I pray that You would do the same for them. As they stay by the stuff and rear the family, assist them. Keep them morally pure. Make them strong. Give them courage.

I ask all this in the name of Him who is able to keep us from stumbling, and to make us stand in the presence of Your glory blameless with great joy . . . the only God our Savior, through Jesus Christ our Lord. Amen.

11

Facing the Unforeseen

How far you go in life
depends on your being tender with
the young, compassionate with the aged,
sympathetic with the striving, and tolerant of the
weak and the strong. Because someday in life you
will have been all of these.

—GEORGE WASHINGTON CARVER

I have admired those words for years. They reflect a perspective easily forgotten in a dizzy schedule of demands and deadlines. It is easy in such a scene to become short-sighted, to think that now is forever. But those who sustain a close companionship with wisdom tend to be more tender, compassionate, sympathetic, and tolerant than those whose world revolves around themselves.

With wisdom comes depth and stability. When families navigate through life under full sail with wisdom at the helm, they may not miss all of the storms, but they will have the strength to persevere. They can face the unforeseen without the fear of sinking. Let's face it, life for any family is no exact science. About the time we think we've got a fix on the compass and the journey looks predictable, we encounter a shallow reef that surprises us and forces us to alter our course.

Life As It Is . . . Not As We Would Imagine

As I boil life down to the nubbies, it seems there are four primary factors I must contend with: people, events, decisions, and results. They seem simple enough, forthright and predictable . . . but they are none of the above.

People

It is our tendency to think that most folks are kind, thoughtful, reliable, unselfish, and stable. Nice thought . . . I wish it were so. But reality forces us to be honest and admit that people are sinful, selfish, and often in trouble. There are times, certainly, when rays of goodness shine through, but those are the exceptions. Anyone who works with people and/or families must accept those painful realities. Imperfect people spawn imperfect families. These imperfections multiply and complicate family struggles.

Events

It is an idealistic dream to think that events in life are predictable. No one knows what tomorrow holds. Chances are good it will include a surprise or two. Events are unpredictable —and occasionally worse than we would expect. Though I would love to write otherwise, I am too committed to truth and too close to the dark drama of human nature to do so. Trouble is all around. Problems are abundant. Things we would be tempted to think would never happen to us can and sometimes do. When they do, they are often worse than we could have imagined.

Decisions

Let me limit this category to Christians for the sake of illustration. We would imagine that Christians would make decisions based on God's will. We might even think that those decisions would represent a clear vertical perspective and a willingness to obey the Lord, no matter where He may lead. That has not been my observation. More often than not, decisions are horizontal and rarely based on biblical principles.

Before you resist that, consider your own life. May I hazard a guess? Chances are good that in most of the decisions throughout your past you looked out for yourself. More often than not you relied on human reasoning rather than some principle from God's Word. Odds are you prayed only superficially, if at all. Having counseled people—mostly Christians—for over twenty years, it has been my observation that a major reason they found themselves in their predicaments is because they had made decisions strictly from a horizontal perspective, rarely based on biblical principles.

Results

In light of the above, it shouldn't surprise anyone that families must endure complex, hurtful consequences. Life gets painful, complicated, and interwoven, doesn't it? No one lives to himself, no one dies to himself. *And no one sins unto himself.* Sinful acts in my life affect my wife, my children, my church, my friends, even my extended family. If those sins are extreme enough, they affect my neighbors and my world at large. No one can deny the ramifications of disobedience. The impact of those consequences can be devastating.

When you mix all of this into a busy family, adding more people, in-laws, hang-ups, bad habits, a lack of biblical orientation, and a full spectrum of human opinions, it isn't difficult to see what a mess we can get ourselves into. You can see right away that when a gen-u-ine "Type A" test hits the family broadside, rather than strengthening us in our walk, it dislodges us, since our inner moorings have become so fragile. The unforeseen can take a terrible toll on us if we are the type who lives in a bubble of beautiful idealism. Wise are those who live realistically.

In spite of our sinfulness, weakness, and tendency to serve ourselves, we need to keep in mind that God remains all the things we are not. Since this is true, *He* can (and will) give us everything we lack when the unexpected hits us head-on. Rather than frighten you, I want this chapter to help you prepare for what may be around the corner of your life. If I knew specifically, I would address it specifically. Since I do not, I can only provide general assistance. But I do plead with you to take these things seriously. In less than twelve hours you could be seized with a heart attack—or lose someone very special and precious to you. It is possible you will have to endure some calamity before this month is over, some awful tragedy that today seems unthinkable. It may be your sad experience prior to your next anniversary to hear your mate say those awful, dreaded words, "I want out" . . . or your adolescent admit, "I think I'm pregnant" or, "I'm on drugs."

The unforeseen can be painful, but it is *not* impossible.

Life As It Was . . . Not As We Would Expect

In times like this I am so grateful we have the Bible. Isn't it terrific that I don't have to dig into my imagination and dream up some imaginary story and hope it helps? How much better to cite a real-life event from biblical days and then identify with the plot. God has given us all of the details we need to equip us to face the unforeseen without fear. We want to do that in this chapter by observing the events in the life of a man whose world not only fell apart in a matter of hours, it caved in on him.

An Enviable Family

Had you and I been driving the streets, looking for the ideal family back in ancient days, we would have stopped when we came to the residence with the Job family name on the mailbox. They lived in the land of Uz. We really know very little about them. Scholars guess and preachers imagine, but no one knows for sure a great deal about Job's family prior to the storm that knocked them off their feet. But that is not important. What seems most significant to us at this moment is that the man was a model father:

> *There was a man in the land of Uz, whose name was Job,*
> *and that man was blameless, upright, fearing God, and*
> *turning away from evil (Job 1:1).*

What a man . . . what a father! His family reflected his splendid leadership. How great it must have been to have had a father like that. A good reputation. Integrity. Close walk with God. A man who deliberately rejected evil. On top of that, he had a large family; he and his wife, plus ten children . . . all grown.

> *And seven sons and three daughters were born to him. His*
> *possessions also were 7,000 sheep, 3,000 camels, 500 yoke*
> *of oxen, 500 female donkeys, and very many servants;*
> *and that man was the greatest of all the men of the east*
> *(vv. 2–3).*

Job also operated a rather large ranch with sizable herds of various animals, and a great retinue of servants to wait upon his every need. Obviously, Job and his family were financially fixed. When we read that he was the "greatest of all the men of the east," we can be sure his name was a household word.

As a dad, I find it encouraging that Job took his family relationships seriously. See the next two verses.

> *And his sons used to go and hold a feast in the house of*
> *each one on his day, and they would send and invite their*
> *three sisters to eat and drink with them. And it came about,*
> *when the days of feasting had completed their cycle, that*
> *Job would send and consecrate them, rising up early in the*
> *morning and offering burnt offerings according to the num-*
> *ber of them all; for Job said, "Perhaps my sons have sinned*

and cursed God in their hearts." Thus Job did continually (vv. 4–5).

The grown siblings got along well. Here was a family that stayed close. They celebrated birthdays together. They enjoyed the holidays together. They laughed with one another, enjoying big family dinners from time to time. They shared the Red Plate together! It is an enviable scene of harmony and happiness. Those parents had done a great job. When adult kids remain close, a lot of credit goes to mom and dad.

I don't know what you appreciate most about a good father, but *consistency* would certainly be high on my list. I think this man represents that, according to the final four words of the statement we just read. He was not perfect by any means (though the first verse in his biography may tempt you to believe he was nearer to it than many), but he was a good man and a consistent father. His heart was tender toward God. And even when the children had moved and left the nest, he continued to represent them in prayer to God. That, by the way, is worth remembering as our kids are launched into life.

A Series of Calamities

Suddenly life changes. You can almost hear the joy and harmony screeching to a halt with the words "now it happened. . . ."

Stop right here. Job stood with his toes on the verge of the unforeseen. But, you see, that is how it occurs. It was a morning like any other morning in Job's life. The sun rose like every other dawn. His day began and looked like any other day. There had been no angelic skywriting the day before announcing some impending calamity. There had been no night visions that stabbed him awake. No audible voice warning, "Beware!" Just another day, sunrise—sunset.

But how tragically different this one would be. Job would never be the same.

FACING THE UNFORESEEN

Several years ago the Argentine tennis pro, Guillermo Villas, was being interviewed. He was the athlete so many in his country admired at the zenith of this career. He seemed so strong, secure as the Rock of Gibraltar. Yet, with vulnerable honesty, he admitted, "Fervently, I think that many times one feels oneself to be secure and suddenly one's world falls down like a pack of cards in a matter of seconds." That's how it is when the unforeseen hits a family. One's world falls down!

That's precisely what happened with Job. He woke that morning, anticipating another day like all the rest. He stretched, yawned, got dressed, and ate breakfast. He looked out the window, expecting it to be like any other day, but before nightfall he had lost it all. Four unexpected messengers brought back-to-back news of tragedy with hardly any breathing time in between. For Job, it meant the loss of everything he owned and everyone he loved.

> Now it happened on the day when his sons and his daughters were eating and drinking wine in their oldest brother's house, that a messenger came to Job and said, "The oxen were plowing and the donkeys feeding beside them, and the Sabeans attacked and took them. They also slew the servants with the edge of the sword, and I alone have escaped to tell you." While he was still speaking, another also came and said, "The fire of God fell from heaven and burned up the sheep and the servants and consumed them; and I alone have escaped to tell you." While he was still speaking, another also came and said, "The Chaldeans formed three bands and made a raid on the camels and took them and slew the servants with the edge of the sword; and I alone have escaped to tell you." While he was still speaking, another also came and said, "Your sons and your daughters were eating and drinking wine in their oldest brother's house, and behold, a great wind came from across the wilderness and struck the four corners of the house, and it fell on the young people and they died; and I alone have escaped to tell you" (vv. 13–19).

Job's world fell down like that proverbial "house of cards." If we live to be one hundred years old, we will never be able to enter into the grief of the man at this point. Without one word's notice, he lost his livestock, his servants, his financial security, and finally, his family. Imagine it! There he is, standing beside ten fresh graves on a windswept hillside, a hollow-eyed victim of the unforeseen.

Those tragic scenes still occur. A phone call, "We are sorry to inform you, but your parents were on board Flight 282 that crashed this morning en route to Dallas."

The physician frowns . . . chooses his words very carefully. "I need to tell you that there were complications at the birth." And perhaps a few days later they tell you, "There is brain damage." Or, "We have every reason to believe your baby has Downs Syndrome."

Two police officers come to your door and admit that after all the searching, they have not found a trace, not even a slight clue, of your little girl. Your stomach churns with the word "lost" . . . by now it has been thirty-six hours. "She has apparently been kidnapped," they sigh. Your world is reduced to one and only one pursuit.

Or your dad pulls you out of junior high school one day. While in the car on the way home, he haltingly tells you he has decided he is not going to stay married to your mother any longer. He asks you not to cry. You feel more like screaming.

I know a couple who, after enjoying dinner out together, drove into their driveway and found a note attached to the gate. Some policeman had scribbled a few words of explanation, which led them to a hospital. Their twenty-one-year-old son, a specimen of health when they left earlier that evening, had suffered a brain aneurysm while on his way to his girlfriend's home . . . and was dead. I know a wife who drove home on a rainy night. She pushed the automatic garage door opener, and as the door lifted that night, she saw the full-length profile of her husband. He had hanged himself earlier that afternoon.

To borrow from Job's story, that is when the Sabeans attack, when the fire falls, when the Chaldeans raid. That's when the wind blows against your house. That's when the unforeseen is no longer a theoretical chapter in a book . . . it becomes your personal nightmare and refuses to go away.

It happens to someone every day. The newspaper recently carried the story of a woman who had spent six years traveling around the world buying unique antiques. She was preparing to set up her own business. A week, *just one week* before she was to open her store, the stab of a wayward bolt of lightning set off an electrical fire in a block of stores. Several shops in a row, including hers, went up in smoke. The goods, being priceless and irreplaceable, were insured for only a fraction of their value. For that matter, what insurance settlement could ever compensate a middle-aged woman for six years of her life searching and collecting those priceless valuables? Like a house of cards . . .

I read about a young pharmacist named Ron who ran a drugstore with an older partner. When Ron bought into the business, his more experienced colleague told him the store had recently been the target of a series of holdups. Young drug addicts looking for drugs and cash preyed on places like theirs. Late one evening, when Ron was closing, a teenaged junkie pulled a small-caliber handgun on him and nervously asked for drugs and money. Ron didn't try to be a hero. He was far more willing to lose a day's receipts than his life. As he turned to open the cash register, his hands were trembling. Dizzy with fear, Ron stumbled and reached for the counter to support himself. The nervous junkie assumed he was going for a gun. He squeezed the trigger and fired one bullet—only one—then ran. But that single round went through Ron's abdomen and lodged in his spinal cord. The doctors removed the bullet, but the damage had been done. Ron would never walk again.[46]

That's how the unforeseen happens. Just that quick. Like you've read about in the newspaper for years. Only one day it happens in *your* store . . . at *your* school . . . to *your* family. And when it does, the unthinkable becomes reality. It is always, always the same. It is sudden, it is surprising, it is worse than you expected, and it is inescapable. After you wrestle with the thought that it is just a dream, the reality of it leaves you reeling.

Semitic scholar Gleason Archer describes Job in vivid terms:

> Job's initial reaction was one of boundless grief and sorrow. Reeling under the impact of these successive strokes of financial loss, the loss of all his faithful servants (many of whom must have been dear to his heart), and above all, the loss of all his beloved children, he was led to expressions of mourning characteristic of the ancient Near East: he tore up the clothes he was wearing at the time he heard the news, and he shaved his hair from his head (in lieu of tearing it out with his hands, as the alternative custom prescribed). As the victim of such unparalleled misfortunes, he felt too crushed in heart to put up any false front of cheerful courage.[47]

I have noticed a curious thing. People much prefer to talk about the patience of Job. But most folks have not allowed themselves sufficient time to ponder the *grief* of Job. Let's take the time to do that.

> *Then Job arose and tore his robe and shaved his head, and he fell to the ground and worshiped (v. 20).*

Like any father who has lost his children, he was crushed in agony. It was absolutely overwhelming. And why shouldn't it have been? Nothing on earth meant more to that man than those children he had raised.

I am disappointed that someone, somewhere, many years ago, introduced the ridiculous idea that if you know the Lord, you don't grieve. That even if you lose something or someone significant you shouldn't weep. With my whole heart, I disagree! Granted, we don't grieve "as those who have no hope." But no tears? No grief? I find that unthinkable. Since when does becoming a Christian make a person less than human . . . or more than human?

The account does add "he worshiped." Job's expression was not an angry sadness. It wasn't a cynical, jaded grief, where with tight fists shaken toward heaven he screamed, "How DARE you do that to me!" It was an "Oh, my Lord and my God! How do I possibly go on?" He blessed the name of the Lord, but we can be sure at the same hour he mourned the loss of his family.

I don't know how you're put together, but I hope it is realistically. Such a trait will keep you from gravitating toward fanatical extremes. Believing Christians must remain thoroughly human, totally authentic. Not until we express our grief fully do we fully recover. As Job grieved and looked to God for strength in his worship, he uttered those immortal words:

> *"Naked I came from my mother's womb,*
> *and naked I shall return there.*
> *The LORD gave and the LORD has*
> *taken away.*
> *Blessed be the name of the LORD."*
>
> *Through all this Job did not sin nor did he blame God*
> *(vv. 21–22).*

Did you note that? There is no sin in his grieving. He felt the hammering blows of loss. He went through it all, and having done so, he learned that he was not alone. It took going *through it,* however. C. S. Lewis was correct: God shouts to us in our pain.

One would think this man had endured enough. Surely he had experienced his quota of grief and calamity. We want to think God somehow made everything right again, setting Job right back on his feet and restoring his fortunes. Wrong. The agony persisted. If you know the story, you know that another unforeseen affliction struck.

> *Then Satan went out from the presence of the LORD, and smote Job with sore boils from the sole of his foot to the crown of his head (2:7).*

It's not enough that he loses farm and family . . . now he loses his *health,* his last physical shred of hope. The dear guy is covered with boils!

When I was a little boy I had a paper route, and during that time I developed a boil on the inside of my forearm, just below the elbow. I remember that as I bounced along on my bicycle, throwing my route, just the bouncing alone hurt so badly that I had to take my hand off the handle bar and steer it with one hand. I remember not being able to throw the papers with both hands because the force of the throw was too painful.

But I only had one boil. Just one. And I'll tell you, when I was a little boy and read for the first time that Job had boils from the soles of his feet to the crown of his head, I could understand Mrs. Job's counsel to her husband, "Why don't you just curse God and die! That's enough." Don't be too harsh on the wife here. Remember that she had lost ten children, too.

My comment reminds me of a very curious fact. Quadriplegic Joni Eareckson Tada has helped all of us better understand the world of the disabled. I've heard her say that approximately three out of four marriages break up when the home is invaded with the pressures brought on by handicapped, brain-damaged, or other developmentally disabled children. Marital conflict is not unusual in homes that have endured the unforeseen tragedies of life. And here's a case in point. In previous years I have been unfairly critical of Job's wife. Who knows what we would have said in her place? As George Washington Carver wrote, we need to be "sympathetic with the striving." Someday we may be there.

Job is in such physical misery that he broke off little pieces of pottery with which he scraped himself. Perhaps the itching from the boils was maddening. Maybe it was to scrape away the encrusted puss that oozed from the angry red ulcers that covered his body. I would imagine his wife looked at him one awful day, having just returned from the gravesites where the two of them wept together, thinking, *How can we go on? Death would be better.*

His answer is a noble one. I admire him all the more!

But he said to her, "You speak as one of the foolish women speaks. Shall we indeed accept good from God and not accept adversity?" In all this Job did not sin with his lips (2:10).

In our day "the gospel of prosperity" is flourishing. We have been led to believe that a good God does only good, that all those things that flow from His hand come with comfort in mind, relief from pain, and smiles of pleasure. On top of all that, we are told He tosses in picnics at a lovely beach, healthy children, full bank accounts, an easy-living lifestyle, and an Alice-in-Wonderland retirement.

Give me a break! Few teachings are further from the truth. Some of God's dearest saints and most trusted disciples are (and have been) people of pain.

One man provides a wise and balanced perspective:

> God has created a world in which many more good things than bad things happen. We find life's disasters upsetting not only because they are painful but because they are exceptional. Most people wake up on most days feeling good. Most illnesses are curable. Most airplanes take off and land safely. Most of the time, when we send our children out to play, they come home safely. The accident, the robbery, the inoperable tumor are life-shattering . . . but they are very rare exceptions. When you have been hurt by life, it may be hard to keep that in mind. When you are standing very close to a large object, all you can see is the object. Only by stepping back from it can you also see the rest of its setting around it. When we are stunned by some tragedy, we can only see and feel the tragedy. Only with time and distance can we see the tragedy in the context of a whole life and a whole world.[48]

The wife saw the object; Job saw the setting. In preparing for the unforeseen, one of the most helpful things parents can do is to assist one another in gaining perspective, reminding one another of the full picture, the many days in life that have been blessed, the many illnesses that have been cured, the many days when there have been weddings—not divorces—many more joyful moments of life and birth than the agony of loss and death. Cynthia and I often encourage each other in this manner. We don't deny the pain of what has happened. We just refuse to focus only on the valleys.

A Process of Recovery

When I think through some kind of process of recovery, several thoughts come to my mind. Four, in fact. They are all illustrated in Job's reaction.

The first stage of recovery is the *agony of humanity.* We saw that earlier as we watched it occur in Job's life. There is deep emotional pain, too deep for words. And let me add, there is often the added (usually irrational) feeling of guilt. *Somehow, I'm responsible for what has occurred.* I don't think I've met a parent of a disabled child who hasn't struggled with, "What did I do to cause it? Is this God's way of getting back at me?" Guilt is a terrible factor in the human battle.

Painful though it is, our full expression of agony must be allowed to run its course if we hope to recover fully.

The second stage of recovery is *the struggle with theology.* In Job's case, that struggle is revealed in Job's wife's words, "Do you still hold fast your integrity? Curse God and die!" (2:9).

What was the trouble? Mrs. Job's theology was viewed one way, her husband's another. There is struggle when emotions are high and those views clash.

I know of a family where the mother of several children is going blind. She struggles severely with the theology of that hardship, more so than her husband. I know another home where a crippling disease plagues a member of the family. Both the mom and dad are haunted by the tragedy. The other children are healthy. But one isn't. "Is that fair of God? I thought He was good." All kinds of theological questions assault us when some unforeseen calamity becomes a reality:

> *Where is God when I hurt?*
> *I know a lot of people much more wicked who prosper.*
> *Why would He permit such a thing?*
> *Have I believed incorrectly?*

I thought God answered prayer!
Perhaps my unbelieving teacher in college was right.
Didn't God promise that we'd be protected?
He said He'd provide a "way of escape." He didn't!

Theological struggles accompany times like this. Having a small, caring group of people who come up close and bring encouragement is so helpful. They escort us through the maze of theological land mines if we'll only let them.

The third step in the process of recovery is what I call *the acceptance of reality.* In Job's case, he passed this test with flying colors. He posed this question to his wife, "Shall we indeed accept good from God and not accept adversity?" Now *there's* a statement I'd love to have the prosperity-gospel gurus preach on! We don't live in an easy world. We don't serve an indulging God. Humanly speaking, life isn't fair nor is it Fantasyland. Contrary to our constitution, all men are not created equal. If you and I want to prepare ourselves for the unforeseen, we must maintain an intimate companionship with the real world. Furthermore, we must be ready to accept *whatever.* That's why I tried to set the record straight at the outset of this chapter regarding people, events, decisions, and results. By reminding ourselves of those four axioms, facing the unforeseen isn't nearly so devastating.

The fourth step is *freedom from iniquity.*

"Shall we indeed accept good from God and not accept adversity?" In all this Job did not sin with his lips (v. 10).

Earlier in this account (1:22) we read of Job's refusal to shake his fist at God. I say again, the man was a model worth emulating.

One of the most important questions we can ask when some unforeseen tragedy brings us pain and suffering is whom we will permit it to serve—God or the devil? Will it cause us to become alive in wisdom or paralyzed by bitterness? We're back to our attitude, aren't we? It is not the circumstance itself, but our reaction to it that makes any event a tragedy or a triumph. How quickly we choose one of two routes: blame or self-pity! Both lead to a dead end. Blame makes us bitter. Self-pity makes us lonely. Nobody wants to be around a feel-sorry-for-me victim. And while I'm addressing common reactions, something needs to be said against one person's telling another that the calamity came as God's punishment. If that is indeed the reason, it's been my observation that God reveals it to no one other than the sufferer. Let's be careful not to play the role of the self-righteous prophet, substituting rationalization for reality.

Years ago I heard about a Kansas preacher who returned home after visiting New England. One of his parishioners met him at the train.

"Well," asked the preacher, "how are things at home?"

"Sad, real sad, pastor. A cyclone came and wiped out my house."

"Well, I'm not surprised," said the rather blunt parson with a frown. "You remember I've been warnin' you about the way you've been livin'. Punishment for sin is inevitable."

"It also destroyed *your* house, sir," added the layman.

"*It did?*" The pastor was horrified. "Ah me, the ways of the Lord are past human understanding."

A Remarkable Restoration

The wonderful part of the Job story is that it has a fantastic ending. We have to look way ahead into chapter 42 of Job's journal to see how everything worked out. It's a scene where relief comes, where healing finally happens, and all the tragedy is turned into triumph. Job, on his face before God, says:

> I have heard of Thee by the hearing of the ear; but now my eye sees Thee; therefore I retract, and I repent in dust and ashes (42:5–6).

He has learned some lessons. He's grown deeper. He's trusted God. He has struggled with four so-called counselors who came with their strong, judgmental comments. And through the process he has finally found a place of quiet understanding. He senses the nearness of God . . . His presence . . . His unchanging love. God finally has become the man's "hiding place" through which Job has found grace to persevere.

> *In a time of trouble, in a time forlorn,*
> *There is a hiding place where hope is born.*
>
> *In a time of danger, when our faith is proved,*
> *There is a hiding place where we are loved.*
>
> *In a time of sorrow, in a time of grief,*
> *There is a hiding place to give relief.*
>
> *In a time of weakness, in a time of fear,*
> *There is a hiding place where God is near.*
>
> *There is a hiding place, a strong protective space,*
> *Where God provides the grace to persevere;*
> *For nothing can remove us from the Father's love,*
> *Tho' all may change, yet nothing changes here.*[49]

And look at what happens:

And the LORD restored the fortunes of Job when he prayed for his friends, and the LORD increased all that Job had twofold (42:10).

Can you imagine the joy? The ecstasy of relief? There was this great family reunion, brothers and sisters came. The works!

Then all his brothers, and all his sisters, and all who had known him before, came to him, and they ate bread with him in his house; and they consoled him and comforted him for all the evil that the LORD had brought on him. And each one gave him one piece of money, and each a ring of gold. And the LORD blessed the latter days of Job more than his beginning, and he had 14,000 sheep, and 6,000 camels, and 1,000 yoke of oxen, and 1,000 female donkeys (42:11–12).

The Lord blessed the latter days of Job more than the beginning. God doubled the man's income! (I'm not making any promises, I'm just reading Job's story.)

And He doubled his livestock! Not seven thousand sheep, but fourteen thousand; not three thousand camels, but six thousand, and twice the number of oxen, twice the number of donkeys.

And he had seven sons and three daughters (v. 13).

He gave him the same number of children because, let's face it, twice the number would not have been a blessing! Ten children to love again. Ten kids to give the family completion. Here he is, seasoned with wisdom and surrounded by loved ones. Finally, he dies, "an old man and full of days" (v. 17). The unforeseen is now the well known. He departs relieved and rejoicing in God's presence.

Life As It Will Be . . . Not As We Would Prefer

Let me set the record straight now that we have come to an end of this emotionally draining chapter. Life is not going to be as we prefer.

We prefer no surprises. Wouldn't it be great (we think) for God to say, "At the beginning of this next year, no surprises." And then He unloads the truck by telling us everything about the next 365 days on the first day of January. What a jolt! We'd want to run and hide if we suddenly saw every day of the whole year stretched out in front of us. How gracious of Him to make it unpredictable . . . to unroll each year one day at a time!

We prefer no adversity. But I must state the truth: Life will continue to be painful and adverse. We want the neighbor to have the heart attack, not one of our family members. We bargain with God by promising we will help our neighbor out. We want someone else's child to have the trouble, not ours. We will bring in the meals and we'll provide the affection and we will even carpool, if necessary, to assist in the growing-up years. "But don't afflict my child, Lord." Again, I remind you, adversity may not skip you or yours this year.

FACING THE UNFORESEEN

We prefer pain at a distance. We want pain kept at arm's length. But it doesn't work like that, does it? Going through the pain makes for wiser families, I've noticed.

Suddenly I am reminded of our heavenly Father and His plan for His Son. Life rocked along fairly predictably for about three years. Then almost out of the blue, talk of the Cross began. Jesus told His twelve that it had to be. They couldn't imagine such a thing! The whole purpose of the Cross seemed to the disciples nothing but a bad nightmare. They saw tragedy written all across the blood of Christ. God saw triumph. They saw iron nails and big pieces of timber at that awful place, the place called The Skull. But when God saw Him lifted up to die, to pay the price for our sins, the awful tragedy became a magnificent victory. In years to come, the disciples not only understood the Cross, they proclaimed it. What they once resisted and ran from, they ultimately embraced and died for. Christ's crucifixion, once unexpected and unforeseen by Jesus' closest followers, proved to be the most significant event in all of time.

I encourage you to continue being tender with the young, compassionate with the aged, sympathetic with the striving, tolerant with the weak and the strong—and, if I may add one more—ready for the unforeseen.

Someday, you will not only have been all of these, you will have become wiser because of it.

12

Enduring the Unbearable

We are deep into the tough issues of family life. Some questions regarding the rearing of children and the cultivation of family relationships are relatively simple to answer. Not these . . . the things we're struggling through in this last section of my book don't have easy answers. In fact, many of the issues we're addressing are so complicated they defy one-two-three type solutions. How tempting it is to offer pat, well-rehearsed answers to people struggling with complex problems! Though they sound sincere on the surface, when put to the test, they are hollow.

All this reminds me of the businessman who took a dinner flight across the country. After the plane reached cruising altitude, the flight attendants began serving everyone the meal. As the man picked up his fork to eat his salad, he noticed a big black roach just beneath a lettuce leaf. Disgusted and infuriated, he didn't wait to return home to write a hot letter of complaint; he used the hotel stationary where he stayed during his trip. In fact, that same night he unloaded his fury in writing to the president of the airline and dropped it in the mail early the next morning.

Upon his return home at the end of the week, he was surprised to find a special-delivery letter awaiting him. It was perfectly typed on the sophisticated letterhead of the airline—and from the president himself. It dripped with diplomacy. Apologetically, the president assured the executive that immediate action was being taken. "I have temporarily pulled that particular aircraft off the line. We will strip the upholstery from all the seats and remove the carpet off the floor. New fabric has been ordered. It will not return to service until everything is in perfect condition." He continued, "The flight attendant who served you your meal has been reprimanded. Her job, I can assure you, is in jeopardy. You have my word that such an embarrassing incident will never occur again. We hope you will continue to fly on our airline" . . . signed by the president.

Well! The businessman was impressed. *That's more like it,* he thought. However, he noticed something unusual. Quite by accident, the secretary who had typed the president's letter had inadvertently included the businessman's complaint letter in the same envelope. As the man looked over his original letter, he noticed that a note at the bottom had been written to the secretary in the president's own handwriting. Obviously penned in a hurry, it said, "Send this guy the standard roach letter."

So often we reply to people who have very real problems with our "standard roach letter." We sound so concerned and sincere. With kindness we say a lot of nice-sounding stuff, which may impress the struggler. He may walk away, shaking his head, thinking how helpful we have been . . . only to realize later he'd really received a set of religious cliches that offered false, empty hope. Words were said, but wisdom was missing.

I never want to be guilty of that. At no time in this book do I wish to write anything that lacks authenticity or fakes compassion. Most of all, I do not want to leave the impression there are quick, slick solutions to all domestic difficulties. I'll be absolutely candid with you, there are times when I am at a loss to provide an answer. On such occasions I refuse to hop on the bandwagon of simplicity and toss out verses from the Bible or write some psychological gobbledygook that leaves me sounding like the answer man and you looking like you're unspiritual and lacking in faith.

Some situations cannot be solved by a person or some nice-sounding principle. They must be endured until God steps in and brings relief.

We have already given serious thought to dealing with the unpleasant—when a growing-up child chooses to rebel. Next, we thought about facing the unforeseen—the tragic circumstances that hit us unannounced and fracture the family's lifestyle. In this chapter we want to go deeper and consider those times when families are forced to endure the unbearable. The scene isn't pretty. I want to assure you, I have no "standard roach letter" that will deceive you into thinking that there is a simple solution to life's complexities. I will not hurriedly add "just trust the Lord" or "you need to pray more." But I can affirm this, God knows, God cares, and God's wisdom can be applied, no matter how bleak things seem.

The Unbearable is Inescapable

In the last few years my heart has gone out to a number of families. One is the Berg family whom I read about in the newspaper.

> When David Berg walked into [the hospital] . . . five years ago, he looked like an advertisement for a health club.
>
> A tan and muscular 6-foot-4, 205 pounds, Berg, then 22, had been running and working out daily with weights.
>
> In just a month, [he] was scheduled to begin his senior year at the University of South Dakota, where he was an honor student and biology major studying to become a veterinarian. In the waning days of summer vacation, Berg had planned elective surgery at the hospital to take care of a nagging groin problem. The procedure was considered so routine

that his doctor told him he could expect to go camping on the Kern River two weeks after surgery.

He never made it.

These days, Berg lies in a hospital room in Inglewood, looking pale and fragile. At 125 pounds, he is so weak he can no longer sit up in bed. Heavily sedated to control muscle spasms, Berg lies flat on his back and gazes with seemingly frightened blue eyes at a world his neurologist says is only a blur to him. . . .

Every six hours the monotony is interrupted by a nurse who connects a thin plastic tube to an opening in his stomach, so that he can be fed juice or liquid food. When Berg soils his diapers, he must lie in them until a nurse comes, because he is mute and can communicate only by small gestures such as blinking his eyes. . . .

An error in administering an anesthetic deprived Berg of oxygen for about 20 minutes and left him with severe brain damage.

David's father, 63, who gave up his Brentwood law practice . . . to take care of his son, is the most frequent visitor to the hospital room. Berg said that unlike someone in a coma, his son is worse off because he is aware of his plight.

He added that for a parent, the death of a child would be easier to take.

"With death there's a finality and as time goes on the memory gets a little dimmer," he said. "The essence of the tragedy is this, it's a continuing one. It goes on and on."[50]

I call that enduring the *unbearable*.

And have you thought about Laura Bradbury lately? Have you prayed for Laura? You may remember that little Laura disappeared on October 18, 1984. Kidnapped? Who knows? Her parents are sure that is what happened. She's still gone. They had her birthday party recently. Put "party" in quotes, because the Bradbury family will tell you it wasn't much of a celebration. It is just not the same without Laura. Will she ever come back?

I call that enduring the *unbearable*.

I could go on for pages. I think of the family I heard about last week who were recently told, "Your son is a drug addict.

You need to face it! You need to know it!" Stunned, they began to probe for the facts. The deeper they have dug to find out about his life, the more the tentacles reach into other lives. Not only is he a drug addict, he's a pusher. Not only a pusher, he's a practicing homosexual with AIDS—and running from the law. And all of this is new information to his parents. Don't blame them. Just call it, well . . . enduring the *unbearable*.

Or how about a family that was once intact, happy, carefree. About a mile from our church, at a busy, well-lighted intersection, the lives of the wife and all three of their children were snuffed out in an instant—their car struck head-on by a drunken driver. When the family didn't arrive home at the expected hour, the father went looking for them. He drove up to the same intersection and happened upon the accident. He stared in disbelief. In one terrible moment, he had lost those who meant the most to him. He returned that same night to an empty house and years of memories. The loneliness . . . the awful loneliness.

I call this man's situation enduring the *unbearable*.

I often recall Samuel Taylor Coleridge's moving words:

> *Alone, alone, all, all alone*
> *Alone on a wide, wide sea*
> *And never a saint took pity on*
> *My soul in agony . . .*
>
> *O Wedding-Guest! this soul hath been*
> *Alone on a wide, wide sea:*
> *So lonely 'twas that God Himself*
> *Scarce seemed there to be.*[51]

Ever been there? Are you there now? So alone, feeling pain so unbearable that your prayers just sort of bounce off the ceiling? Job, the sufferer, sized it up correctly.

> *Man, who is born of woman, is short-lived and full of turmoil (14:1).*

ENDURING THE UNBEARABLE

One paraphrase says:

How frail is man, how few his days, how full of trouble! (TLB).

It is possible life has been very good to you. You have all your children. You have your health. You have a reputable family heritage. You have a fine job . . . financial security . . . few worries. You look forward to a future even brighter than your past. You find it almost impossible to identify with these stories. They seem like little more than headline fodder for the media. You're not arrogant, just a stranger to such struggles.

If so, you especially need to ponder several verses from Psalm 102. The one who wrote these words understood. Not only had he been there, but at the time he penned the psalm he was there. Whatever his family was going through had so gripped him he had to write out his feelings to God. I'm so glad they found their way into the ancient Psalter, preserved for all of time. The opening lines drip with emotion:

Hear my prayer, O LORD!
And let my cry for help come to Thee.
Do not hide Thy face from me in the day of my distress;
Incline Thine ear to me;
In the day when I call answer me quickly.
For my days have been consumed in smoke,
And my bones have been scorched like a hearth.
My heart has been smitten like grass and has withered away,
Indeed, I forget to eat my bread.
Because of the loudness of my groaning
My bones cling to my flesh.
I resemble a pelican of the wilderness;
I have become like an owl of the waste places.
I lie awake,
I have become like a lonely bird on a housetop
(Psalm 102:1–7).

He felt like a little chirping sparrow that has lost its song. How fragile! "I find myself all alone, clinging to the shingles of a rooftop. My situation is inescapable."

A few lines later, he adds:

"My days are like a lengthened shadow; and I wither away like grass" (v. 11).

"I am now the most miserable man living," wrote a famous American leader. "If what I feel were equally distributed to the whole human family, there would not be one cheerful face on earth. To remain as I am is impossible. I must die or be better."[52] You may be surprised to know the man was none other than Abraham Lincoln.

Years later, in the darkest days of the Civil War, Lincoln wrestled constantly with the specter of unrelenting depression. The unbearable, you see, can strike anyone. No one is immune. Not even a nation's president. Here is this marvelous man with magnificent character, feeling absolutely alone. Yet, like the immortal psalmist who of all people, we might think, had no reason to feel alone, he is indeed *feeling all alone.* Surely, the president ought to sleep well because of his protection, because of his wise counsel, to say nothing of his financial security. Yet there he was, tossing and turning through the night, haunted by dark and debilitating thoughts.

The Unbearable Seems Unendurable

Let me invite you to a family scene that puts flesh on these abstract thoughts. From the psalmist's words we return to a history book in the Old Testament, the ancient account of 2 Samuel 18. If you know your Bible, right away you realize we are returning to the biography of a king. King David . . . but his situation is anything but kingly.

Family Background

A little background is necessary. David hasn't laughed for weeks. I personally don't believe David really laughed beyond the Bathsheba affair. The way of the transgressor is not only hard, it's grim. From that time on, his life was a study in tragedy. The shame and the humiliation of that moral failure so gripped him he perhaps felt guilty just thinking of ever laughing again. He had done it all. Deception. Murder. Adultery. He had soiled his record in God's eyes and lost his reputation in the public's eyes. Yet, by grace, God had preserved him from stoning, and the people had allowed him to remain as their leader. But, as I've pointed out in earlier chapters, the king's family began to deteriorate.

You'll recall a son of David, a young man with a rebel heart whose name was Absalom. What a handsome charmer! Hair like a raven's—solid black, long and full. But Absalom's life had been scarred by his father's neglect. David, too busy with duties of the kingdom, failed to give Absalom the time and attention he needed. No need to repeat the details we reviewed at length back in chapter 7.

Years passed before father and son talked. Finally, David allowed his son to return to Jerusalem and live there. Feelings between the two remained strained. Absalom took the authority given by his father and ran wild with it. He cultivated the friendship of a growing number of people who became more loyal to him than to David. He deliberately stole the hearts of the people from the king. Ultimately, he led an insurrection against his father's throne. Rather than killing his own kin, David fled for his life. And Absalom, in a bewildering twisted period of history, took the throne—though he didn't deserve it and certainly hadn't earned it.

Time passed, and as is often true, the tables were turned. Absalom became the object of David's attention again as the tide of the young man's rebellion shifted. In predictable poetic justice, we find Absalom running for his life. And David, having had sufficient time to rethink his strained relationship with his now grown son, longed for an opportunity to rebuild the bridges of yesteryear.

David, out of guilt, out of brokenness, for whatever reason, pulls his commanders aside prior to combat and commands them not to harm Absalom.

> *And the king charged Joab and Abishai and Ittai, saying,*
> *"Deal gently for my sake with the young man Absalom."*
> *And all the people heard when the king charged all the com-*
> *manders concerning Absalom (2 Samuel 18:5).*

He made it clear. He didn't want one warrior who carried a sword, whether he rode on horseback or fought on foot, to hurt his boy.

Absalom was an enigma. He won the hearts of many. He confused some. He angered a few. But, without a doubt, he *enraged* one . . . Joab. This man had been David's confidant and military commander. He was the consummate faithful, albeit cruel, commander all through Absalom's early years. Joab had seen the whole scenario unfold in David's palace. He had observed Absalom on the run. He watched from a distance as the handsome deceiver stole the hearts of the people. And he was enraged that Absalom had the audacity to overthrow the throne that belonged to King David alone. He hated the delayed discipline, the absence of justice. So when David gave his command to preserve Absalom, Joab closed his ears. If there was one thing Joab wanted, it was Absalom hanging from a noose.

> *Then the people went out into the field against Israel, and*
> *the battle took place in the forest of Ephraim. And the peo-*
> *ple of Israel were defeated there before the servants of David,*
> *and the slaughter there that day was great, 20,000 men. . . .*
> *Now Absalom happened to meet the servants of David. For*
> *Absalom was riding on his mule, and the mule went under*
> *the thick branches of a great oak. And his head caught fast*
> *in the oak, so he was left hanging between heaven and*
> *earth, while the mule that was under him kept going (2*
> *Samuel 18:6–7, 9).*

Sometimes Scripture is a little humorous, isn't it? Here is Absalom galloping full speed like the Lone Ranger into the sunset, and all of a sudden—GUNK! His hair gets caught on a fork in the tree, and he is hanging in thin air, totally vulnerable, as his mule continues on down the path. Now is Joab's moment! However, the edict of the king is in everyone's else's mind. Look at what is recorded:

> When a certain man saw it, he told Joab and said, "Behold, I saw Absalom hanging in an oak" (18:10).

Joab's ears must have perked up like an uptight German Shepherd on patrol when he heard that name. His mind raced with thoughts of revenge. Now was his chance to vent his spleen.

Absalom's Death

> Then Joab said to the man who had told him, "Now behold, you saw him! Why then did you not strike him there to the ground? And I would have given you ten pieces of silver and a belt." And the man said to Joab, "Even if I should receive a thousand pieces of silver in my hand, I would not put out my hand against the king's son; for in our hearing the king charged you and Abishai and Ittai, saying, 'Protect for me the young man Absalom!' Otherwise, if I had dealt treacherously against his life (and there is nothing hidden from the king), then you yourself would have stood aloof."
>
> Then Joab said, "I will not waste time here with you." So he took three spears in his hand and thrust them through the heart of Absalom while he was yet alive in the midst of the oak. And ten young men who carried Joab's armor gathered around and struck Absalom and killed him (vv. 11–15).

Back at the palace, David knows nothing. The king's heart is not on winning a victory on the battlefield nearly as much as on saving the life of his son. Somehow in the process of remorse, David has come to terms with a number of things.

It happens to a parent in times of quietness, doesn't it? A lot of things pass in review as you get a little older in life and see your children from another perspective. The river seems to widen and things begin to look different. The silt settles, the water clears up. You realize wrong that was done against them.

No longer is it all their fault. You realize your neglect; your failure becomes overwhelmingly more obvious than theirs. You realize the guilt you're living with. A strange thing happens: restoring a relationship becomes infinitely more important than winning any more battles.

David wanted Absalom back by his side. He wanted a close relationship, closer than ever before. Little does he realize it would never be. By now, Absalom was a corpse hanging from an oak tree.

The dialogue that follows is intriguing, as Joab and two soldiers discuss who should bring the news to the king. One of Israel's warriors desperately wants the assignment, but the other is given the nod.

> Then Ahimaaz the son of Zadok said, "Please let me run and bring the king news that the LORD has freed him from the hand of his enemies."
>
> But Joab said to him, "You are not the man to carry news this day, but you shall carry news another day; however, you shall carry no news today because the king's son is dead."
>
> Then Joab said to the Cushite, "Go, tell the king what you have seen." So the Cushite bowed to Joab and ran. Now Ahimaaz the son of Zadok said once more to Joab, "But whatever happens, please let me also run after the Cushite."
>
> And Joab said, "Why would you run, my son, since you will have no reward for going?"
>
> "But whatever happens," he said, "I will run." So he said to him, "Run." Then Ahimaaz ran by way of the plain and passed up the Cushite (vv. 19–23).

So what we have is a foot race back to David's palace. Ahimaaz wins it. Just let your mind imagine the scene. Here's the king waiting at the gate. (Tell me he wasn't anxious!) Why? The man was in an *unbearable* situation. He was waiting . . . like you would wait for a phone call from your family who happened to be in the precise town where the tornado struck. You're not sure. You're "at the gate" worried sick. It's the kind of anxiety you have in a war when your son is in combat on foreign soil. You live in the mental anguish of a knock at the door or the ringing of your phone late some night. It's that kind of unbearable anxiety.

David is waiting, pacing back and forth between the gates. He sees the runner in the distance and his heart skips a beat.

> *Now David was sitting between the two gates; and the watchman went up to the roof of the gate by the wall, and raised his eyes and looked, and behold, a man running by himself. And the watchman called and told the king. And the king said, "If he is by himself there is good news in his mouth." And he came nearer and nearer (vv. 24–25).*

David is doing his best to think positive. "I know if one man is running, he has good news for me. I'll await his coming."

> *Then the watchman saw another man running; and the watchman called to the gatekeeper and said, "Behold, another man running by himself." And the king said, "This one also is bringing good news" (v. 26).*

"There's another man with good news. We've got good news from both runners! It will be wonderful!"

> *And the watchman said, "I think the running of the first one is like the running of Ahimaaz the son of Zadok" (v. 27).*

Maybe he was a popular track star in those days . . . "It looks like Ahimaaz is running."

> *And the king said, "This is a good man and comes with good news" (v. 27).*

But all the positive thinking in the world wouldn't change the message. That anxious dad is about to hear the unbearable. Let's identify with the man. Let's feel the surge of his erupting emotions. Even though the scene occurred centuries ago, it remains vividly portrayed in living color.

> *And Ahimaaz called and said to the king, "All is well." And he prostrated himself before the king with his face to the*

*ground. And he said, "Blessed is the LORD your God, who
has delivered up the men who lifted their hands against my
lord the king" (v. 28).*

In other words, "You've won the battle, King David. You
have the throne again. The enemy has been defeated. We won!
The civil war has ended at last. You're back in authority, O
King!"

Look at the king's response—in case you're wondering what
was uppermost in his mind:

*And the king said, "Is it well with the young man
Absalom?" And Ahimaaz answered, "When Joab sent the
king's servant, and your servant, I saw a great tumult, but I
did not know what it was" (v. 29).*

Right about that time the other messenger, the Cushite,
arrived.

*And the Cushite said, "Let my lord the king receive good
news, for the LORD has freed you this day from the hand of
all those who rose up against you."*

*Then the king said to the Cushite, "Is it well with the young
man Absalom?" And the Cushite answered, "Let the enemies of my lord the king, and all who rise up against you
for evil, be as that young man!" (v. 31–32).*

Those words hit David like a wrecking ball. He was stunned.

David's Grief

In the Hebrew Bible, the chapter ends at that verse. The
nineteenth chapter begins with the next verse. It is the emotional beginning of a chapter of grief. Few biblical scenes are
more heartrending! An aching, wailing, lonely cry echoes from
the king's chamber. Like Coleridge, David feels "alone, alone,
all, all alone." This, by the way, is the same man who wrote:

*The LORD is my shepherd,
I shall not want.
He makes me lie down in green pastures;*

He leads me beside quiet waters.
He restores my soul;
He guides me in the paths of righteousness
For His name's sake.
Even though I walk through the valley
of the shadow of death, I fear no evil . . .

(Psalm 23:1–4).

But now he walks in that valley. "The king was deeply moved," we read. *Rah-gaz!* It is a Hebrew verb that means "to quake, shake, and shudder." Harris, Archer, and Waltke write: "It's agitation growing out of some deeply rooted emotion like writhing in birth pangs."[53] It is a literal trembling due to misfortune. David visibly shook with grief.

I watched the late news the other night and winced as I saw a grieving father clutching at the casket containing the corpse of someone from his family. He reached for the box. He pulled at it. He ripped a part of it with his fingers. Finally, he sat down and covered his head and WAILED aloud. That is the word *Rah-gaz.* It is enduring the *unbearable.* For a never-to-be-forgotten example, read the following—slowly.

And the king was deeply moved and went up to the chamber over the gate and wept. And thus he said as he walked, "O my son Absalom, my son, my son Absalom! Would I had died instead of you, O Absalom, my son, my son!" (v. 33).

If you have never been there, you can't imagine. It is absolutely unbearable. The mind is flooded with memories: *I remember holding you in my arms. I played with you. I watched you grow. I had dreams for you. Then distance came. You wanted to be closer, but I didn't take the time. In a foolish moment of passion, I ruined my life. You got caught in a no-win vise. You ran. I fought. I wanted you back! You retaliated. I longed to make it right. And just when we were close to reconciliation . . . O my precious son, you're gone. GONE!*

The victory of that day turned to mourning. Who cares if David's flag flies again at Jerusalem? Absalom was dead. The triumphant soldiers slipped quietly into the city. No cheers. No songs. Why? Because Absalom is gone. The king's palace is draped in crepe. The loudest sound in the city was not the warrior's cheer, it was the king's cry. You could hear it for blocks. You don't think so? Look at the fourth verse:

> *And the king covered his face and cried out with a loud voice, "O my son Absalom, O Absalom, my son, my son!" (19:4).*

Yet his wailing cry couldn't bring the boy back. Nothing hits a family harder than heartbreaks that can't be resolved.

How do you handle the unbearable?

What do you do when it is *you?*

It can happen, you know. It happens to the noble as well as the lowly. It happens to the rich and famous as well as those who are obscure and poor . . . to the president as well as the homeless.

So it is with the king. The man is crushed. His bones are scorched, hot as a hearth. Tears sting. There's no hope. He'll never see Absalom alive on earth again. We're back to the psalmist's words, "days . . . consumed . . . bones scorched . . . heart smitten. . . ."

It looked as though David would never recover. His grief appeared to be unending.

The Unbearable is Not Unending

Joab's counsel to David could better be described as *confrontation.* I remind you, Joab had seen it all from earliest days. He had had it up to his eyebrows with Absalom. From his perspective rebellious Absalom ruled the throne, not David. The father wasn't in charge, the son was, this "fugitive from justice." There's been enough of that. So, when Joab heard that David was paralyzed by guilt, immobilized by grief, he rolled up his sleeves and did the hardest thing. He talked straight to David.

> *Today you have covered with shame the faces of all your servants, who today have saved your life and the lives of your sons and daughters, the lives of your wives, and the lives of*

your concubines, by loving those who hate you, and by hating those who love you. For you have shown today that princes and servants are nothing to you; for I know this day that if Absalom were alive and all of us were dead today, then you would be pleased. Now therefore arise, go out and speak kindly to your servants, for I swear by the LORD, if you do not go out, surely not a man will pass the night with you, and this will be worse for you than all the evil that has come upon you from your youth until now (19:5–7).

Even though David was grieving over the unbearable, he needed to hear those words. Joab's counsel could be summarized in three direct pieces of advice. First: *Face the truth.* "Don't let the sorrow of this death eclipse the truth." Second: *Reject self-pity.* "All your thoughts are upon yourself, your loss, your son. Your self-pity, prompted by guilt, cannot erase the fact that you never had a good relationship with your boy." Third: *Affirm those closest to you.* "The warriors who fought for Israel are closer to you than your own son was. Your lingering grief over Absalom doesn't seem fair to their grieving families. Some of them died while fighting for you, David."

It takes a strong-minded Joab to bring us back to reality. Face the truth. Reject self-pity. Don't forget those who are close to you. In our overwhelming grief over the loss of one family member, it is easy to forget those who survive (often within our own family) and still need our affirmation more than ever.

The Stanley Patz family comes to my mind. Do you remember this family? They lived in lower Manhattan. They had a son named Etan.

Stanley Patz wonders what kind of a ballplayer his son would be now. Julie Patz wonders if she would still recognize Etan if he suddenly walked through the door.

On the misty morning of May 25, 1979, Julie stood on the third-floor fire escape watching her 6 1/2-year-old son proudly march off to the school bus stop by himself for the first time.

In the bustle below on Prince Street she quickly lost sight of the small boy with a "future flight captain" cap squashed down over his blond hair.

Etan P. is still missed. . . .

Julie Patz, 42, ticks off the emotional stages a family goes through when a child is missing: terror, guilt, anger, despair, paralysis.

"There's no such thing as synchronized grief," she said. Each family member—Etan has a 15-year-old sister and an 8-year-old brother—deals with the loss in his or her private way.

One day soon after Etan disappeared his baby brother, Ari, came up to his mother and asked: "When are we going to smile again?"

Ari tried to fill the gap by "becoming Etan," Julie recalled.

Although not quite 3, Ari "toilet-trained himself overnight," his father said. The toddler began dressing himself in Etan's clothes and would eat only the foods Etan liked to eat. He climbed into the upper bunk where Etan had slept.

Retelling this, Julie struggled to maintain her composure, troubled by the guilty conviction that Ari and Shira needed more love and attention than their frantic parents were able to give then.

As a kindergartner, Ari went on an eating binge and became obsessed with body-building. He was determined to grow strong enough to defend himself against the nameless, faceless "they" who kidnapped his brother.

Panic gripped Ari when he turned 6. Six was when something terrible happened to you; 6 was when Etan disappeared.

"On his seventh birthday, Ari went through an incredible sense of relief that he'd made it through this dangerous year," his mother said.

Jealous of the attention her family received, classmates used to taunt Shira (Etan's sister) cruelly. "They would say things like, 'Gee, I wish my brother would disappear so I could be in the paper,'" her mother said.

Some of Shira's closest friends dropped her because they found it too depressing to be around her, Julie added. Shira refused to join the rest of the family in interviews. Her mother explained that she is "angry and resentful" over the "persisting intrusion" of the case on her young life.[54]

In part, that's Joab's point. "Life must go on. You must wake up, David. You have an entire army walking quietly in the streets, longing to see your presence, to hear your voice, to feel your affirmation. You owe it to them." I'm pleased to add that David did as Joab suggested.

Let me be painfully honest with you. For many years I used to say that if something ever happened to one of my children—if we lost one, for example—I would just give up. But now that I'm older and have had time to consider, I no longer feel that is true. I don't think that would be best. Grieved though I may be, and as long as it would take me (I think longer than most) to get over it, I think my calling, my ministry to people, and affirming and supporting other members of my family would require me to go on. For me to hide in my own world of mourning, to turn all my thoughts inward and allow myself to be consumed with self-pity and grief for the balance of my days would prove to be counterproductive. My life would have to go on. God's plan is larger than any one loss, grievous though it is.

The implications of this are far-reaching. It applies in numerous areas—it could be divorce, the kidnapping of your child, losing your child to drug addiction or to death. Life cannot stop. You've got to go on! For you to reduce your life to the tight radius of your own world is not only selfish and unfair to you, it is unfair to your family, your friends, and all the others to whom you can minister in the brokenness of your future years. God greatly uses crushed and broken vessels! Joab may have been heartless, cruel, and severe, but his counsel was right on target.

The good news is that David pulled out of his emotional nose dive.

So the king arose and sat in the gate. When they told all the people, saying, "Behold, the king is sitting in the gate," then all the people came before the king (v. 8).

The Unbearable Can Be Endured

How do I equip myself for that kind of tragedy? How do I, today, press on? What would help people like us to go on with our lives? What "tools" must we have to handle that phone call, to answer that knock at the door, to discover that my child didn't get off the school bus? What can I do to steel myself for that moment?

I need a walk that is realistic. As long as I sit in my private, protected world and think: What a terrible thing happened to the Bradburys. What an awful effect on the Berg family. How difficult it must be to be in the Patz family in lower Manhattan. How tough it must be to go through divorce. How tragic it must be to have your son addicted to drugs or to get the call from the police that says, "It was a head-on collision, and he was drinking." As awful as things may be, so long as I sit and say, "It won't be me," I am not prepared to handle it. Force yourself to realize "it could be me next." Families need a walk that is realistic. Not fearful, understand, but realistic.

I need a friend who is honest. Those kinds of friends don't suddenly pop on the scene. They take time to find . . . to nurture. Are you cultivating a friend who is honest, who will know when it is time to put his or her arm around your shoulder and say, "Hey, it's time. You've grieved for months. Now, let's go on." We all need friends like that.

I need a Savior who is reliable. Do I ever! If I live to be an old, old man, I will never understand how anybody endures the unbearable without the Lord. That includes you, my friend. I don't know how you do it! If you are trying to do so, why not stop. Come to the Cross. Come to Christ and say, "In my overwhelming need, in my desperate loneliness and all of my brokenness, Lord Jesus Christ, I need You. Come into my life."

Years ago someone gave me a small card that he frequently passes on to others. It is a simple prayer, "Lord, help me to remember that nothing is going to happen to me today that You and I together can't handle" (Psalm 68:19). That's what the Lord can do. We all need a reliable Savior.

I need a faith that nothing can shake. Emphasis on NOTHING. Even when I do not know why, I can endure with a faith like that . . . even if I never find out why!

ENDURING THE UNBEARABLE

Helen Rosevere was, for many years, a British medical missionary. She found herself trapped in the Congo uprising. When the Mau-Mau revolutionaries invaded, she was victimized. This innocent woman of God was assaulted, raped, and humiliated. Her life clung to a faith that refused to be shaken. While recovering from that unbearable event, Helen and the Lord grew closer than they'd ever been before. She wrote a statement in the form of a question that every person reading this chapter needs to ask himself or herself. It is a question she claims she received from the Lord. He asked her:

> Helen, can you thank Me for trusting you with this experience, even if I never tell you why?

May our all-knowing God give us the courage to ask that question, the honesty to answer it, and the wisdom to apply it when *our* family must endure the unbearable.

13

Anticipating the Unusual

Charlie Steinmetz was a crippled dwarf. But what he lacked physically he made up for mentally. When it came to the subject of electricity, Steinmetz was a wizard. No one in his day knew more about it than he.

Henry Ford realized that when he hired the man to help in the building of those massive generators and turbines that would run his first automobile plant in Dearborn, Michigan. Once everything was in place, the assembly line worked like clockwork. Thanks to the electrical genius, cars began to roll off the line and profit began to pour into Ford's pocket. Things ran along smoothly for months.

Suddenly, without warning, everything ground to a halt. Ford Motor Company went dark. One mechanic after another was unable to locate the problem, much to Ford's frustration. Finally, he contacted the brains behind the system. Steinmetz showed up and immediately went to work. He fiddled around with some switches and a gauge or two. He tinkered with this motor and that one . . . pushed a few buttons and messed with some wires. He then threw the master switch and wouldn't you know it? Lights blinked on, engines began to whirl, and things were back to normal.

Within a few days, Charlie Steinmetz mailed Henry Ford a bill . . . for $10,000. Ford couldn't believe it. He was wealthy, but paying such an exorbitant amount of money was out of the question, especially for what appeared to be such a small amount of work. He sent the bill back with a note attached, "Charlie, doesn't it seem a little steep to charge me $10,000 for tinkering around with a few wires and switches?"

Steinmetz rewrote the bill and sent it back. It read:

| For tinkering around on the motors | $10.00 |
| For knowing where to tinker | $9,990.00[55] |

The dwarf came up with a giant of an idea. Sometimes, what appears to be rather simple and ordinary represents that which is invaluable.

For a dozen chapters I have been taking a rather unsophisticated, even unimpressive approach to the subject of the family. My personal opinions and counsel have not been that valuable . . . my tinkering has hardly been worth ten bucks. But during the process the Spirit of God has been illuminating our minds with the truth from Scripture . . . and He has this uncanny way of knowing where to tinker, which makes His insights priceless. Perhaps He has hit a nerve or two regarding discipline and your need to be more consistent. Maybe the counsel on affirmation, encouragement, and relationships was what you needed to hear most. And then when we got deeper into the tough side of family life — dealing with the rebel or facing the unexpected or enduring the unbearable — you really sensed the still small voice of God hitting pay dirt. If something you have read has helped, I am grateful and He gets the glory.

We're nearing the end now, but we're not through yet. There still remains a couple of areas that need to be probed. Hopefully, you will find them just as relevant and on target as the others. In this particular chapter I have in mind the family's need to anticipate the unusual. To make it more personal — *your* family's need to anticipate the unusual.

I should warn you ahead of time . . . God really knows where to tinker.

In God's Family: An Unusual Operating Procedure

God has an amazing way of keeping us guessing.

He's full of surprises! About the time we think we've got things nailed down into a manageable routine, He introduces the unusual.

Wise is the family that lets God be God . . . that anticipates His right to throw an inside curve when everyone would normally expect it high and outside. Remember, His ways are past finding out! He breaks the mold more often than not.

There are a couple of passages in both the Old and New Testaments I want us to look at before we center our attention on one particular family. Let's return to the Book of Job . . . chapter 5.

The scripture I have in mind is one of those "who," "what," and "why" passages from the Bible. The "who" is God. The "what" has to do with His operating procedure. The "why" explains the purpose.

> *But as for me, I would seek God, and I would place my cause before God (v. 8).*

That's the *who* of the passage. The writer says, in effect, "I will go before my God and simply lay my circumstances before Him." He continues by mentioning *what* it is that God does.

> *Who does great and unsearchable things, wonders without number (v. 9).*

Wonders means "miracles." The writer says he would go before God and place his circumstances at His disposal, because He alone is the one who does great, unsearchable, even miraculous things. They are also limitless. God never runs out of ideas. For example:

> *He gives rain on the earth, and sends water on the fields, so that He sets on high those who are lowly, and those who mourn are lifted to safety. He frustrates the plotting of the shrewd, so that their hands cannot attain success (vv. 10–12).*

How unusual. How strange. How surprising. He does the unexpected. Have you had that happen in your life? Have you seen Him frustrate things in other people's lives? I'm referring to those who are so shrewd, so crafty, who think they are cool as they plot against you . . . but He brings them down to nothing. Furthermore:

> *He captures the wise by their own shrewdness and the advice of the cunning is quickly thwarted. By day they meet with darkness, and grope at noon as in the night. But He saves from the sword of their mouth, and the poor from the hand of the mighty (vv. 13–15).*

Now for the *why*. Why does God do all that?

> *So the helpless has hope, and unrighteousness must shut its mouth (v. 16).*

I love the way that reads. This is describing God's unpredictable, unexpected style. He sees the helpless and gives them hope by doing the unusual. He turns to the wicked and says to them in His own inimitable way, "Now keep quiet!" Remember that. We'll see how it ties in later on.

Look next at Romans 11:33. This comes as a conclusion to the great section on God's sovereign hand in people's lives. Paul has built his thoughts toward a climax, leading to a great doxology of praise. This is one of the earliest verses I ever committed to memory. To this day, I refer to it again and again.

> *Oh, the depth of the riches both of the wisdom and knowledge of God! How unsearchable are His judgments and unfathomable His ways!*

Isn't that great? When it comes to God's decisions, we cannot search them out. When it comes to His ways, we cannot find the depths. We can never fully comprehend His game plan. And yet, I meet people all the time who still try. Wasted effort! As one of my mentors in seminary used to say: "We need to stop trying to unscrew the inscrutable." God's agenda includes the inscrutable, the amazing, the miraculous, the great, the unsearchable, the unfathomable. Puny folks like us think we can put it together and then explain it to someone else. Wrong! *We cannot do it!* Why? Because God is infinite. He is incomprehensible. He is full of surprises. He is in the business of rescuing the helpless and causing the wicked to shut their mouths.

Of all the things I love about my heavenly Father, I think I love His creativity the most . . . *usually!* There are times I think it might be better to have my future predictable, but looking back, I'm always grateful He didn't tell me ahead of time. And how amazing are His decisions! How absolutely unique His ways! I give Him praise.

Allow me a few moments to take a quick stroll with you through some stories of the Bible and remind you of several amazing, unusual events. A good place to start would be the time God freed a body of people from Egyptian bondage. They were helpless and leaderless. They were good at only one thing — making bricks. Despondent and depressed, they had experienced things only getting worse for four hundred years. Four centuries, however, do not thwart His power or His purpose. His unexpected plan? He comes up with an eighty-year-old leader (how's that for a surprise?) who has the audacity to stand in front of the most intimidating man in the nation, the Pharaoh of Egypt. The result? God breaks the grip of Egyptian bondage.

After marching out of Egypt scot free, the Hebrews journey as far as the Red Sea. Their circumstance has all the appearance of the end, and once again, their unsearchable, unfathomable, inscrutable God takes over. The Red Sea is rolled back, allowing them to walk across on dry ground. Unexpected. Miraculous!

And just as soon as the Hebrews get across, boom! The same water that gave them protection consumes the enemy.

As the Hebrews arrive at Canaan, they face Jericho with its formidable walls. Impossible situation . . . except that God has no problem with walls around Jericho or any city, for that matter. He just has His men walk around it seven times, and it collapses. Unexpected. Unusual. Who would have ever guessed it?

Oh, by the way, did I tell you He fed them by an angelic catering service? Manna, which the psalmist calls "angel's food." And guidance? In the morning, a cloud; in the evening, a pillar of fire. The unexpected presence of God . . . for forty years. There are a hundred similar stories I'll not take the time to mention.

When we get to the coming of the Savior, we have another unusual, amazing situation. How do you bring the perfect Son of God from heaven to earth without contaminating Him in sin — yet maintaining His true humanity? Surprise, the virgin birth! What a genius plan.

When Jesus saw five thousand-plus people who were hungry and in need of food, he had absolutely no problem putting together five loaves and a couple of anchovies for a full meal. How? He fed people in a most unexpected, unusual manner.

When it came time to offer the sacrifice for sin, God chose a most unusual lamb . . . the Lamb of God, His Son! His death paid sin's penalty and after that unusual solution — payment by death — He brought Him back from beyond. The Resurrection was another unusual, miraculous plan. The Bible is full of such things. Those who know this Book fairly well have to confess the unusual, the inscrutable, and the unfathomable weave their way from cover to cover.

About now you are thinking: I thought this was a book on the family. What's the point of all these stories with unusual endings? My primary interest is not in historical accounts or remarkable Bible stories. It is to encourage you to begin believing God for the unusual in your family's life. God hasn't stopped doing the unusual, you know.

I think there are some folks reading these lines at this moment who are on the verge of the unusual, yet you don't know it. In fact, it would probably surprise the life out of you if you realized at this very moment what God's ultimate plan was for you and your family! If you're not careful, however, you'll let the predictable lull you to sleep. Wake up! God's ways are unpredictable. As I said earlier, He knows where to tinker in all our lives.

An Ancient Family: A Study in Surprises

I've chosen a story that you and your family may be able to identify with, at least I hope so. Most of all, I hope you are open. I challenge you to think outside the familiar realm. I hope you're ready to act. My prayer is that nothing will keep you from believing that God may want to use your family in a most unusual way. The real question is: ARE YOU OPEN . . . ARE YOU WILLING TO COOPERATE?

One of our problems in identifying with these biblical examples of the unexpected is that we don't consider ourselves on their level. We shrug and think: *Who am I? Just a little nobody living in the twentieth century.* When I'm reading about these great men, women, and families of ancient days, how easy to think it couldn't happen today. All we need is a nudge . . . somebody to convince us it is possible. I like what one man wrote about the Taft family:

> People need an atmosphere in which they can specialize, hone their skills, and discover their distinctiveness. The biographies of the great are sprinkled with accounts of how some teacher or some kindly employer looked closely enough to see a spark no one else saw and for periods, at least, believed in their ability to perfect that gift when no one else did. The Taft family, for instance, was evidently good at pushing their children to cut their own swath and to find a specialty of which to be proud. When Martha Taft was in elementary school in Cincinnati she was asked to introduce herself. She said, "My name is Martha Bowers Taft. My great-

grandfather was President of the United States. My grandfather was United States senator. My daddy is ambassador to Ireland. And I am a Brownie."[56]

I love that answer! You may feel like all you are in God's vast plan is a little Brownie or an insignificant Cub Scout. But let me remind you that as a Christian you are a child of the King! As a believer in Christ, you are a son or daughter of the living God. Hold your head up high, He isn't through with you! His plan includes doing the unusual. Furthermore, He isn't finished using *families* to model His miracles. God still desires to impact our generation with remarkable families of faith. And that includes you and your family. If you discount that, count on it, you will not anticipate His unusual plan, nor will you be ready for it when it comes your way. You'll find an excuse to pass the baton on to someone else and let *them* run the adventuresome race instead of you. I challenge you: Don't let that happen!

These thoughts lead me to refresh your memory about the family of Noah. Even though the overall narrative is familiar, the details of the unusual episode are not that well known to many. Strangely, it seems we know just enough of the story to have overlooked a major message it communicates to families in every generation — even yours!

A Difficult Time in Which to Live

In what kind of world did Noah live? In a world much like ours . . . difficult and cynical. Hardened toward spiritual things.

Then the LORD saw that the wickedness of man was great on the earth, and that every intent of the thoughts of his heart was only evil continually. And the LORD was sorry that He had made man on the earth, and He was grieved in His heart. And the LORD said, "I will blot out man whom I have created from the face of the land, from man to animals to creeping things and to birds of the sky; for I am sorry that I have made them" (Genesis 6:5–7).

Dreadful days. Vicious. Violent. Days of moral contamination and compromises. Everywhere the eye looked there was evidence of corruption. Depravity on parade.

But there was one exception — and this is where the story gets exciting. One man, one *family,* made the difference. We read . . .

But Noah found favor in the eyes of the LORD (v. 8).

Now, if there has ever been a passage of Scripture that proves an environment does not dictate character, this one is classic. Noah's life was like a beautiful tulip blooming in a junkyard. In the midst of human corruption, here was a godly man rearing a faithful family.

These are the records of the generations of Noah. Noah was a righteous man, blameless in his time; Noah walked with God (v. 9).

That means he was righteous, in right standing, before God.

Noah was . . . blameless in his time (v. 9).

No one could point a finger of accusation at him.

Noah walked with God (v. 9).

I don't know about your family tree, but it may not be much to brag about. You may look back at your roots and not find many great men and women in your heritage. Instead of using that as an excuse to be like all the rest, realize *God wants to begin with you.* You may have a past that is sordid and checkered, full of fractured relationships and broken lives. You may have made an unholy mess of your life. But the encouragement you need to focus on is the contrast, "BUT Noah." This is the place of beginning.

I remember one of the first times my wife and I shared our home and children with an unwed mother. We were living in a small house in another state. During the months of this young woman's pregnancy, before the birth and adoption of her baby, a beautiful romance developed with a young man in seminary, training for a lifetime of ministry. The two fell deeply in love. As time passed, it was clear to him that after the baby was adopted (it was not his child), they should marry. He saw beauty in her character . . . and believe me, there was plenty of it there. He chose to look beyond her failure and sin.

I'll never forget the large sign he placed in her room before she came back to our home for the days of recovery after the birth and adoption of her child. The sign read, "Today is the first day of the rest of your life." Families need to remember that!

That's the place to start when God plans to do the unusual. If you are anchored to past failures, you'll never be used greatly in God's plan. Never. If you listen to people who are always holding you down, then you'll never break free from the predictable. You will discount even the possibility of God's doing the unusual through you or your family.

BUT Noah was different. He was ready for whatever God had in store for him. Was he in for a surprise or what!

Frightening Prophecy . . . Creative Plan

And the LORD said, "I will blot out man whom I have created from the face of the land, from man to animals to creeping things and to birds of the sky; for I am sorry that I have made them" (v. 7).

Then God said to Noah, "The end of all flesh has come before Me; for the earth is filled with violence because of them; and behold, I am about to destroy them with the earth" (v. 13).

"And behold, I, even I am bringing the flood of water upon the earth, to destroy all flesh in which is the breath of life, from under heaven; everything that is on the earth shall perish" (v. 17).

I call that a frightening prophecy. Such an event had never occurred before and would never happen again. It was a one-time-only event on earth, when all flesh was to perish . . . and the Lord's plan was to involve Noah's family.

Noah's mouth must have dropped open as he heard of the judgment of God. But before he could ponder that for long, he was told of a creative project that was to get under way soon. It was so extensive it would keep him and his family busy for 120 years.

> Then the LORD said, "My Spirit shall not strive with man forever, because he also is flesh; nevertheless his days shall be one hundred and twenty years" (v. 3).

I take it from that statement that God's plan of judgment was going to take over a century to run its course. For twelve long decades from the time God met with Noah until the flood, there would be numerous opportunities for Noah to warn people and for his neighbors to respond. I call that gracious. God says, in effect, "I'll give everyone 120 years to repent . . . during which time, Noah, you and your family will be My models."

Here was the surprise that would involve their time and concentration:

> "Make for yourself an ark of gopher wood; you shall make the ark with rooms, and shall cover it inside and out with pitch. And this is how you shall make it . . ." (vv. 14–15).

We have just a thumbnail sketch here of the ark's construction and design. I'm sure Noah talked at length with God about the details of construction. In our terms, "Let's make the ark 450 feet long, 75 feet wide, and 45 feet high." That's quite a barge to be built in a man's front yard!

Whitcomb and Morris, in a very insightful volume, *The Genesis Flood,* have provided some helpful information by describing the capacity of the ark:

> The Ark had a carrying capacity equal to that of 522 standard stock cars as used by modern railroads or of eight freight trains with sixty-five such cars in each![57]

How would you like to see that in your neighbor's driveway?

Every time I think about the ark, I remember something that happened on our church site in Fullerton. I was preaching through the letter to the Hebrews. When I got to chapter 11,

I read of God's telling Noah to build the ark. I realized there was no way the congregation and I could comprehend the size of that vessel without my going outside and literally walking it, measuring the precise distance in our parking lot. So one morning I got one of my yellow pads of paper and drew an outline of the ark dimensions very carefully. Wanting to picture how far those distances were I went out to our vast lot and began to step off 450 feet, counting each pace. Out of the corner of my eye (as I continued pacing very deliberately and counting), I noticed one of our neighbors who does not attend our church, walking his dog.

He looked at me and I looked back at him and smiled. The next thing I knew he and his dog had crossed the street and were right by my side.

"Uh, g'morning," he said.

I said, " . . . 53, 54, good morning, 55, 56."

He said, quietly with a frown, "What are you doing?"

I answered, "59, 60 . . . I am measuring the ark . . . 61, 62, 63 . . . "

I was smiling. He wasn't. Before long I turned and began to pace off the width, counting as I walked.

"The ark, huh?"

"Yep," I grunted, "like Noah's ark."

Then he said, "You people aren't gonna start building one of those things out *here,* are you?"

I cracked up! People don't want an ark built across the street from their house.

Peter calls Noah a preacher of righteousness. The Greek term used (in 2 Peter 2:5) for "preacher" is the word for *herald* — or *announcer.* All the time Noah and his family were driving nails and cutting wood, he was making an announcement to a wicked generation. You say, "Come on, not that many people would even notice." Not notice a barge $4^{1}/_{2}$ stories high? To make things even more strange, Noah's family probably lived no less than five hundred miles from the closest body of water.

Not too many people build huge ships in Nebraska or Iowa. Of course people would notice! What an unusual, weird project!

On top of that, there had never been rain. Did you know at that time the earth was not watered by rain but was watered by dew? Prior to the flood, people had never seen rain and most had never laid eyes on a large lake—to say nothing of a great ocean. Yet here's a family doing the unusual, busy as beavers, constructing this mammoth sea-going barge. Can you imagine the mockery of people who saw Noah, his wife, and his kids building this thing in their front yard?

The delivery of wood alone would be enough to finish you off. "Mabel, don't look now, but Noah's getting more wood. What a strange family! That thing is never gonna end. The guy has really flipped!" It's enough to make us smile even today, but what a wonderful step of faith! I can't help but wonder about the Noah family as they sat down for supper together. What they talked about . . . how they prayed . . . how they felt. They were called upon to do the unusual as a family. The mold-breaking significance of it all is enough to blow your mind if you put yourself in their sandals.

Let's do that. God is tapping some father on the shoulder this very day, saying, "I don't want you to stay where you are in the same career. I want to change and use your skills to serve Me." If you're not careful, you'll read all this about Noah and his family and miss God's message to you.

God may be saying to some couples, "I want you to adopt a child. I know you already have your family . . . but I want you to rear this very special child in a godly atmosphere, because I want you to be a unique model of My unusual plan."

Ever heard of Carolyn Koons? I'm sure many of you have. She tells quite a story! The remarkable thing about Carolyn's experience is not only that it is true but it breaks the mold. She, as a single woman, a professional teacher, went to Mexico on a brief ministry trip. While there she saw a little boy among many in a group. Her heart went out to Tony. Ultimately, she adopted him and reared him. Great step of faith . . . unusual. Her story has now been put into a book titled *Tony*.

Everybody applauds Carolyn *today,* "Good for you, Carolyn. You did what God wanted. It makes a lot of sense. What faith . . . a single lady, adopting a little boy. Even though you couldn't speak the language. We're proud of you, lady!" But back then, can you imagine how many people must have said, "Uh, Carolyn, we're getting a little concerned about you. Are you real sure you're doing the right thing?" You see, the unusual always looks wonderful after the fact. *Then* it's a great testimony of God's unsearchable, unfathomable, and unusual mighty plan.

But before the fact? Some sneer, others snicker.

Cynthia and I know a couple whose lives are spent working with incorrigible adolescents. We're talking tough kids! Neither one has had any training in judo. They don't look rough or sound mean. I doubt that either one could fight very well. Nor were they "streetwise" when they began this ministry. They were so shielded and protected I doubt they had heard much profanity. What a marvelous, godly couple! In the years that have passed they have been used of God to bring any number of those tough, mistreated, abused fellows and gals, raised on the street, to a knowledge of the Savior. Why? Because that couple, the most unlikely couple you would ever expect to do such a thing, said, "Yes, Lord, we will trust YOU. We'll risk doing the unusual."

I'm asking you in this chapter to break the mold . . . to think about risking like Noah and his family risked. I'm asking you to stop standing around the car lot of life, kicking tires. I picked up that thought from David Seamands, in his helpful book, *Healing for Damaged Emotions:*

> I remember some years ago talking with a salesman in a used car lot. As we looked out the showroom window, we saw a man who was going around kicking tires on the cars. He was also raising the hoods and banging the fenders. The salesman said disgustedly, "Look at that guy out there. He's a wheel-kicker. They are the bane of our existence. They come in here all the time, but never buy cars because they can't make up their minds. Now watch him out there. He's kicking the tires. He'll say the wheels are out of line. He'll listen to the motor

and say, 'Hear that knock?' Nobody else can hear the knock, but he can hear it. Something is always wrong. He is afraid to choose; he can never make up his mind, so he always finds an excuse."

Life is filled with wheel-kickers, people who fear failure, fear making the wrong decision. What happens to such people as they approach the Christian life? Believing is a great risk; it's very hard. Decisions tear them up. Faith comes hard. Witnessing is difficult. Launching out in the Holy Spirit and really surrendering to God is almost a trauma. Discipline is difficult. The fearful people live on *if onlys:* "If only this or if only that, then I would be okay." But since the *if only* never comes to pass, they usually never accomplish what they would like to. The fearful are the defeated and indecisive.[58]

Is yours a tire-kicking family? Am I writing to a few parents who tend to listen for the knocks that aren't there, who are afraid of the peril, who think of the *if onlys,* who focus mainly on the dangers? Please take notice! You will not know what it means to trust God for the unusual until you deal directly with that age-old, traditional fear of risk. It is a *killer.*

Obedience, Deliverance, Blessing

The best part of the Noah story is its beginning: "Thus Noah did" . . . and its conclusion: "so he did." Just imagine: Here is Noah, walking quietly with God.

The Lord speaks to him: "Build an ark."

"I'll do it, Lord. But, uh, what's an ark?"

God explains, "Build it this size, this shape, and use these materials as you follow My instructions."

"Got it. Now, where do I start?" (Notice . . . no hesitation.)

"Start here with this, this, and that."

"Right!"

And he does it! We need to keep in mind that no one had ever built an ark before. Noah (who never read Genesis 6) doesn't know what is coming next. All he knows is that God has spoken. And even though the plan is unusual, he's gotta do it. That is what makes this story so exciting. There wasn't a tire kicker in the entire Noah family. They were pumped, full-bore ready and willing.

Is that happening in your family's life? Why not? What in the world are you waiting for? Why is it so hard for us today to believe that God can still do the impossible? When did He stop leading people down unusual paths? As we've seen, His Book is *full* of stories like that. And those in the inspired record who experienced the fullness of His power stepped in with total obedience.

> Then the LORD said to Noah, "Enter the ark, you and all your household; for you alone I have seen to be righteous before Me in this time" (Genesis 7:1).

Finally, once the floating zoo is full of animals, Noah goes in and his family steps in behind him. The Lord slams the door shut. The 120 years have passed. All the neighbors are standing outside the ark . . . probably still laughing and jeering. Suddenly, for the first time in their lives, the people outside feel rain on their shoulders. For the first time, they are envious of Noah's family, but it's too late. Scripture preserves us from the horror Noah's family went through as they stood arm in arm inside the ark, listening to the cries of their neighbors and friends on the outside, screaming to get in.

I am not trying to be dramatic by playing on your emotions. This is a story of incredible judgment and supernatural rescue. To borrow from that statement out of Job we looked at earlier, while the helpless (Noah's family) were given hope, God shut the mouths of the wicked (the neighbors).

In the centuries to come, there would be another ark. But this one would be in the shape of a cross. It was built for One . . . the only One qualified to be on it. Every drive of the nail, every agonizing groan from Jesus' throat, told the observer, "You're going to be sorry. You're making an eternal mistake if you don't believe in Me." Our dear Savior paid the penalty for sin so that all who would believe in Him would have deliverance from an eternal judgment. In every sense of the word, He was willing to do the unusual to accomplish the incredible.

And would you believe, most people today still mock, still deny? Let's face it, the majority of the world has never been right when it comes to spiritual things. If you find yourself among that majority, saying, "Ah, I could never believe in that Savior on a Cross," then be sure of this, you're in company with a lot of people who also are wrong. Get smart. Believe. Accept God's rescue offer! If you will, this statement can come true in your life:

> *But as many as received Him, to them He gave the right to become children of God, even to those who believe in His name (John 1:12).*

Open your eyes! Judgment is coming. By refusing to get in the ark of His provision—the Cross—you will experience God's judgment. The door will be shut, and it will be too late.

Back to Noah's family. Judgment fell. It was awful. Every living creature on the earth perished outside the ark. But God marvelously delivered His friend and his family. Over a year later, God directed:

> *"Go out of the ark, you and your wife and your sons and your sons' wives with you.*
> *"Bring out with you every living thing of all flesh that is with you, birds and animals and every creeping thing that creeps on the earth, that they may breed abundantly on the earth."*
> *So Noah went out, and his sons and his wife and his sons' wives with him (8:16–18).*

Ultimately, the ark emptied. It had accomplished its purpose. The wood with which it was constructed became no more significant than the lumber which had formed the Cross following the Lord's crucifixion. The event was history, but the enduring offer of hope lingers to this day. The tragedy is that so few accept it.

Look at the first thing Noah did: He built an altar. He and his small family, all alone in the wide, empty world, gathered around that altar. It was a statement of their trust, their confidence in an unchanging God. Their world was now completely different. It now had climates. And seasons. Unfamiliar mountains soared on the horizon. Sloping valleys looked eerie in the misty distance. There was a whole new world stretching out before them and not another sound on its surface except those from scattering animals and birds in the sky. Noah and his family fell before God at that altar. How they must have prayed! Their words lifted to heaven as a soothing, sweet aroma, right into the nostrils of the Lord. And the Lord reassured His friend.

> *I will never again curse the ground on account of man, for the intent of man's heart is evil from his youth; and I will never again destroy every living thing, as I have done.*

> > *While the earth remains,*
> > *Seedtime and harvest,*
> > *And cold and heat,*
> > *And summer and winter,*
> > *And day and night*
> > *Shall not cease (vv. 21–22).*

What a promise!

A Rainbow and a Reminder

To make the promise sure, God gave him a reminder:

> *I set My bow in the cloud, and it shall be for a sign of a covenant between Me and the earth (9:13).*

Do you have any idea how few people know the origin of rainbows? I love telling them! My favorite place to do so is on an airplane. As we see a rainbow in the sky, I love to lean over and say to the guy next to me, "God put that there, you know." That usually makes him jump . . . he doesn't know whether to spit or wind his watch. Usually, he looks out the window as though God is going to suddenly appear or something. "That's right!" I continue. "There's a promise in the Book of Genesis that states He'll never again flood the earth." That has opened more opportunities to talk about Christ! Rainbows provide an ideal setting for such discussions.

By the way, do your *children* know why there are rainbows? Not if you haven't told them. Why not ask your children this evening before you go to bed if they know where rainbows came from and why they keep reappearing. It will lead to a great conversation.

I love the statement in verse 16:

> *When the bow is in the cloud, then I will look upon it, to remember the everlasting covenant between God and every living creature of all flesh that is on the earth.*

God is saying, in effect, "I will see the rainbow and say, 'Ah, that reminds Me of Noah and the flood, and I'll never do it again.'" Your children need never worry. A heavy windstorm and rain will stop. There will never be another world-wide deluge.

Charles Schulz captured the idea of this promise in one of his "Peanuts" cartoons. Lucy and Linus are looking out the window, watching it rain. Lucy begins the conversation:

Lucy: Boy, look at it rain . . . what if it floods the whole world?

Linus: It will never do that . . . in the ninth chapter of Genesis, God promised Noah that would never happen again, and the sign of the promise is the rainbow.

Lucy: You've taken a great load off my mind . . .

Linus: Sound theology has a way of doing that![59]

I like Linus's style, don't you? Such adult confidence! "Sound theology has a way of doing that!" Believe me, our children love it when they can find a practical truth in the Bible to count on.

Do you know what everyone in your family needs the most when tough times hit? Sound theology! You and they need a good solid dose of biblical truth to put down secure anchors, especially if you decide to risk. The adversary will tempt you to doubt, to hold back, to kick a few tires, to think, "We're not gonna make it." Relax. Always remember, God's unusual plan ends with a rainbow of new hope. And people who trust Him are especially honored and protected.

In The Family . . . Some Practical Suggestions

Enough of ancient history. This isn't a book about Noah and his family but about you and yours. I've thought a lot about how all this applies today. Three specific ideas surface in my mind.

1. *Remind your family that the unusual is God's standard procedure.* I suggest you do that today. Don't wait until after He leads you to risk. Do it before the fact. Remind your family the Bible is full of individuals and families who broke the mold of the predictable as they accomplished the incredible. Begin anticipating what unusual project He may have in mind for you. Make it a part of your table talk at supper tonight. Children *love* such ideas!

2. *Keep in mind that God is still looking for families who model faith.* This might be worth talking over with your mate to begin with. Introduce the thought by asking a few gutsy questions:

"Are we a couple who models faith? How?"

"In what way do we demonstrate confident trust in God?"

"Are we afraid for our family to risk? Why?"

God's plan is not that all Christians gather in one section of the world and live there in a well-protected bubble of affluence. His plan is that we shake salt and shine light all across this earth. He is still interested in families who model His message. Sitting at your table may be a future hero in miniature. Does your child know how special he or she is? Are you challenging him . . . believing in him . . . encouraging him to soar, to live above the level of mediocrity?

The history books are full of stories of gifted persons whose talents were overlooked by a procession of people until someone believed in them. Einstein was four years old before he could speak and seven before he could read. Isaac Newton did poorly in grade school. A newspaper editor fired Walt Disney because he had "no good ideas." Leo Tolstoy flunked out of

college, and Werner von Braun failed ninth-grade algebra.
Haydn gave up ever making a musician of Beethoven, who
seemed a slow and plodding young man with no apparent
talent—except a belief in music.

There is a lesson in such stories: different people develop
at different rates, and the best motivators are always on the
lookout for hidden capacities.[60]

Parent is a synonym for motivator. Let's keep doing it!

3. *Fight the tendency to prefer security to availability.* In other
words, quit hanging on to today's comfort. It will keep you
from anticipating tomorrow's challenge.

You might think I was raised to think like this. I was not. My
dad was the super-cautious, extremely responsible type. Time and
again I saw him opt for the safe and secure rather than the risky.
My philosophy of living by faith was first cultivated by my observations of Orville, my older brother. What a man!

I'll never forget when my brother (now a veteran missionary
in Buenos Aires) drove his family back from Mexico where they
had been serving the Lord on the mission field for a period of
time. This was back in the 1950s, shortly before they moved to
South America. They drove up into our driveway in a beat-up
old Chevy. My dad, God bless him, could hardly believe his
eyes. He was a man who just didn't believe that you could make
it if you didn't have a pile stashed away in a savings account, a
full tank of gas, two spare tires, a parachute, an extra set of
underwear, and a tool box. You know the type. Needless to say,
that was not Orville's philosophy. Thank goodness, it still isn't.

After dinner that evening my dad nervously said to my
brother, "Uh, Orville, let me ask you straight: How much
money do you have?" (They were planning to drive on to
Kansas in a day or two.)

"Aw, Dad, don't worry about it," my brother replied. "It
isn't important."

"No," Dad said, "I saw those slick tires you've got on the
back of your car . . . and I want to know . . . how much money
do you really have? I'm concerned for you and your family."

"You really want to know?" asked Orville, with a twinkle in his eye. He smiled as he slipped his hand into his pocket and dragged out a nickel—one thin nickel—and rolled it across the table. All of us in the family watched that sucker roll from Orville's fingers to my dad's lap.

I'll never forget the moment! With mouth wide open, my father grabbed it.

Dad exclaimed, "You're kidding!"

"No," was my brother's reply. "Isn't that *exciting?*"

One nickel! I thought my dad was gonna have a coronary. So it was—and still is!—in Orville's family. On a regular basis, they anticipate the unusual. What an adventuresome life they have lived for God's glory. Four grown children—all now happily married—and how beautifully God has met their needs.

Now you may not want to go quite that far . . . but let me tinker around in this sensitive area and ask: Does your family have any idea of what it means to come anywhere close to living by faith? Are your children ever in a place where they must trust God? He always comes through, you know. He honors those who do the unusual and trust Him to accomplish the incredible.

My wife and I dearly love a particular family . . . a dad and mom, Dave and Kaya, and *seven* kids. Not long ago they told us of a time in their earlier years as a family when they were forced to trust God through some unusual circumstances. At that time in their lives they were financially strapped. They literally didn't have another meal to put on the table! That morning their dad prayed with them as the mother scraped together the last bit of flour and milk to bake them biscuits. After they ate them, the dad said to the family before he left that morning to work as a carpenter: "Children, God *must* provide for us today. This is absolutely all we have to eat. But He loves us dearly. We are going to trust Him to provide for our needs." I doubt that the children even had lunches that day to take with them to school.

Later that morning a friend happened to drop by and said, "I understand that Dave is now working as a carpenter."

"Well, yes, that's true," said Kaya, his wife.

They chatted briefly, and before Kaya knew it, the lady started hauling in bags and bags of groceries. By the time the friend finished, there were bags loaded with food stacked all over the kitchen counter—even a little bag of Oreo cookies poking from the top of the last bag.

Dumbfounded, yet full of tearful gratitude, Kaya told the visitor what had occurred during their morning time of prayer with the family—how she was a direct answer to prayer. The woman, of course, had no idea. The Lord had just prompted her to carry out that mission of mercy. She was extra thrilled. Well, Kaya had the joy of filling up their shelves with groceries. What an amazing provision! Finally, she put the Oreo cookies in a special cookie jar and set it on the counter, knowing her family's love for Oreos.

When Dave came tooling in that evening, he saw the jar stuffed with cookies and said, "Good night, Kaya! We have only a little bit and you just bought all these Oreo cookies?"

She replied, "No, Dave, *not a little bit.*" And with grand gestures, she opening the pantry and displayed shelf after shelf of groceries. Guess whose kids understand the excitement of walking by faith?

What are you and your family doing to demonstrate faith . . . to risk trusting God? Are you really open to anticipating the unusual? Are you sincerely honest when you say you are available to model faith? C'mon, stop all that tire-kicking! Risk!

The Lord knows where to tinker, doesn't He?

14

Accepting the Undeniable

A book like this one on the family evokes many emotions.
Some who read it feel affirmed, encouraged, and reassured.
Others, however, are a bit confused, wondering how they can
change horses in midstream. Still others are a bit disappointed,
wishing I had addressed a particular issue I may have passed
over. Of all the feelings that surface, however, none is more
prominent than guilt . . . a guilt that oozes from the "if only"
sore. Looking back, many parents long for the impossible,
namely, a chance to raise their family all over again.

For years I have said that I know of no more guilt-giving
assignment than parenting. Do it long enough and, even
though you gave it your best shot, you can look back over the
years and locate any number of flies in the ointment.
Accepting the undeniable fact that you blew it is among life's
most painful thoughts.

A few years ago, when I brought a series of talks to our
church on some of the same subjects I've written about in this

book, I received the following letter from a fine lady who is also an honest mother:

> Dear Pastor Swindoll,
>
> My husband and I are particularly enjoying your current series on the family. We are hungry for biblical truths in this area as we face problems with an irresponsible older son.
>
> He was twelve when I came to know the Lord, about a year later he accepted Christ, and about a year and a half later my husband became a Christian. When our son was sixteen, we listened to your "You and Your Child" tape series and realized a number of areas where we had, with good intentions yet in ignorance, not followed God's principles for raising our children. Since that time we have done everything we know to reconstruct a damaged spirit—with very little success.
>
> We will be very disappointed if you finish the series without touching on some principles for how to regroup after we've "blown it."
>
> We have experienced beautiful healing in other areas of our lives, and we're confident of God's grace and instruction as we have struggled with this painful problem. We are praying you will offer a few insights we so desperately seek.

For her and thousands of other parents like her, I want to begin this final chapter by stating four very realistic facts. While these observations are neither new nor novel, they are easily forgotten by those of us who care about our children and struggle with the painful thought that some things we did could have caused irreparable damage. Let's call these things . . .

Inescapable and Painful Realities of Being Human

It would be wonderful if we lived a cut above humanity—soaring through life on graceful wings. But we do not. Speaking of that, there are some statements that appear in Isaiah 53 which most of us never apply to the family, even though we could. Because these statements provide an ideal backdrop to my initial comments in this chapter, I'd like us to ponder the prophet's familiar words:

*Surely our griefs He Himself bore, and our sorrows He car-
ried; yet we ourselves esteemed Him stricken, smitten of
God, and afflicted. But He was pierced through for our
transgressions, He was crushed for our iniquities; the chas-
tening for our well-being fell upon Him, and by His scourg-
ing we are healed. All of us like sheep have gone astray,
each of us has turned to his own way; but the LORD has
caused the iniquity of us all to fall on Him (Isaiah 53:4–6).*

In that vivid prophetic account of Messiah's suffering and
death, we find no less than four references to universal human
needs:

- **our griefs**
- **our sorrows**
- **our transgressions**
- **our iniquities**

Pretty tragic scene, isn't it? And before you're tempted to think
of yourself (or your child) as an exception, take note of "All of
us . . . have gone astray, each of us has turned to his own way
. . ." This brings me to my first of four facts.

1. We Are All Imperfect . . . and That Includes Our Offspring.

Conscientious parents tend to live under an enormous
weight of guilt because they feel wholly responsible for their
wayward children. That is, quite honestly, an unrealistic and
unreasonable thought. Furthermore, it is unbiblical. No one
individual is *wholly* responsible for another's wayward ways.
Like us, our children have wills of their own. They are like we
are, sinners who turn to their "own way." To put it bluntly,
children come to us from birth as damaged goods. As we
learned back in chapter 4, they possess a bent toward evil that
comes as part of the "birth package." Restoring those damaged
goods is quite a task. By "damaged," I mean spiritually damaged from birth. And no matter how sincere our efforts or diligent and untiring our energies, we must never forget we are

dealing with a person who is far from perfect. If you forget that, your frustration will be increased in the parenting process. Rather than being defeated by thinking you may slip up and scar a perfect model, think of parenting as doing your best to patch up a broken one. That will keep you from running scared as well as harboring all the blame.

2. We Cannot Change the Past . . . and That Includes the Way We Reared Our Children.

All of us—yes, every parent I have ever met—would love to step into the time tunnel and return to the Island of Second Chance. We would give anything to relive those years and correct the failures and mistakes we committed the first time around. All such fantasy wishes need to be erased. They can *never* be fulfilled! The parenting process offers only one try per child, one day at a time, never again to be repeated. Someone once said, "Life is like a coin; you can spend it any way you wish, but you spend it only once." That is never more true than with rearing children. About the time we get fairly good at it, our kids are all young adults and gone. Having come closer than ever to perfecting the process, we suddenly realize nobody is listening! Which means we're qualified for one major role: grandparenting (when it becomes our right to break all the rules and spoil those darlings!). It's a funny world.

All this brings me to a third fact, which is going to hurt.

3. We Are Personally Responsible for Our Wrongs . . . and That Includes Mistakes Made In Ignorance.

Let's presume I don't know much about driving a car, yet I drive it on a long trip at sixty-five miles an hour with only a quart or two of oil in the crankcase. Chances are good I will burn up the engine. I have never yet met a mechanic who gives drivers a discount for burning up an engine because they didn't realize it needed more oil. Most mechanics I know don't hesitate to charge you the full price, even though you were unaware of causing the problem.

Here's another example. If I don't know how to judge distances and I hit someone at high speed, I am still responsible for the accident. Inexperience doesn't relieve me from the wrong. So it is with rearing children. You may do the wrong thing in ignorance, but it was wrong, my friend, and you are responsible.

Now the reason I bring this to your attention is not to increase your guilt. You don't need that. It is to help all of us face the fact that blaming someone else *never* solves a problem. We're very good at that. We got the tendency from Adam, remember?

"The woman you put here with me—she gave me some fruit from the tree, and I ate it" (Genesis 3:12, NIV).

Interesting, isn't it? And even the woman, when faced with her wrong, said,

"The serpent deceived me, and I ate" (Genesis 3:13, NIV).

"It was that snake, Lord." We hurl, we blame, we point fingers in another direction at any number of scapegoats: strained circumstances, financial difficulty, a mate that ran away, a strong-willed child, poor toilet training, bad habits we learned from *our* parents, the list is endless. But we cannot escape the fact that we are responsible for our wrongs. Until we face that, we will not get on the path of recovery and renewal. God holds out an enormous amount of hope and forgiveness if we will simply face the music. I mean, the whole symphony! Remember the prophet's stinging statement? "Each of us has turned to his *own* way."

My fourth fact offers a great deal of relief. In so many words, it says this: The car can be fixed even though I burned up the engine. The accident can be taken care of even though I was to blame.

4. We Have the Hope of Healing Because All Our Wrongs Fell On Christ . . . and That Includes Domestic Failures.

You didn't miss that last line in Isaiah's words, did you?

The LORD has caused the iniquity of us all to fall on Him (v. 6).

That, my friend, falls under the category of G-R-A-C-E. God's magnificent grace brings the hope of healing. But let me hasten to connect this thought with the previous one on personal responsibility. Healing of damage done in the home is not automatic. Nor is it usually quick. It starts with the recognition—and *confession*—of wrong, and that is difficult.

As Paul Tournier correctly observes:

> It is not easy to break free from our psychological reactions. The first requisite, of course, is to recognize them. But that is not enough. . . . That is why true liberty is not to be found without the confession of our sins and the experience of divine forgiveness.
>
> This experience leads at once to dedication, to a decision in every circumstance to choose God's will.[61]

Sally Dye makes a similar statement as she points out:

> Facing the truth is the only way to break out from behind the . . . mask. . . . It seems that one has to acknowledge falling short, accept cleansing for unacceptable emotions and actions, and appropriate the real [acceptance] provided by God's grace, realizing that God loves, forgives, and accepts everyone who comes to Him with a humble heart.[62]

These comments remind me of a statement recorded by the apostle Paul in 2 Corinthians 13:7 (NIV). Paul, referring to the Corinthians as his children (he had begotten them in the faith, prayed for them, and nurtured them), later wrote to them:

> *Now we pray to God that you will not do anything wrong. Not that people will see that we have stood the test but that you will do what is right even though we may seem to have failed.*

The King James version concludes: ". . . though we be as reprobates." Think of those words in a family context. We, as parents, will come off at times wrong, looking like failures. Be that as it may, we still possess this deep-down desire that our children become and do what is right.

The *Living Bible* offers this paraphrase:

> " . . . *for we want you to do right even if we ourselves are despised.*"

Paul's "parental" desire for them? That they do no wrong—of course! His reason? Not that he might be approved and applauded (he had truly let them go—their conduct and lifestyle were now independent of his image or reputation), but that he might realize his goal for them: "that you will do what is right."

My point? Parents want only the best for their offspring. We want this even though we may not have done everything right. This positive desire helps prompt parents to admit their failures, which can start the process of healing.

Guidelines for Recovery and Renewal

I'm convinced there are some specific guidelines set forth in Scripture that will help after we have "blown it." They can serve as the road leading to recovery and renewal, even complete healing. But first, let's consider—

Negatively: Things That Won't Help

First: *It will not help for any parent to think "everything is my fault."* I repeat, no problem that occurs in a home between a parent and a child is completely one-sided. The same is true in a divorce, in sibling rivalry, or in a broken romance. It is always a two-way street.

In the book of Galatians, Paul pictures the Lord as our parent.

For you are all sons of God through faith in Christ Jesus. . . . But when the fullness of the time came, God sent forth His Son, born of a woman, born under the Law, in order that He might redeem those who were under the Law, that we might receive the adoption as sons (Galatians 3:26; 4:4–5).

The only method God employs for bringing humans into His forever family is *adoption*. Obviously, there can't be a physical birth into His family; it must be a spiritual one. You were physically born into your earthly home. You are spiritually adopted into your heavenly home. God is your heavenly Parent while you live on this earth as a Christian.

Let me go a little further. Keep reading:

And because you are sons, God has sent forth the Spirit of His Son into our hearts, crying, "Abba! Father!" (v. 6).

Abba was among the early words uttered by a little child who spoke Aramaic. "Daddy, daddy." Spiritually speaking, the Spirit of God was there, as you were born into God's eternal family, leading you to say "Abba." So you have a "daddy" relationship with your Father. He continues:

Therefore you are no longer a slave, but a son; and if a son, then an heir through God (4:7).

Not only are we adopted, not only do we call Him "Daddy," we are, in turn, called God's adopted *child,* and we are made *heirs* of the family. I call that being in the innermost circle of a relationship with our eternal Father God. But then, Paul rebukes those folks for not living like the King's kids!

But now that you have come to know God, or rather to be known by God, how is it that you turn back again to the weak and worthless elemental things, to which you desire to be enslaved all over again? (v. 9).

What is the domestic point of all this? Even though Christians have the perfect Parent, we still choose to do wrong. Frankly, that gives me hope. Even the ideal Parent (our heavenly Father) has children who have wayward wills. Even when we get perfect counsel and wise direction from our heavenly Father, we occasionally go our own way. So it is in an earthly family. One of our children may receive good counsel from us—not perfect, because it is coming from imperfect vessels, but reliable, wise counsel—yet choose to ignore it and rebel. If that happens, it is wrong—it is *damaging* to your esteem as a parent—to think YOU are completely at fault.

A Christian physician writes:

Parents are admonished to bring up children properly.
Children are admonished to respond wisely to parental cor-

> rection. If both play their part all will be well. But it takes a
> parent-child team working in harmony to produce this happy
> result. . . .
>
> You cannot ever control another human being, even if
> that human being is your own child.[63]

Yes, some of the fault was yours. You have done wrong because
you're imperfect, but it is incorrect and unhealthy to think it is
all your fault. That simply doesn't help.

Second: *It won't help to be simplistic with verses or principles
from the Bible.* Please understand I am not belittling the words
or principles of Scripture. God has spoken in His Word, and we
are to adapt our lives accordingly. We can stake our very lives
on the unshakable claims of the eternal, inerrant Word of God.
That fact, however, does not give us license to be careless or
simplistic with principles from Scripture. For example, you'll
remember my referring to Proverbs 22:6 in the early chapters of
this book.

> *Train up a child in the way he should go, even when he is
> old he will not depart from it.*

God's Word offers general principles and guidelines, but
there is no magical rabbit's foot power here. You don't rub it
three times a day and find automatic fulfillment. If I may quote
the verse a little differently, I think you'll get the slant of what
I'm getting at: "Train up the child in the way he should go,
even when he is old he will usually not depart from it."

Ah, some of you say, "But it doesn't say *usually*." But wait,
it doesn't say "invariably" either. Nor can you force it to say
that on the basis of the Hebrew text. As a matter of fact, the
Hebrew is less specific than the English. There is a general principle here: Normally speaking, more often than not, good parents produce good children. And more often than not, poor
parenting produces a youngster who grows up with a poor self-
esteem. You and I do ourselves no favor to read an inflexible
law into this verse. That is what I mean by being "simplistic"
with Scripture.

I have known several families where the parents created a domestic disaster. They drank heavily, argued openly, neglected their children, and ran around on each other. Yet their children turned out well. In fact, *quite* well. They flourished in school, landed good jobs, seemed to have decent friends, and now appear to have stable marriages in which they handle their own children in a reasonably balanced and responsible manner. I'm also acquainted with families in which the parents were warm, firm, wise, and giving, who have at least one child in serious trouble. My wife and I know one couple whose marriage is a model of godliness, faithfulness, and Christian compassion. The unexplainable mystery is that three of their four adult children have been through painful divorces.

There are general rules. Good parents are less likely to produce problem children than bad parents. Please, as a thinking adult, as a growing Christian learning to think for yourself, be careful about wiping a simplistic salve across the Bible, inadvertently adding "never" and "always" to its proverbs and principles. When God says "never," He means never. When He doesn't, we shouldn't. A simplistic view of Scripture does not help. On the contrary, it hurts and leads to disillusionment.

Positively: Things That Will Help

My mind returns to that grand Book of Isaiah—this time chapter 58. Trust me, I'm fully aware of the historical context of Isaiah 58. This is not a chapter written directly to families or parents. Nor is it written directly to Americans living in the twentieth century. Originally, this was a powerful message addressed to the ancient people of Judah approximately eight hundred years before Christ. The prophet is writing about a fast. Isaiah is pleading for an attitude of repentance before Jehovah. The initial interpretation is to the Jew who lived in a country rapidly on its way down the tube. It was only a matter of time before the Babylonians would invade and conquer.

Just as we have looked carefully at other scriptures written to other people in other eras and applied the truths to the family today, I would like to do the same with Isaiah 58. What was written to Judah is definitely applicable, especially to families today. So please understand that contextually we're lifting this from its original harbor. We're moving it like you would move a large ship, and by application only, sailing it into another harbor.

The heart of Isaiah is heavy with a burden for his nation. He realizes that the people have begun to dig their own graves. Looking at the social and moral vultures feeding on the vitals of his nation, Isaiah writes with deep passion. He doesn't hold back as he exhorts them: "God has proclaimed that we fast. God has proclaimed that we repent, that we come before Him in dust and ashes . . . in sackcloth. And this fast that God has commanded us to observe will bring us into His favor. Obey Him!"

Guess what? Those words meant nothing to Isaiah's audience. They were like water on a duck's back. Those in Judah went through the empty motions of a hypocritical fast. They put on a religious mask, but underneath they remained unrepentant. So the prophet, presenting God's message, rebukes them for their hypocrisy.

Is this not the fast which I chose, to loosen the bonds of wickedness, to undo the bands of the yoke, and to let the oppressed go free, and break every yoke? (58:6).

I freely admit I don't know a lot about farming (I have never once been behind a pair of plowing mules), but I know a little bit about a yoke. I've seen yokes in use. I have observed that a yoke is seldom built for one; usually a yoke is for two. Isaiah pictures his nation yoked with wickedness. He challenges them to get out from under the yoke of wickedness, drop it aside, and come back to God to ask for His forgiveness. "He'll bring back the oppressed if you break the bands of that yoke. He will set the captives of wickedness free. Break loose from that irksome, godless yoke and come before the Lord in utter humility, and He will honor your repentance." That's the idea here.

Allow me to stop long enough to apply that to today's family. Some parents have been yoked with their children in a most unhappy relationship. The child, as he or she has grown older, has become increasingly more distant. Offenses have been created, some innocently, some deliberately. In either case, there are lingering offenses. If I may apply Isaiah's words quite pointedly, you have been "yoked" with an offense in the relationship with your child—some of you worse than others.

God speaks to you through the prophet's words and says, "O courageous, sincere parents, I have a plan that will break the bonds of the yoke." Now we are ready to see how it works. You might want to take a deep breath. What you are about to read won't be easy to accept. The counsel of Scripture is not a slight tap on the shoulder. It is truth to live by . . . to change one's actions. It is a howling reproach to all who have blown it. Are you ready?

To begin with: *Humble yourself.*

> *Is it not to divide your bread with the hungry, and bring the homeless poor into the house; when you see the naked, to cover him; and not to hide yourself from your own flesh? Then your light will break out like the dawn, and your recovery will speedily spring forth; and your righteousness will go before you; the glory of the LORD will be your rear guard (vv. 7–8).*

He is saying "humble yourselves!" to parents today who wish to apply this on a family level. You didn't hurry through those verses and miss his reference to "hiding yourself from your own flesh," did you? And did you see the hope in his promise of "recovery"? It's all there! Perhaps you should read verses 7 and 8 again.

I believe the greatest barrier in breaking most long-standing domestic yokes is nothing more than pride. Parents can be awfully proud—too proud to say, "Sweetheart, a number of years ago offenses grew between us. Today, looking back on those years, I realize I was more wrong than right." Or, "You know, son, as I think back to those days when our problems multiplied, obviously I wasn't all wrong, but I was more wrong than you were. And I humbly declare before you and before God my responsibility in this broken relationship. Please forgive me."

If you read and apply this correctly, you'll begin to change your attitude toward your wayward, distant child. You'll begin to divide your bread because he's hungry. You'll give him a home again and bring the poor into your house. You'll see the nakedness of his condition and you'll want to have a hand in clothing him. There will be a change in your heart toward the hurting. And don't doubt for a moment that your distant child is hurting. Trust me, when the lights are out at night and he lays his head on the pillow and attempts to go to sleep, left alone with his memory, he remembers the days when there was a wonderful harmony between you and him. I'm not trying to play on your emotions. This is not mere sentimentality. These words—the poor, the homeless, the naked, the hungry—are words of deep emotion stirred up by unresolved hurts.

God says to the parent who is willing to humble himself, "Reach out, lay aside the pride." And when you attempt to run in the other direction and crawl back behind your mask, He promises, "The LORD will be your rear guard." I may be stretching it a little by saying this, but I think there's a reason He is a rear guard here and not a *forward* guard. Our natural tendency is to run backwards—to escape from such humbling situations. Our pride causes us to rancor when we know that we're to deal with things this difficult. We recall all of their wrong and so few of their rights. That's not humility. Take some sound advice: Leave their wrongs to God. Never try to take vengeance. You're responsible for your wrongs. God will deal with them about theirs.

Let's go further:

Then you will call, and the LORD will answer; you will cry, and He will say, "Here I am" (v. 9a).

Here is the next guideline to follow: *Pray!* Yes, pray. It is one of those disciplines we do too little of as it relates to our family relationships. Mom . . . Dad, can you remember the last time you prayed for your adult offspring by name, now that he or she has left the nest? It has been a long time, hasn't it? Start today. Begin to pray specifically. Call on the Lord. *Cry out* to Him on behalf of your son or your daughter. Be fervent in your intercession. You may not even know where they are, but you know where God is. He is right there. He never left. He will say, "I'm here, I hear your cry . . . let Me help."

Now for the really tough part. The third guideline can be stated in three words: *Remove the yoke!*

> *If you remove the yoke from your midst, the pointing of the finger, and speaking wickedness . . . (v. 9b).*

Talk about descriptive! What do you feel when you see someone point a long, bony finger at you? You feel blame. He says, "Don't do that! Remove the yoke. Stop pointing a finger. Stop speaking wickedness every time his or her name comes up. Change your attitude. Change your response!" Removing the yoke conveys the idea of getting rid of an irksome attitude, the lingering offense, all the finger-pointing and name-calling. This could apply to your sons-in-law or daughters-in-law as well as to your own flesh and blood. His point? Quit blaming your family members.

Next, *make yourself available and vulnerable!*

> *And if you give yourself to the hungry, and satisfy the desire of the afflicted, then your light will rise in darkness, and your gloom will become like midday (v. 10).*

People who have blown it are often living in darkness, in the shadows of bad memories. We feed that by finger-pointing, by name-calling, by building case after case against a son or daughter. The Lord's counsel is right on: Make yourself available, be vulnerable before them.

He then promises:

> *And the LORD will continually guide you, and satisfy your desire in scorched places (v. 11a).*

Parents, you want the same thing your child wants. You want peace. You want a bridge built across the chasm of broken relationships. Isaiah calls that chasm "scorched places." The Lord can make such places fruitful again. God's Word says the Lord will . . .

> *give strength to your bones; and you will be like a watered garden, and like a spring of water whose waters do not fail (v. 11).*

What a beautiful, soothing metaphor! How therapeutic! It's a picture of fruitfulness, abundance, and harvest as opposed to scorched barrenness. A long-standing broken relationship is like a scorched desert . . . but the Lord says it can become a verdant valley if you will make yourself available and vulnerable.

Finally, *trust God to bring about change.* Read this verse slowly, carefully.

> *And those from among you will rebuild the ancient ruins; you will raise up the age-old foundations; and you will be called the repairer of the breach, the restorer of the streets in which to dwell (v. 12).*

Do your part and God will do His. He will bring about change in another. And you will be called what? The blamer? No. Name-caller? No longer. Offender? No . . . no more. You will be given a new title, parent: Repairer of the breach. Restorer of relationships. What a wonderful new identity!

For years I've recalled my mother's saying: "People can't change people." If I may amplify: Parents can't change adult kids. But God does. It is His specialty. The only one you can work on is the one inside your skin. You have to leave with God the change in the heart of your offspring. This reminds me of a proverb that describes someone whom we have hurt:

> *A brother offended is harder to be won than a strong city, and contentions are like the bars of a castle (Proverbs 18:19).*

Now *that's* vivid. Their resistance is as strong as thick, iron bars on castle windows. They are reluctant to respond, they will be gun-shy, defensive. Remember, they may not jump at the chance to forgive you right now. But in time, that moment may come.

Essentials Along the Way

May I close by offering three essentials in carrying out this process?

1. You must go with the right motive.
2. You must be patient.
3. You must do it in God's strength.

Going the extra mile. That's what much of this chapter has been about. Instead of intensifying the offense, I've suggested that we humble ourselves—a major key in unlocking the rigid yoke of offense. Next, instead of blaming, pray. Call on the Lord for help. And rather than resisting, be available. Yes, go more than the extra mile.

Sometimes a parent will feel led by God to conduct a search for an adult child whose lifestyle has become shameful. Such a search is never successful if the parent goes with plans to blame or condemn. There must be a humility, a willingness to negotiate . . . to confess . . . to forgive . . . to accept.

Max Lucado relates a touching, true story of love demonstrated to the extreme. Though it occurred in a poor village in Brazil, it illustrates the extent to which a parent sometimes feels the need to go in order to restore a relationship.

> The small house was simple but adequate. It consisted of one large room on a dusty street. Its red-tiled roof was one of many in this poor neighborhood on the outskirts of the Brazilian village. It was a comfortable home. Maria and her daughter, Christina, had done what they could to add color to the gray walls and warmth to the hard dirt floor: an old calendar, a faded photograph of a relative, a wooden crucifix. The furnishings were modest: a pallet on either side of the room, a wash basin, and a wood-burning stove.
>
> Maria's husband had died when Christina was an infant. The young mother, stubbornly refusing opportunities to

remarry, got a job and set out to raise her young daughter. And now, fifteen years later, the worst years were over. Though Maria's salary as a maid afforded few luxuries, it was reliable and it did provide food and clothes. And now Christina was old enough to get a job and to help out.

Some said Christina got her independence from her mother. She recoiled at the traditional idea of marrying young and raising a family. Not that she couldn't have had her pick of husbands. Her olive skin and brown eyes kept a steady stream of prospects at her door. She had an infectious way of throwing her head back and filling the room with laughter. She also had that rare magic some women have that makes every man feel like a king just by being near them. But it was her spirited curiosity that made her keep all the men at arm's length.

She spoke often of going to the city. She dreamed of trading her dusty neighborhood for exciting avenues and city life. Just the thought of this horrified her mother. Maria was always quick to remind Christina of the harshness of the streets. "People don't know you there. Jobs are scarce and the life is cruel. And besides, if you went there, what would you do for a living?"

Maria knew exactly what Christina would do, or would *have* to do for a living. That's why her heart broke when she awoke one morning to find her daughter's bed empty. Maria knew immediately where her daughter had gone. She also knew immediately what she must do to find her. She quickly threw some clothes in a bag, gathered up all her money, and ran out of the house.

On her way to the bus stop she entered a drugstore to get one last thing. Pictures. She sat in the photograph booth, closed the curtain, and spent all she could on pictures of herself. With her purse full of small black-and-white photos, she boarded the next bus to Rio de Janeiro.

Maria knew Christina had no way of earning money. She also knew that her daughter was too stubborn to give up. When pride meets hunger, a human will do things that were before unthinkable. Knowing this, Maria began her search. Bars, hotels, nightclubs, any place with the reputation for street walkers or prostitutes. She went to them all. And at each place she left her picture—taped on a bathroom mirror, tacked to a hotel bulletin board, fastened to a corner phone booth. And on the back of each photo she wrote a note.

It wasn't too long before both the money and the pictures ran out, and Maria had to go home. The weary mother wept as the bus began its long journey back to her small village.

It was a few weeks later that young Christina descended the stairs. Her young face was tired. Her brown eyes no longer danced with youth but spoke of pain and fear. Her laughter was broken. Her dream had become a nightmare. A thousand times over she had longed to trade these countless beds for her secure pallet. Yet the little village was, in too many ways, too far away.

As she reached the bottom of the stairs, her eyes noticed a familiar face. She looked again, and there on the lobby mirror was a small picture of her mother. Christina's eyes burned and her throat tightened as she walked across the room and removed the small photo. Written on the back was this compelling invitation. "Whatever you have done, whatever you have become, it doesn't matter. Please come home."

She did.[64]

A yoke is not broken by pointing a finger of blame or manipulating our child to say, "Well, really, I was all wrong. It was all me." You go with the simple motive of declaring your concern and you patiently let God go to work on the heart of your child. It may take months, perhaps years. After all, the offenses were built over the years. Scar tissue has a thickness about it that can be tough and calloused. You'll need supernatural wisdom, which means you go in God's strength.

I realize I've built a real case back in chapter 9, defending the father of the prodigal who let his boy go without chasing after him. This story may appear contradictory, but it is not. It merely underscores, again, the need for wisdom. Sometimes parents are led to stay . . . to wait . . . to let the wayward child come to his senses. On other occasions, there is the need to go, to reach out, to seek reconciliation.

As a result of writing this chapter, I have had to take care of some homework in my own family. My children are still in their twenties and thirties; yours may be in their thirties or forties . . . and that's even harder. But always remember, they're never too young and they're never too old to build bridges. When we do, great things happen.

In her fine book, *Children Are Wet Cement,* Anne Ortlund tells a wonderful, true story:

> Only a few months ago Ray and I made a date with Nels [their son] and drove out into the hills overlooking Newport Beach.
>
> "Nels," said Ray "I've goofed a lot as a dad. I love you very much, but I've said and done a lot of dumb things through your fifteen years. I know I've hurt and not helped lots of times, and I just want you to know that I'm sorry."
>
> There was a long silence. Nels didn't quite know how to respond.
>
> "Are you leading up to something?" he asked.
>
> "Not a thing," said Ray. "I just wanted to say that for all the times I've blundered and hurt you and done or said stupid things to you, to put you down or make life tougher for you, I really am sorry. I just wanted to apologize."
>
> I chimed in from the back seat of the car. "Nels, we didn't do dumb things on purpose, but we know we've been far from ideal parents. We've blown our tempers; we've misjudged you; we haven't always handled you wisely—and that's been tough on you. We get intense and overzealous, overpicky on some issues, and we completely overlook other issues. We're just plain ol' dumb human beings. But our goofs have an influence on how you turn out—that's the scary part."
>
> Ray said, "We think you're just turning out great. But whatever scars you've got, they're our fault, not yours. And don't think we don't realize that."
>
> "That's okay," said Nels. "I think you're great."
>
> "We sure are crazy about you, Nels," I said.
>
> "We're so proud of you," Ray added. "You're terrific—in spite of us."
>
> "You're great parents," said Nels.
>
> Over the seats of the car there were pats and smiles and squeezes. That was it—and pretty soon we drove down the hill and home again.[65]

There is no "right way" or "quick 'n' easy process" in building bridges. You initiate the process . . . you just step in, tell the truth, admit whatever was your fault, and seek to make things better. What an essential factor is your *attitude*. Stay submissive.

WEATHERING THE STORM

Our family has had several dogs during our years together. Some have been small and nervous, others large and placid. A few have gotten into fights with other dogs. I've noticed a curious "signal": When the dog being overpowered finally realizes it cannot win the fight, it finally submits and surrenders by lying down at the other dog's feet, baring its vulnerable throat and belly to the attacking dog above it. In this position it could get seriously hurt in an instant, but interestingly, that's how the dog is spared.

Parents, I'm asking you to risk getting "seriously hurt" by accepting the undeniable. If you have wronged your family, the wisest move you can make is to admit it. Hide from the truth no longer! In all sincerity, I plead with you to bare yourself before God first and then before the one in your family that you've wronged . . . then watch God work. You could be amazed at the outcome. Rather than being attacked, you'll be spared. God will honor your transparent honesty. And best of all, your name will be changed from Offender in the Family to Repairer of the Breach.

I don't know of a more beautiful name for a parent . . . especially for one who has blown it.

Conclusion

Our journey together has been a longer one than I original-ly had in mind. We took the scenic route, which required a few extra miles. The benefits of doing so, however, far outweigh the time we could have saved by taking a shorter course. I have been reminded of some vital truths and, hopefully, you have as well. We have taken a fresh, objective look at the family. The time we have spent together has heightened my awareness of the importance of the home and has deepened my gratitude for its existence. Since we asked Wisdom to be our guide, we have continually listened to her counsel, viewed the scenes through her perspective, and formed conclusions based on her principles. She has been an insightful instructor and escort.

Neither time nor space allowed me to reach into more areas of domestic turmoil. I am well aware of the high-priority sub-jects I was not able to address, which causes me to regret that Wisdom's voice must remain silent on those topics so far as this book is concerned. My only comfort is that other equally reliable volumes are readily accessible—and more will be writ-ten in days to come.

As I said in my opening remarks, the family is "in." Its pop-ularity is on the increase. This resurgence of interest pleases me, for I know of no realm of life that can provide more com-panionship in a lonely world or greater feelings of security and purpose in chaotic times than the close ties of a strong family. As tough as it may be to maintain this closeness, I say again: It is worth every ounce of effort.

It still brings a smile to my face every time I see a family reunited at airports. Watching them engage in caring conversa-tion and arm-in-arm affirmation renews my hope for our coun-try. It is a beautiful sight to behold, especially in a day when so many authorities still predict the family's demise. Nonsense! There are tens of thousands of homes across our land where love draws lives together like a magnet, then launches them into society with indomitable courage.

I was reminded of that in an unforgettable story CBS correspondent Charles Kuralt uncovered and captured on camera. He happened upon the Chandlers, a large black family in Prairie, Mississippi. Read it and weep joyfully with me.

> A long road took nine children out of the cotton fields, out of poverty, out of Mississippi. But roads go both ways, and this Thanksgiving weekend, they all returned. This is about Thanksgiving, and coming home.
>
> One after another, and from every corner of America, the cars turned into the yard. With much cheering and much hugging, the nine children of Alex and Mary Chandler were coming home for their parents' fiftieth wedding anniversary.
>
> GLORIA CHANDLER: There's my daddy. [*Gloria rushes to hug him.*]
>
> Gloria Chandler Coleman, master of arts, University of Missouri, a teacher in Kansas City, was home.
>
> All nine children had memories of a sharecropper's cabin and nothing to wear and nothing to eat. All nine are college graduates.
>
> Cooking the meal in the kitchen of the new house the children built for their parents four years ago is Bessie Chandler Beasley, BA Tuskegee, MA Central Michigan, dietitian at a veteran's hospital, married to a Ph.D. And helping out, Princess Chandler Norman, MA Indiana University, a schoolteacher in Gary, Indiana. You'll meet them all.
>
> But first, I thought you ought to meet their parents. Alex Chandler remembers the time when he had a horse and a cow and tried to buy a mule and couldn't make the payments and lost the mule, the horse, and the cow. And about that time, Cleveland, the first son, decided he wanted to go to college.
>
> ALEX CHANDLER: We didn't have any money. And we went to town; he wanted to catch the bus to go on up there. And so we went to town and borrowed two dollars and a half from her niece, and bought him a bus ticket. And when he got there, that's all he had.

CONCLUSION

From that beginning, he became Dr. Cleveland Chandler. He is chairman of the economics department at Howard University. How did they do it, starting on one of the poorest farms in the poorest part of the poorest state in America?

PRINCESS CHANDLER NORMAN: We worked.

KURALT: You picked cotton?

NORMAN: Yes, picked cotton, and pulled corn, stripped millet, dug potatoes.

They all left. Luther left for the University of Omaha and went on to become the Public Service Employment Manager for Kansas City. He helped his younger brother, James, come to Omaha University, too, and go on to graduate work at Yale. And in his turn, James helped Herman, who graduated from Morgan State and is a technical manager in Dallas. And they helped themselves. Fortson, a Baptist minister in Pueblo, Colorado, wanted to go to Morehouse College.

FORTSON CHANDLER: I chose Morehouse and it was difficult. I had to pick cotton all summer long to get the first month's rent and tuition.

So, helping themselves and helping one another, they all went away. And now, fifty years after life began for the Chandler family in a one-room shack in a cotton field, now, just as they were sitting down in the new house to the ham and turkey and sweet potatoes and cornbread and collard greens and two kinds of pie and three kinds of cake, now Donald arrived—the youngest—who had driven with his family all the way down from Minneapolis. And now the Chandlers were all together again.

ALEX CHANDLER [*saying grace*]: Our Father in heaven, we come at this moment, giving thee thanks for thou hast been so good and so kind. We want to thank you, O God, for this, for your love and for your Son. Thank you that you have provided for all of us through all these years. [*Mr. Chandler begins weeping.*]

Remembering all those years of sharecropping and going hungry and working for a white man for fifty cents a day and worrying about his children's future, remembering all that, Alex Chandler almost didn't get through this blessing.

CONCLUSION

ALEX [*continuing grace*]: In Jesus' name, amen.

And neither did the others. [*Family members wiping tears away.*]

The Chandler family started with as near nothing as any family in America ever did. And so their Thanksgiving weekend might have been more thankful than most. [*Chandler family singing "I'll Fly Away."*]

"I'll Fly Away" is the name of the old hymn. It is Mr. Chandler's favorite. His nine children flew away, and made places for themselves in this country; and this weekend, came home again. There probably are no lessons in any of this, but I know that in the future, whenever I hear that the family is a dying institution, I'll think of them. Whenever I hear anything in America is impossible, I'll think of them.[66]

I am convinced that stories of families like the Chandlers—strong families—are tucked away in pockets of our nation's population along hundreds of other back roads, blue highways, and busy cities. They represent places of quiet determination where character is being forged and where our future is being shaped. They do not make the headlines, but it doesn't matter. What does matter is that mothers and dads are staying at the unheralded, relentless, and often thankless task of building their home by wisdom, establishing it by understanding, and, by knowledge, filling each room with precious and pleasant riches.

Enough children reared in places like that will provide all that is needed to turn this nation around. The secret rests with the family . . . your family and mine.

Notes

1. *Time,* 28 September 1987, 56.

2. Malcolm Muggeridge, *Jesus Rediscovered* (Wheaton, Ill.: Tyndale House Publishers, 1971), 3.

3. Nick Stinnett, "Six Qualities that Make Families Strong," chapter 1 in *Family Building: Six Qualities of a Strong Family,* ed. Dr. George Rekers (Ventura, Calif.: Regal Books, 1985), 38.

4. John Walvoord and Roy Zuck, *The Bible Knowledge Commentary,* 1 (Wheaton, Ill.: Victor Books, 1987), 274.

5. Charlie W. Shedd, *You Can Be a Great Parent,* formerly titled *Promises to Peter* (Waco, Tex.: Word Books, 1970), 16.

6. Giora Dilberto, "Invasion of the Gender Blenders," *People Weekly,* 23 April 1984.

7. Alvin Toffler, *The Third Wave* (New York: Bantam Books, 1982), 123.

8. *Theological Dictionary of the New Testament,* 3, ed. Gerhard Friedrich and Gerhard Kittel (Grand Rapids, Mich.: Wm. B. Eerdmans, 1964), 176.

9. Richard Halverson, *Perspective* (Grand Rapids, Mich.: Zondervan Publishing House, 1957).

10. *Saint Augustine's Confessions,* trans. with an introduction by R. S. Pine-Coffin (Harmondsworth, Middlesex, England: Penguin Books, Ltd., 1961), 45.

11. Dan Benson, *The Total Man* (Wheaton, Ill.: Tyndale House Publishers, 1977).

12. Shedd, *Great Parent,* 12–13.

13. William B. Franklin, from *A Father's Love,* Peter S. Seymour (Kansas City, Mo.: Hallmark Cards, Inc., 1972).

14. "Ships" by Ian Hunter, © 1979 SBK April Music Inc. and Ian Hunter Music Inc. All rights controlled and administered by SBK April Music Inc. All rights reserved. International copyright secured. Used by permission.

15. Charles R. Swindoll, *Strike the Original Match* (Portland, Ore.: Multnomah Press, 1980), 24–25.

NOTES

16. Alan Loy McGinnis, *Bringing Out the Best in People* (Minneapolis: Augsburg Publishing House, 1985), 19–20. Used by permission.

17. Elisabeth Kubler-Ross, *On Death and Dying* (New York: Macmillan Publishing Co., 1969). Used by permission.

18. James Dobson, *Hide or Seek* (Old Tappan, N.J.: Fleming H. Revell Company, 1974), 182–183. Used by permission.

19. Dorothy Nolte, as quoted by Anne Ortlund in *Children Are Wet Cement* (Old Tappan, N.J.: Fleming H. Revell Company, 1981), 58.

20. James Dobson, *The Strong-Willed Child* (Wheaton, Ill.: Tyndale House Publishers, 1978), 145.

21. "Would You Have Kids Again?" from Ann Landers column, © *Los Angeles Times* Syndicate.

22. Albert Siegel, *Stanford Observer,* as quoted in *The Wittenburg Door* (San Diego, Calif.: Youth Specialities).

23. Dr. Winship as quoted by J. Oswald Sanders in *A Spiritual Clinic* (Chicago: Moody Press, 1958), 90.

24. Theodore Roosevelt in an address before the First International Congress in America on the Welfare of the Child, March 1908.

25. Dennis Waitley, *Seeds of Greatness* (Old Tappan, N.J.: Fleming H. Revell Company, 1983), 73–74. Used by permission.

26. James Dobson, *Straight Talk to Men and Their Wives* (Waco, Tex.: Word Books, 1980), 58–60. Used by permission.

27. Charlotte Elmore, "An IQ Test Almost Ruined My Son's Life," *Redbook,* April 1988, 50–52. Used by permission.

28. From the promotional leaflet of The Original Red Plate Company, 1835 Whittier Avenue, Costa Mesa, Calif., 92626. Used by permission.

29. Dorothy Corkille Briggs, *Your Child's Self-Esteem* (Garden City, N.Y.: Dolphin Books edition, 1975), 2–3.

30. William Barclay, *The Daily Study Bible: The Letters to the Galatians and Ephesians* (Edinburgh, Scotland: The Saint Andrew Press, 1962), 211.

31. J. Oswald Sanders, *Spiritual Leadership* (Chicago: Moody Press, 1967), 59.

32. C. F. Keil and F. Delitzsch, *Commentaries on the Old Testament, Proverbs of Solomon,* 2, ed. Franz Delitzsch (Grand Rapids, Mich.: Wm. B. Eerdmans, n.d.), 214.

33. Briggs, *Self-Esteem,* 9.

34. Socrates, 469–399 B.C.

35. Earl F. Palmer, *The Enormous Exception* (Waco, Tex.: Word Books, 1986), 145.

NOTES

36. David Elkind, *The Hurried Child* (Menlo Park, Calif.: Addison-Wesley Publishing Co., 1981).

37. Susan Ferraro, "Hotsy Totsy," *American Way,* inflight magazine of American Airlines, April 1981, 61. Used by permission.

38. Douglas S. Looney, "Bred to Be a Superstar," *Sports Illustrated,* 22 February 1988, © 1988, Time Inc., 56–58. All rights reserved. Used by permission.

39. D. L. Stewart, "Why Fathers Hide Their Feelings," *Redbook,* January 1985, 32.

40. J. Allan Petersen, "Expressing Appreciation," chapter 4 in *Family Building,* ed. Dr. George Rekers (Ventura, Calif.: Regal Books, 1985), 103–106.

41. The Family, *Preserving America's Future:* A Report to the President from the White House Working Group on the Family, 2 December 1986, 2. Used by permission of Gary L. Bauer, chairman.

42. Alexander Whyte, *Whyte's Bible Characters from the Old Testament and the New Testament* (Grand Rapids, Mich.: Zondervan Publishing House, 1952, 1967), 218–219. Used by permission.

43. Carle C. Zimmerman, *Family and Civilization* (New York: Harper & Brothers, 1947), 776–777.

44. John White, *Parents in Pain* (Downers Grove, Ill.: InterVarsity Press, 1979), 201, 204–205.

45. William J. Kirkpatrick, 1838–1921, "Lord, I'm Coming Home."

46. Harold S. Kushner, *When Bad Things Happen to Good People* (New York: Schocken Books, published by Pantheon Books, a division of Random House, Inc., 1981), 21–22.

47. Gleason L. Archer, *The Book of Job* (Grand Rapids, Mich.: Baker Book House, 1982), 35.

48. Ibid., 138–139.

49. "The Hiding Place" by Bryan Jeffery Leech. © 1973, 1974 by Fred Bock Music Co. International copyright secured. All rights reserved. Used by permission.

50. Ralph Cipriano, "Downey Man Brain-Damaged During Routine Surgery, Huge Payment Can't Erase Medical Tragedy," *Los Angeles Times,* 1–2 June 1985, 1, 3. Used by permission.

51. Samuel Taylor Coleridge, "The Rime of the Ancient Mariner," in *The Oxford Book of English Verse,* ed. Sir Arthur Quiller-Couch (London: Oxford University Press, 1940), 653, 667.

52. Abraham Lincoln to John Todd Stuart, 23 January 1841, Springfield, Ill., in Roy P. Basler, ed., *The Collected Works of Abraham Lincoln,* 1 (New Brunswick, N.J.: Rutgers University Press, 1953), 229–230.

NOTES

53. *Theological Wordbook of the Old Testament,* 2, ed. R. Laird Harris, Gleason L. Archer, Jr., Bruce K. Waltke (Chicago: Moody Press, 1980), 831.

54. Tamara Jones, "When Are We Going to Smile Again? Boy's Family Torn between Mourning, Waiting," *Los Angeles Times,* 26 May 1985, 4. Used by permission of The Associated Press.

55. David A. Seamands, *Healing for Damaged Emotions* (Wheaton, Ill.: Victor Books, 1981), 23. Used by permission.

56. McGinnis, *Bringing Out the Best,* 35.

57. John C. Whitcomb, Jr. and Henry M. Morris, *The Genesis Flood* (Philadelphia: The Presbyterian and Reformed Publishing Company, 1964), 67–68.

58. Seamands, *Damaged Emotions,* 18–19. Used by permission.

59. Reprinted by permission of United Feature Syndicate, Inc.

60. McGinnis, *Bringing Out the Best,* 34.

61. Paul Tournier, *The Strong and the Weak* (Philadelphia: The Westminster Press, 1963), 198–199.

62. Sally Folger Dye as quoted by Anne Ortlund in *Children Are Wet Cement,* 178.

63. White, *Parents in Pain,* 44, 58.

64. Max Lucado, *No Wonder They Call Him the Savior* (Portland, Ore.: Multnomah Press, 1986), 157–159.

65. Ortlund, *Wet Cement,* 183–184.

66. Charles Kuralt, *On the Road with Charles Kuralt* (New York: The Putnam Publishing Group, 1985), 306–309. Used by permission.

Discussion Guide

Welcome! Come in, come in, it's good to see you. Just make yourself at home—that's it, kick off your shoes—and we'll begin discussing *The Strong Family* in a moment. Before we do, though, let me put some of your minds at ease about what I mean by a "strong family."

In the past, good families were always taught to hide their problems. This, in turn, led to the misconception that strong families were problem-free families. The Good Housekeeping Seal of Approval was awarded to only those whose manicured lawns and regular church attendance projected a spotless image of perfection. Never mind what went on inside those model homes—the bitter marital rifts, little or no communication, and even darker problems such as alcoholism or abuse.

Today, fortunately, the myth of trouble-free households is being replaced with the truth about families and problems—they're inseparable! Strong families experience many of the same heartaches and conflicts as the not-so-strong. It's how they handle them that makes the qualitative difference.

> The "good" family of yesterday claimed it had no problems; today's healthy family expects a variety of problems. The "good" family of the past never admitted any need for help; today's healthy family is healthy because it is able to admit to need and seek help in the early stages of the problem. In fact, it might even be said that the healthier the family today, the sooner it is likely to admit its weakness and work on it publicly, a direct turnaround from a couple of generations ago when the best families were problemless.[1]

That is what I mean by a strong family—one that admits need and seeks help, just like you're doing right now by reading this discussion guide. Sure, you're not perfect, nor will you be when you finish this book, but you'll be wiser, healthier, and better prepared biblically to build a truly strong family.

Solomon once said, "Two are better than one because they have a good return for their labor. For if either of them falls, the one will lift up his companion. But woe to the one who falls when there is not another to lift him up" (Eccles. 4:9–10). What mom or dad doesn't "fall" in their parenting practically every day? Even now, many of you are pretty skinned up and frustrated. That's why, although the questions may also be done at home alone or as a couple, we've designed them to be used in a small group setting—a safe haven of understanding, encouragement, and fellowship in God's Word where you can lift up others as well as be lifted up yourself.

To ensure a good return from your group's labor, here are a few helpful tips to remember:

• *Choose a leader.* Select a proven leader who understands the dynamics of a small group. Someone who will facilitate, not dominate.

• *Stay small.* Nothing is more frustrating than to be in a "discussion" group that always runs out of time before half the people can share. Stay small, four or five couples at most. Anything much beyond that will be self-defeating.

• *Be committed.* The unity and intimacy of the group will never develop if only some of the people come some of the time. Show your love and commitment for the others by being there, on time, each week.

• *Prepare.* This is a tough one for busy parents. Believe me, I know. But you want a strong family, right? OK, then, what's it going to cost for you to have some uninterrupted time to prayerfully read each chapter and answer its corresponding discussion questions? Getting up earlier? Going to bed later? Maybe giving up an activity so you can take this one on? Decide now, and then let nothing separate you from that time—not principalities or powers, nor height, nor depth, nor any other created thing. Remember, too, to have a notebook or journal handy during your preparation and the small group session to record your questions, answers, and insights.

• *Share.* Be open. Put away your pat answers. Resist pontificating on everyone else's problems and just share the truth of what you think and how you feel. It will feel a bit awkward at first, it always does. But you can overcome that all the more quickly if everyone will commit to confidentiality.

Last, use the following questions as you see fit to spark discussion each time the group gathers. God bless!

CHAPTER 1 An Endangered Species?

1. Take a moment to measure the health of your home using the six qualities from Dr. Stinnett's study. (Husbands and wives, if you really want to be challenged, do this exercise separately and then compare answers.) On a scale from 1 to 10, 1 meaning almost extinct, circle the number that best represents the strength or weakness of each trait in your family.

Committed to the Family

1   2   3   4   5   6   7   8   9   10

Spend Time Together

1   2   3   4   5   6   7   8   9   10

Good Family Communication

1   2   3   4   5   6   7   8   9   10

Express Appreciation to Each Other

1   2   3   4   5   6   7   8   9   10

Have a Spiritual Commitment

1   2   3   4   5   6   7   8   9   10

Able to Solve Problems in a Crisis

1   2   3   4   5   6   7   8   9   10

Using the same scale from 1 to 10, what number would you choose to signify the overall strength of your family? _____

Finally, rearrange the six qualities, starting with your strongest on top and working all the way down to the weakest.

2. All six traits from Dr. Stinnett's study reflect the health of the parents' marriage. As we saw from Genesis 2, and as research has affirmed, domestic strength begins with the bond between the husband and wife. Spouses, write out your thoughts on the following questions separately, then share them together: How strong is your marriage today as compared to before you had children? Has the busyness of raising children devoured all your time and energy so that you barely have leftovers or anything at all to give to your spouse? What practical steps are needed to protect and nurture your marriage? Now, discuss your plans with the group and listen for any other good ideas you might glean.

3. To sustain domestic strength, we're to practice the four principles from Deuteronomy 6. Did your parents model one principle in particular that impacted your life? How?

4. In what specific ways are you hearing the truth and teaching that to your children? How are you reflecting a fervent love and reverent fear of God? It may be something you do each day, each week, or once a year. Whatever you do that's true, honorable, right, pure, lovely, and worthy of praise (Phil. 4:8), put down on paper. When you're finished, ask yourself, How strong can I expect my family to be if nothing changes?

CHAPTER 2 Masculine Model of Leadership

1. Preoccupied, passive fathers and gender blending are trends in today's society that undermine the biblical concept of masculinity. Can you name a few others? Men, have you ever felt confused by the difference between the ways cultural norms and biblical truth define your role as a husband or father? Cite some examples and any conclusions you may have reached.

2. Husbands and wives, what image of masculinity did you grow up with? Who or what influenced your perception the most? Have your ideas changed significantly since becoming a

Christian? Since reading this chapter? Spouses, are unspoken expectations about what it means to be a father causing conflict in your marriage? What might some of those expectations be?

3. Dad, if someone measured your love for your children by just the physical affection you show each one, how strong would that love appear? In what meaningful ways can you improve that outward show of love?

4. St. Francis of Assisi once said, "Preach Jesus, and only when necessary, use words." What has your behavior, not merely your words, proclaimed to your children about the following areas: prayer, concern for the unsaved, compassion for the poor, commitment to the church, knowledge and obedience to God's Word? What have you imparted about yourself to your children lately?

5. Appropriate physical touching is not all that's required of a good father. He must also learn how to exhort and encourage his children with the touch of his words. Are your words heavy-handed or gentle? Calloused or sensitive? Angry or affirming? . . . With your spouse's help, list the encouraging phrases you say most often in the routine exchanges at home. What are some of the hurtful words that need to be weeded out from your family conversations?[2]

CHAPTER 3 Positive Partner of Support

1. Can you give a specific example from your own life that testifies to the riches you inherited from your mother? A particular character trait? An unerasable memory? A lasting, deep relationship? Some other treasure?

2. Wives, do you struggle with hidden doubts about the value of your role as a mother? Has it been hard for you to stay at the task for lack of encouragement or a positive role model to follow? What strengthens and motivates you to steadfastly continue? How can you hold on to that strength and motivation?

3. Mom, are you too busy to be tender? Has work, soccer games, piano lessons, choir practice, and housekeeping left you frazzled and irritable? Busyness tends to do that, you know. Sensitivity is for slowpokes. And slowpokes always get trampled in the fast lane. What legacy did you leave your children this past week? The memory of a mother who was curt, tense, always distracted? Or one who was perceptive and empathetic?

4. Genuine faith lived out in the home is not something that can be easily distilled and extracted for others to inspect. It goes deeper than dinnertime prayers or family devotions. Authenticity is modeled, lived, and taught by example, not by words. That takes incredible strength from a supernatural source, as any Christian parent knows. So, Mom, are you taking good care of yourself spiritually? Or have all the demands of home pushed your time alone with the Lord to the edge of nonexistence? What spiritual disciplines have you been able to consistently practice this last month? If changes are needed, how will you implement them?

5. Husbands, here's your chance to be that positive influence Chuck talked about in the last chapter. This week, you and the kids put your heads together and identify at least two examples of how Mom has demonstrated transparent tenderness, authentic spirituality, and the other three traits discussed in this chapter. Then take her out to dinner and sincerely affirm this great lady for the specific ways she has fulfilled her role as a positive partner of support.

CHAPTER 4 *Your Baby Has the Bents!*

1. What are the two major mistakes Chuck mentions that preoccupied parents tend to make? Can you see your parenting style reflected in either one? How?

2. Mom and Dad, can you accurately describe the unique bent God has given each of your children? Or are you more familiar with the prefabricated mold you expect them to conform to based on your hopes and expectations?

3. In your notebook, make a copy of the following chart for each one of your children. Then inventory with as much detail as you can their individual physical, spiritual, emotional, and intellectual bents. Don't stop working on this after your first attempt. Keep adding and refining throughout the week.

Child's Name:	
Good Bents	*Bad Bents*

How about using the insights you've gained from the last exercise to affirm your children? This next week, set aside some time with your family to focus on a different child each night. Begin the time by praying a personalized version of Psalm 139:13–16 from the Bible. To do this, simply insert that particular child's name and personal pronouns into the passage where appropriate. After you've prayed, share how you've seen God's workmanship revealed in that son or daughter through his or her good bents. You might even encourage the other children to chime in at this point and affirm the positive traits they appreciate.

CHAPTER 5 *Shaping the Will with Wisdom*

1. Chuck said that discipline should leave the child feeling loved and valued. Overall, did the way your parents handle discipline communicate these feelings to you? If not, what did their discipline say? What would you do the same or differently with your children?

2. Think back to the last time you physically disciplined each of your children. Now reread Chuck's list contrasting abuse and discipline. Is there anything from that left column that characterizes what happened in those instances? What about your words? Were they prompted by love to build your child's self-esteem? Or did they injure, leaving behind festering wounds of shame and resentment?

3. As Chuck shared, the Swindoll home strove to be consistent about the way it disciplined by establishing three specific guidelines. With your spouse, prepare a set of written guidelines for your own home. Share these guidelines with the group.

4. Corporeal punishment and verbal instruction. Children need both, but parents often neglect one in favor of the other. Some punish their children for doing wrong without ever instructing them, from God's Word, how to do right. Other parents just preach meaningless sermons and threaten, which their kids never take seriously because they don't back them up with concrete action. Children need both types of discipline. Which of the two do you need to emphasize to achieve more balance in your discipline? Share this within the group, and find out what practical insights they can offer.

CHAPTER 6 Enhancing Esteem

1. What kind of self-esteem did your parents instill in you? Is there a particular tape of your parents' approval or disapproval that you keep replaying in your mind? When is it the loudest? Is it possible to silence that tape or are we just stuck with it?

2. Husbands and wives, what does your love for your spouse reveal about your own self-esteem?

3. I've got good news! You've already begun implanting a healthy self-esteem in your children by drawing out and praising their good bents. Remember? In what other ways are you fostering in them a sense of worth, love, and competence?

4. Do you see any signs of poor self-esteem in your children? Have any signs emerged lately that indicate a budding inner strength? How did you respond when you saw it?

5. Every child needs help compensating in one area or another. What are those difficult challenges for your children?

In what specific ways can you assist each one to achieve his or her goals?

CHAPTER 7 *Challenging Years of Adolescence*

1. Chuck talks about parents of adolescents needing to be flexible. What would be some examples of how you can show flexibility?

2. Parents, take a walk down memory lane and reflect for a moment on the struggles you went through to find answers to the four essential questions of adolescence discussed in the chapter. Are you sympathetic and supportive toward your children as they grope for their own answers? What are some good ways you've found to communicate this support? Any wrong ways?

3. If you were to choose, which of the four questions would you say your teen struggles with the most right now? Is he dealing with the same issues as Jephthah or Absalom? Or would she identify more with Josiah or Daniel? What insights did you gain from examining those biblical characters to help you support your children?

4. In the section dealing with Jephthah's identity problem, Chuck raised four important questions concerning our role in teaching our kids about friendships. Go back and address each of the four questions.

CHAPTER 8 *Having Fun with Your Family*

1. Parents, does your lifestyle encourage a hurried-child mentality? What are the "hurry up" influences your children face, and what can you do—are you doing—to counteract them?

2. What is the difference between flexibility and permissiveness? Which side do you tend to lean toward most? Why do you feel that is so?

3. Chuck suggested several guidelines for keeping fun in the family. Which was the most helpful to you? Why?

4. Over the years, what key things have helped keep the fun alive in your family?

CHAPTER 9 *Warning the Uninvolved*

1. For forty years Eli served as a priest and judge in Israel. He earned the respect and recognition of everyone—except his own sons. What did Moses do that Eli could also have done to earn even greater respect in his community and his home? (Read Exodus 18.)

2. If Eli had come to you for counsel early in his career, what advice would you have given him to protect his sons from what Chuck called the "hothouse syndrome"?

3. Do you see any similarities between yourself and Eli? Between his approach to work and family and yours? Has work or just plain busyness become a way of avoiding your responsibilities and relationships at home? If things continue just as they are, what do you project will become of your children and your marriage?

4. Have there already been some early warning signs in your children's lifestyles? What are they? How did you respond? Are you ignoring the warnings of others?

5. Two more questions, and they're tough. If you occupied a position of leadership in the church or the community and your children began acting like Eli's sons, would you willingly give up that responsibility to focus all your energies on the home? Do you need to do that now?

CHAPTER 10 *Confronting the Unpleasant*

1. Can you think of any past instances when you confused normal growing up with rebellion in your child? What helps you discern between the two?

2. Have you relinquished your authority in the home to a rebel? Does this out-of-control adolescent constantly intimidate everyone? Are you walking on eggshells, too afraid to take drastic, needed steps? Does public opinion overly concern you? Are you clinging to unrealistic hopes?

3. Are you considering severing your relationship with a rebellious child? Before you do, let's examine the feelings inside you right now that are influencing this decision. Do you feel hurt? Angry? Depressed? Are you feeling guilty for not being a better parent? Put all your feelings down in your notebook without judging the rightness or wrongness of any of them.

Everyone who has dealt with a prodigal son or daughter can identify with your feelings. They're intense, draining. And they make it very hard to think clearly and make wise decisions. Perhaps if you wrote down your reasons for this action it would help you cut through some of the emotions that could be clouding your thinking. Is an eternal principle at stake or simply a difference of opinion or taste? If you feel it is an eternal principle, explain why and support your reasoning with Scripture.[3] Last, share your thoughts with the group. Let them give you some needed feedback to guide and strengthen your decisions.

CHAPTER 11 Facing the Unforeseen

1. At just about any given time, we all know someone who's reeling from the force of the unforeseen. Who would that be in your life, and in what practical ways can you demonstrate care for this person?

2. Has an unforeseen tragedy raised a theological question that keeps weakening your faith in God?

3. "The point of the book [of Job] is not suffering, where is God when it hurts?" Philip Yancey writes in his excellent book *Disappointment With God*. "The point is faith: Where is Job when it hurts? How is he responding?"[4] What is your typical response when you are hurting? Are you quick to blame God and become bitter? Or are you able to accept reality as Job did? (See 1 Peter 2:20.) Is it impossible to equip our children for the unforeseen?

CHAPTER 12 Enduring the Unbearable

1. What have you found most helpful for enduring the unbearable?

2. Like David, parents often get so wrapped up in the grief of unbearable situations that they completely ignore the pain of those closest to them. Children, for example, are often unwittingly shut out from being able to express their pain or receive help. How were severe trials handled when you were a child? Were you ignored? Was the truth of what happened hidden from you? How did that affect you? Would you do anything different with your children if the same thing were to happen today?

3. Can you honestly thank the Lord for trusting you with an unbearable experience, even if He never tells you why you had to suffer through it?

CHAPTER 13 Anticipating the Unusual

1. Are you ready for what God has in store for you? Or is your mind, your heart, and your faith still chained to past failures? Are there people around you that constantly clip your will to fly with their pessimistic nay-saying?

2. Is it possible that God has been tapping you on the shoulder about an unusual project for you and your family? What's been in the back of your mind that you haven't shared with anyone yet?

3. In the practical suggestion section, Chuck fired off three gutsy questions we should look at more closely. It would be good to get both the husbands' and wives' perspectives on these, so answer them separately before you discuss them together.

CHAPTER 14 Accepting the Undeniable

1. Are you burdened with feelings of guilt over your parenting mistakes? How did you react to Chuck's statement, "Rather than being defeated by thinking you may slip up and scar a perfect model, think of parenting as doing your best to patch up a broken one"?

2. "Mistakes will happen, but they won't ruin a family. How we handle them, however, can."[5] Think back to how wrongs were handled in your family as a child. Were confession and forgiveness fostered? Was it a constant free-for-all of blame? Or did everyone refuse to admit their mistakes because of pride? How can you best deal with wrongs in your family now?

3. When was the last time you asked one of your children for forgiveness? Even now, are you resisting humbling yourself about a wrong you've committed recently? If you know *what* you need to confess, the only question left is *when*.

4. Think about your faith from your child's point of view. What do you model to them in seeking forgiveness? What does it teach them about your faith?

5. Congratulations, Mom and Dad, you've fought the good fight and finished the course, as Paul would say. In your last meeting, set aside some time to talk about the significant ways God has used this book, the group, and His Word to strengthen your family.

NOTES

1. Dolores Curran, *Traits of a Healthy Family* (Minneapolis, Minn.: Winston Press, 1983), p. 258.

2. From the study guide *The Strong Family*, coauthored by Lee Hough, from the Bible-teaching ministry of Charles R. Swindoll (Fullerton, Calif.: Insight for Living, 1991), pp. 17–18.

3. Adapted from the study guide *The Strong Family*, pp. 118–19.

4. Philip Yancey, *Disappointment With God* (Grand Rapids: Zondervan Publishing House, 1988), p. 165.

5. From the study guide *The Strong Family*, p. 151.

Scripture Index

Subject Index

SUBJECT INDEX